Acknowledgements

This book is a rare attempt to drag the Treasury out into the light, to cast a more critical eye over its recent history. I say rare, because all too often the Treasury tells its own story. It presents its highs and edits out its lows. We know of its many rescue missions of the UK economy but rather less about its contributions to failure. In my eyes, the Treasury didn't simply salvage the economy from various meltdowns and economic shocks, but was often a causal factor in those same crises. That includes the lost Brexit vote, something the Treasury fought hard to prevent without understanding its own contribution to that very outcome.

This study has had a long gestation period. It began with a project conceived with Catherine Walsh in the wake of the financial crisis back in 2013. We found ourselves wondering how the UK economy had become so intertwined with its financial sector, and was thus so devasted by the banking collapse of 2007–08. In particular, we wanted to know what happened back in the 1980s, when the City began to take off just as UK industry was suffering a rapid retraction. Catherine looked at the budgets and wider documentation. I began trying to interview some of the key players. Fairly quickly, several past chancellors and DTI Secretaries of State agreed to talk. In one particular week I spoke to Margaret Beckett, Michael Heseltine, Geoffrey Howe, Nigel Lawson and Norman Lamont. The research was fascinating, and we produced two interesting articles for prestige journals.

After that I moved on to other projects but still managed the odd related interview when an opportunity arose. Then, in 2016, there was Brexit, Donald Trump's victory and a number of shock election results producing extreme populist leaders across the world. Like many, I was struggling to work out how and why. Although ostensibly writing about other topics, I repeatedly came back to these events and their ongoing consequences. In a way this book is the third of a trilogy of books trying to explain how we got to where we are. Book one, *Reckless Opportunists: Elites at the End of the Establishment* (2018), focused on how the UK's political, corporate and administrative systems were enabling erratic, self-interested leaders such as Boris Johnson to rise to the top. *Political Communication: An Introduction for Crisis Times* (2019) looked more closely at how evolving political parties and media had contributed. In this book, the objects of enquiry are the Treasury, mainstream economics and technocracy.

To explain more, during the EU referendum I was firmly convinced by the arguments put by Remainers

Bankruptcy, bubbles and bailouts

Manchester University Press

The *Manchester Capitalism* book series

Manchester Capitalism is a series of short books that follow the trail of money and power across the systems of financialized capitalism. The books make powerful interventions about who gets what and why, with rigorous arguments that are accessible for the concerned citizen. They go beyond simple critiques of neoliberalism and its satellite knowledges to re-frame our problems and offer solutions about what is to be done.

Manchester was the city of both Engels and Free Trade where the twin philosophies of collectivism and free market liberalism were elaborated. It is now the home of this venture in radical thinking that primarily aims to challenge self-serving elites. We see the provincial radicalism rooted here as the ideal place from which to cast a cold light on the big issues of economic renewal, financial reform and political mobilisation.

Books in the series so far have covered diverse but related issues. How technocratic economic thinking narrows the field of the visible while popular myths about the economy spread confusion. How private finance is part of the extractive problem not the solution for development in the Global South and infrastructural needs in the UK. How politics disempowers social housing tenants and empowers reckless elites. How foundational thinking about economy and society reasserts the importance of the infrastructure of everyday life and the priority of renewal.

General editors: Julie Froud and Karel Williams

Already published:

Bankruptcy, bubbles and bailouts

The inside history of the
Treasury since 1976

Aeron Davis

Manchester University Press

Published by Manchester University Press
Oxford Road, Manchester M13 9PL
www.manchesteruniversitypress.co.uk

British Library Cataloguing-in-Publication Data
A catalogue record for this book is available from the British Library

ISBN   978 1 5261 5977 9   hardback

First published 2022

Typeset
by New Best-set Typesetters Ltd
Printed in Great Britain
by Bell and Bain Ltd, Glasgow

Contents

Contents

– their rationality, their seemingly enlightened cosmopolitan vision, their concerns about the economic devastation that would result from leaving the EU. I felt equally disdainful of the Leave campaign's presentations and behaviour. But when the dust settled, I had this nagging feeling that, like many London-centric professionals, I had got something entirely wrong. For me, economic policy over many years, presented by a succession of centrist political leaders, delivered as 'expert consensus', had contributed. The Coalition government's austerity policies exacerbated deep-seated inequalities and problems. All of which led me back to that earlier 2013 Treasury study.

So, in late 2019 I began interviewing again. The book would begin in 1976, with the IMF bailout and Treasury humiliation, and finish in 2016, with the Brexit vote and another Treasury humiliation. A neat arc. However, the wilderness years of Brexit negotiations and then COVID demanded an additional postscript. Two years later, disrupted by my being head of department, a pandemic, relocating to New Zealand and a new job, somehow the book manuscript was completed. Along the way I have spoken to over fifty people who were intimately connected to the Treasury at some point. These include eight former chancellors and six permanent secretaries to the Treasury, along with many other ministers, advisors and officials. I like to think I found some useful answers.

Acknowledgements

I have to thank many people for helping me put this together. First are those interviewees. Many of them, particularly senior civil servants, were very generous with their time (an almost full list is given at the back of this book). The last third of the interviews were conducted from New Zealand and so involved speaking to people at unsociable hours. Second are those people who have talked with me about these issues, passed on recommended reading and other advice, or just plain supported me when it was needed: Anthony Barnett, Mike Berry, Clea Bourne, Roger Burrows, Aditya Chakrabortty, James Curran, Will Davies, Sahil Dutta, Joe Earle, Lee Edwards, Ewald Engelen, Des Freedman, Julie Froud, Becky Gardener, Dan Hind, Sukhdev Johal, Gholam Khiabany, Anu Kantola, Adam Leaver, Colin Leys, Mick Moran, Jack Mosse, Jón Gunnar Ólafsson, Ann Pettifor, Bev Skeggs, Peter Thompson, Catherine Walsh, Kate Wright and Simon Wren-Lewis.

I'm grateful for the institutional support of Goldsmiths, University of London, where the project started, and to Victoria University of Wellington, where it ended. Thanks especially to my new colleagues Alex Bukh, Jonette Crysell, Xavier Marquez and Kate McMillan, for easing me into New Zealand academic life. Many thanks are due to the team at MUP, who pushed me back to the keyboard, commented on earlier drafts, and kept supporting me over a rather longer period than they expected: Tom Dark, Chris Hart and Karel Williams. I'm also very appreciative of an anonymous real economist who read over the manuscript to try and head off

Acknowledgements

my worst errors of interpretation (they may not have been 100% successful). And, last of all, my close family who, as ever, have had to tolerate my extended absences as I double down on the writing: Anne, Hannah, Miriam, Kezia, Kelly, Neville and Helen.

1

Introduction: the Treasury as saviour?

Picture the scene in mid-March 2020. COVID was spreading rapidly throughout the world. Italian hospitals were being overwhelmed. Countries were implementing shutdowns and border closures. Yet Boris Johnson still thought this was just another harmless flu epidemic and was more preoccupied with a *Times* story about his dog. Meanwhile Matt Hancock, the health secretary, was assuring everyone that there was a robust pandemic response protocol, years in the making … he just had to find it. In the meantime there was a collective crossing of government fingers as ministers prayed for a modest death rate before herd immunity kicked in.[1]

Then, from the chaos, emerges someone with a real plan and a crack team behind him: Rishi – PPE Oxford, MBA Stanford, Goldman Sachs – Sunak. Sunak, the new chancellor and rising star of the Conservative Party, is everything Boris isn't. Eloquent, cosmopolitan, credible and able to look as good in a hoodie as a suit. Behind him stands the Treasury, peopled with the top brains of the civil service. 'Whatever it takes', says Sunak as hundreds of billions are found and committed to the nation's safety. The Treasury rolls out an extensive furlough and business support scheme. This ensures that the economy remains afloat while people can stay safe at home.

It's not the first time a public-facing PM has had to be rescued by their more policy-focused chancellor. The First and Second Lords of the Treasury often come in pairs: think Thatcher and Lawson, Blair and Brown, Cameron and Osborne, May and Hammond. One manages the party-political branding and the ministerial musical chairs, the other works out the complex policy directions and detailed spending decisions.

Over recent decades, chancellors and the Treasury have rescued the nation's economy from the hands of spendthrift ministers, the vanity projects of posturing prime ministers, all-powerful special interests and the regular combustions of world financial markets. Back in 1976, when this book begins, when a bankrupt Britain was being bailed out by the IMF, it was a revamped Treasury that got the public finances under control. Economic stability was regained and international confidence in the UK was restored. In 1992 two Tory chancellors, Norman Lamont and Ken Clarke, stabilized the economy after John Major's foolhardy plan to adopt the euro fell apart. Gordon Brown stepped in to obstruct Tony Blair's equally misguided attempt to do the same. He then helped stave off the impact of the dot.com meltdown (2000) before going on to 'save the world' from the great financial crash (2007–08).

And then there was Brexit. Brexit went against everything the Treasury had believed and worked for. George Osborne tried his best to deter David Cameron from his EU referendum plan. The Treasury then crunched the data to show how disastrous leaving would be. When the vote happened, it stepped in to calm the markets and maintain stability in the years of political deadlock and paralysis that followed. They were, and remain, the 'grown-ups' in government, all the more so now, in an administration flush with populist 'liars' and incompetent 'fantasists' (labels given by former cabinet colleagues who I interviewed).

Well, that's the story that successive chancellors and Treasury officials have been very successful at telling. The liars and fantasists bit apart, I beg to differ. In fact, the overarching thesis of this book is an attempt to even out the balance of this narrative.

It is true that the Exchequer is an impressive institution that is essential to the UK's political economy and stable government. For Martin Wolf, the *Financial Times* chief economics commentator and a Treasury observer over decades:

> Its most important job is to prevent catastrophe and manage crises as best as it possibly can. Over the centuries of course, it has had to cope with a succession of very large crises, the World Wars, the Napoleonic Wars, diseases, the great depression, the great inflation. That's

what it does. At its core, the Treasury is a department dedicated to keeping the show on the road, by which it means the British government and the British State.

To read some of the accounts of more recent crisis management, or to talk to those who were there rescuing the British economy from certain disaster, is to be reminded of its remarkable abilities. Hearing how the collapse of the UK banking system was averted, or about the construction of a furlough and business support scheme in the early weeks of COVID, reveals just how amazing the Treasury can be in a crisis. It is a bedrock of government stability in times of national crisis, a bulwark against the madness of Brexit and other follies.

However, all too often the Treasury has escaped critical academic and public scrutiny when it comes to the ups and downs of Britain's economy. The various bubbles, crashes and depressions, the banking crises, productivity gaps and decline of industry are all blamed on others, from obstructive unions and greedy bankers to inept regulators and politicians. Indeed, the Treasury is presented as the saviour which, like an endlessly patient parent, comes and sorts out the messes of others.

But one also has to remember that the Treasury has a certain amount of culpability for many of these crises (not COVID of course). It has been the prime institution of government responsible for UK economic policy for decades. It has overseen every decision on taxation, financial regulation, privatization, government borrowing and everything else. Although a relatively small department of state, its power and influence has only grown stronger since the 1970s. It has moved beyond controlling government finances to slowly dominating wider economic strategy and then to influencing multiple other policy areas. This power spread through the Thatcher years and was consolidated thereafter. Which makes one wonder how it can possibly be absolved of all responsibility for the debacles of the UK economy during that time.

Of course, there have been highs but also many lows, from botched privatizations to the mass sell-off of social housing, from favouring international finance over national industry to building up vast off-balance-sheet debts, from facilitating huge income inequalities to regional and generational inequalities. And don't forget all those market bubbles that it either ignored or fuelled. Whether consciously or not, the Treasury's elite appointees have acted as a sort of advance guard for the implementation of many of the neoliberal ideas and practices that organize the UK economy today. For me, when all is said and done, the Exchequer did as much to bring about Brexit as did lying, populist politicians and billionaire newspaper owners. They didn't want it (well, Rishi Sunak did) but they sowed the seeds for it over many years.

Why does the Treasury get to make its own story and why aren't fingers pointed at it more often? One key reason is that all too often the institution escapes close scrutiny. Whitehall civil servants, as a professional grouping, prefer to keep out of the public eye; ministers do the media work while they do the actual work. More than that, the Exchequer is a naturally secretive institution. It continually flies under the radar, except when popping up at annual budget presentations or to manage economic crises. It's very much inward- and Whitehall-facing, not outward- and public-facing, as all other departments of government are.

Another explanation is that it hides behind its boffin-like image. It is a place buried in reams of technical data and complex models that rocket scientists would struggle to comprehend. That's the reason, as any insider will tell you, why the Treasury has the brightest and best of Whitehall in its ranks. Lastly, there is the 'dull' factor of the Treasury. If the technical incomprehensibility doesn't get you, the boredom will. Any journalist or academic who manages to gain access to the inner sanctum of 1 Horse Guards Road finds little to excite their future readers.

Thus, most of what we know of the Exchequer and its leaders comes from two sources. One is the various autobiographies of chancellors and the odd former mandarin. These are mainly focused on the personal trials of chancellors as they battle with cabinet colleagues, various economic typhoons and political earthquakes. The hero is usually the author, ably supported by their competent and conscientious officials. A second source is the excruciatingly detailed institutional publications and infrequent academic studies of the Treasury. These are full of dissections of tax and spending patterns, new financial control practices, forecasts, etc., much of it presented via an impenetrable list of acronyms.

Scarce are the books that combine personalities, trends and big picture analysis. There remain few attempts to critically interrogate the Treasury, question its power or remit, or pull apart the consequences of its many conflicts of interest. The odd exceptions to this are to be found in wide-ranging political accounts which also devote substantial space to the Exchequer.[2] Hopefully, this volume will fill some of this gap.

The Treasury as an institution of contradictions

I have never had an official tour of the Treasury buildings at 1 Horse Guards Road, but I have visited a few times and been led to various offices and meeting rooms. It is part of the Government Offices Great George Street ('GOGGS'). From the front entrance it looks out on St James' Park. As with much of Westminster, my memories of the place are of moving through security checkpoints and wandering along mazes of corridors, in various states of repair, sometimes going up or down, to reach a destination. I can imagine ministers and officials through the ages getting lost from time to time, as they sneak back and forth from offices dispersed across Westminster, all without having to walk out into the open streets.

The more I have visited or researched the Treasury, the more I have become aware of its many contradictions. The first is visible to anyone who visits.[3] That is the mix of old and new. Various refurbishments have left in place (or renovated) the ornate stucco ceilings, the dark wood panels, the marble busts, fireplaces and stairwells. But the offices and meeting rooms are now full of modern filing cabinets, ergonomic chairs and tech. It is as if the Treasury wants to convey a double message: of both the weight of a past tradition and a present of modern engagement; of ancient authority and forward-looking futurism.

There are many more contradictions buried in the Treasury's psyche that have helped shape the institution. For one, it is both a finance department and an economics ministry. So, its traditional primary remit is to take control of the government's budget. It is engaged in an ongoing, sometimes brutal battle to restrict department spending. Sir Tom Scholar, the current Treasury permanent secretary, describes *raison d'être* number one: 'Things have got to be paid for, whether by taxation, spending reallocation or borrowing. Everything somehow in the end has got to be paid for.'

But at the same time, it is also responsible for wider economic policy, which often requires spending from those same departments, including on measures to support the economy. This has led some to argue that the Treasury should be split into two departments of finance and economics, as in Germany and the US.[4] As Vicky Pryce, a former head of the Government Economic Services, said to me:

> The real analysis and the real knowledge of what happens in particular sectors, or what you need to do about the

welfare system, or energy or climate change, is elsewhere and is not actually in the Treasury. Nevertheless, the Treasury generally thinks that they can handle it all and they know best ... the Treasury should just be the finance department, which really makes a huge deal of sense in my view.

The Exchequer is thus the government department most responsible for guiding national economic policy. However, since the 1970s (and before 'the Keynesian interlude'), the predominant Treasury consensus has been that the economy is best served by keeping the state out of all forms of economic management. This belief goes well beyond selling off nationalized industries and other state assets. It also manifests itself in a reluctance to support any forms of business or regional development, to favour national industries in trade negotiations or financial regulation, or to invest in grand infrastructure projects. This view within the Treasury is long running, although it has intensified in recent decades. As Nicholas Macpherson, the last Treasury permanent secretary, declares:

The Treasury historically has tended to prefer to leave the allocation of resources to the market rather than to central planning ... the Treasury knows that it doesn't know best, so better to leave decisions to markets. And there's quite a strong antipathy towards trying to rig markets.

Similarly, although responsible for boosting the whole of the UK economy, the Treasury is very much rooted in central London. Not only do officials do most of their work with other department officials inside government, they never leave London and the South-East. For years, the Exchequer has encouraged its upwardly mobile staff to spend time in the private sector, but that almost always means working in London's financial sector or for international bodies such as the IMF or World Bank. Thus, its knowledge of regional economies and non-financial industries is very limited. Ken Clarke, a former chancellor, remarks of his time in the Treasury:

> The officials were absolutely brilliant. It was like being on the high table at an Oxbridge College composed of brilliant people, none of whom would have been capable of running a whelk stall, because they didn't have much experience of the real world in a hands-on way … The Treasury doesn't actually run anything.

Another contradiction lies in the fact that the Treasury has slowly attempted to centralize its control of Whitehall but with a staff that is increasingly junior, transient and reduced in numbers. The Exchequer is still thought to attract brilliant graduates and the best from across the civil service. But it also has an annual staff turnover of 20%, as people move on, often into far more lucrative positions elsewhere.[5] In recent years, under the guidance of small-state permanent secretaries such as Nicholas Macpherson, the Treasury has attempted to regularly shrink its own staff numbers while also being reluctant to give up any of its responsibilities and power levers.

The last contradiction worth teasing apart, and one that drives much of the narrative of this book, is that between the human and non-human elements of economics and institutions. By this I mean that the Treasury, on the one hand, is being operated by individuals in social spaces; and on the other, it is an institution responding to and managing according to rational, pseudo-scientific economic rules and data. In a way, this conflict, between non-human and human reflects the types of account we are used to reading in relation to the Treasury.

One type, coming out of biographies written by former Treasury people and connected journalists, focuses very much on leading decision makers. We learn about the politics, the alliances, the personal predilections of those key players. Economics is subordinate to politics. This makes a certain sense, as most chancellors during the period of this book (and before) never formally studied economics. As George Osborne explained to me when asked about his lack of economics education:

> At the heart of almost all domestic political decisions are basic questions of who are you taking money from and who are you giving money to. That's not really economics; it actually goes to the heart of how you organise a society … So, in the end I always thought of them more as sort of social judgements rather than economic judgements.

A second type emerges from formal Treasury publications and some detailed academic studies that focus on financial trends and procedures.[6] In these, the Treasury is a sort of central processing hub, managing inputs of hard data and ever-more sophisticated economic models, all deployed to observe and respond to economic conditions. This world is one of logical decisions, formal institutional practices, complex algorithms and advanced processor power, in which human decisions play a diminishing part.

This latter view is one that mainstream economists often relate to. Economics is, after all, about markets and self-interested rational decision making that single individuals have little influence over. Indeed, to oppose modern economic thought, along with contemporary developments such as financialization, the platform economy and globalization, appears both ignorant and futile. Standard mainstays of economic thinking become a technical fait accompli. This abstract conception of the process also conveniently enables those involved in making decisions to hide behind faulty models and unmanageable markets and global economic forces.

Various critics of neoliberalism and current manifestations of capitalism can be similarly inclined to diminish the social and human side. Many critiques are based on documenting international capital flows and trends, technical assemblages, big data, super-fast computers and communication, all of which make humans appear almost superfluous.[7]

This book tries to chart a way between these two approaches. I focus on a range of key groups and individuals who played important roles in the recent historical development of the Treasury. I observe and document the periodic trends, fashions and cultures of the institution, its relationship to other government departments, the Bank of England and financial sector, its shifting personnel and remits.

While focusing on individuals, I was also aware of being able to look back on events and larger economic outcomes in Britain with the benefit of hindsight. I wanted to see what links existed between what happened within the Treasury and what then followed in the wider UK economy. I believe very much that nothing that transpired was inevitable or a response to wider market or other forces. Groups of individuals made choices, often based on the dominant economic norms of the time, and often in response to political or financial expediency, though sometimes with grander idealistic goals in mind.

Much of the time, however, there was no grand plan. Some of those I spoke to admitted that they hadn't thought through certain ideas or how key policies would result in the significant outcomes that followed. They showed a certain amount of remorse about the eventual pathways taken. Others simply wanted to defend their decisions at the time and preferred to dwell on more positive results. Others still, who watched rather than participated, were eager to condemn key decisions and policies from afar. Almost all of them, however, wouldn't have predicted then how things were to turn out now.

No one in Margaret Thatcher's Treasury knew just how far privatization would go at the start, or understood quite how monetarism would develop in practice. No one in New Labour was quite aware of how much their policies would contribute to inequality, just as they sought to tackle that same inequality. No one stopped to think of the long-term consequences of continually boosting financial and housing markets over decades, adopting clever new accounting ruses, or strongly encouraging foreign takeovers and investment.

Telling the Treasury history: an institutional perspective

Underlying the logic of this particular history is the view that government institutions matter a lot when it comes to shaping national economies. Behind the big ideas, political personalities and global economic shifts of economic history, it is such institutions that do most to enact economic policy in concrete ways.

This approach to economic history can be situated somewhere between accounts focused on ideas and those tied to global economic trends. In some histories, economics is about changing ideas and philosophies. Most recently, this has involved Hayek, Friedman and their followers usurping Keynesians in producing the dominant paradigm utilized by governments. Political figures such as Pinochet, Thatcher and Reagan then implemented those ideas through their institutions.[8] From another vantage point, economic history reflects larger, global economic forces and international organizations that impose themselves upon national economies. Governing institutions respond to these.[9] They are reactive not proactive.

Between these positions sits a perspective focused more on institutions themselves, be they privately run market exchanges, international bodies or national financial institutions such as central banks and finance departments. They turn theory into applied policies and practices. They respond to international financial trends and multinational organizations to facilitate nation-level changes. They produce regulatory mechanisms, standardized measures and metrics, tools of analysis, and apply economic levers to attempt to generate desired outcomes. Within each nation they produce a very specific variety of capitalism,[10] alternate manifestations of Keynesianism or monetarism, corporatism, neoliberalism or authoritarian capitalism.

As such, as authors such as Krippner[11] or Varoufakis[12] demonstrate, economic histories need also to document key institutions, their practices and working cultures, and the decisions of technocrats. They are as fundamental to a nation's economic history as politicians, ideas and global economic trends. Thus, this book's central focus is on the Treasury as a key driver and facilitator of UK economic history. As I argue, it is the Treasury more than any other institution, public or private, which has shaped modern Britain's socio-economic structures.

Although presented as a historical account, this book doesn't always follow the conventional template of such histories. It starts in 1976 and follows a neat narrative arc up to the Brexit vote, followed by a more speculative Brexit and COVID postscript. Chapter 2 begins with the fallout from the collapse of the nation's finances and IMF bailout in 1976. Chapter 7 leads us through the final economic missteps of the Coalition government that led to Brexit in 2016. However, most of the chapters are more thematic, focusing on grander trends that developed through multiple governments. Each often had an obvious high point, for example, privatization in Nigel Lawson's 1980s, or PFI in Gordon Brown's 2000s, but all developed over longer stretches of time. Each chapter also dwells on groups of individuals who pushed particular policy pathways: the new microeconomists, the ex-City types, the exuberant internationalists, the financial fixers, the professional politicians and the reckless opportunists.

The stories told combine a mix of economic studies, histories and public documents, biographies, academic publications and first-hand accounts. In all I completed some 60 interviews with 55 people over several years. These were not short, sharp, journalist-style interviews on immediate topics. Rather they were reflective discussions, probing past decisions and events, ranging in length from 40 minutes to over two hours. They generated over 420,000 words of transcript material. Each required days of background research as well as generating a further 40,000 words of personal observations.

The broader narrative line goes as follows. Chapter 2 begins with the crucial shocks that bludgeoned the Treasury in the 1970s: near bankruptcy, the 1976 IMF bailout and the arrival of the 1979 Thatcher government. The new administration was intent on tearing things up, starting with the removal of top Exchequer mandarins. But while the Thatcherites knew what they wanted to get rid of (nationalized industries, unions, Keynesianism), they weren't so sure about how everything would happen or what would replace state economic forms of management. That left a rapidly reconfigured Treasury to begin drawing up the map. Behind the sell-offs and political battles, changes in the Exchequer were very significant. One of these was the strengthening of the institution itself, giving it considerable new powers over other Whitehall departments. Another was the rise to power of a new generation of monetarists and economic modellers within the institution, replacing the Keynesians and generalists of before.

These combined changes effectively placed economic policymaking firmly in the hands of the Treasury at the same time as it was rejecting the idea of state economic management altogether. So began the long road, not simply towards free markets, but to the end of government macroeconomic policymaking. Fiscal policy was put on autopilot while monetarist policy came to be reduced to interest rate setting, a lever eventually handed over to the Bank of England. Micro became the new macro.

The question was what was going to replace all that state-managed industrial activity and multiple forms of national economic investment and stimulation? All these things were still needed to keep the economy growing, but who or what was going fill the gap? Chapters 3, 4 and 5 provide the answers.

Chapter 3 argues that one gap-filler was big finance. Successive Thatcherite chancellors, including Nigel Lawson, John Major and Norman Lamont, as well as several junior ministers, all had pre-political careers in London's financial sector. The same can be found when looking into the background of Cecil Parkinson and others who managed the DTI. Thus, when looking for inspiration as to how to usher in the new economy, all these individuals were very much influenced by their prior professional experiences in the City.

Ultimately, many of the nationalized industries were not simply privatized, they were handed over to the control of shareholders in the London Stock Exchange. Likewise, a series of financial regulatory changes, corporate governance reforms and tax shifts benefited the financial sector at the expense of UK industry. New Labour had their own reasons for continuing the trends. The consequences were a massive expansion of UK finance and an equally rapid contraction of manufacturing.

Chapter 4 suggests that Keynesian-style demand management may have been wound down, but in its place came various manifestations of pseudo- or privatized Keynesianism. These both cut Treasury expenditure and stimulated economic activity without immediate public costs. To enable such developments required outside experts and networks that spread across the top business consultancies, accountancies and investment banks. So emerged a group of financial fixers, intermediaries who moved between private and public and back again.

Pseudo-Keynesianism came in several forms. In the 1980s it was privatizations, council house sales and North Sea oil. For Labour in the 2000s, the golden elixir was PFI (private finance initiatives), which allowed huge public investments to be made off balance sheet. For both Labour and Conservatives, there were three more 'magic money trees': deregulated finance, enabling a large new source of private credit creation, puffed-up housing markets, and quantitative easing (QE). As far as the Exchequer was concerned, all these initiatives generated income and stimulated economic activity without showing up as public spending. The hidden downsides were an ever-growing accumulation of long-term individual, corporate and government debt, and a stagnating economy that encouraged financial market trading and rentier behaviour rather than productive investment.

Chapter 5 looks at the Treasury doctrine of internationalism. If one replacement for state economic management was the financial sector, another was international business knowhow and investment. Previously, Britain had done exceedingly well out of free trade and exploiting imperial preference. From the 1980s onwards, the globalization credo was adopted once again by Treasury officials, Thatcherites and New Labour ministers alike. Everything was done to open up the UK economy, to encourage international investment and big foreign multinationals to set up shop.

In some cases, such as car manufacturing, industry and exports were revived very positively. But overall the story has not been so successful. An open economy approach did not help home-grown business innovation and expansion. Instead, more and more of the UK's finance, industry and real estate came to be owned by often transient non-UK multinationals and financiers. As international ownership of UK companies has increased, so manufacturing capacity and profits have been relocated abroad. Investment, productivity and home-grown supply chains have declined. It's easier to buy, break up and sell off a company in the UK than in almost any other advanced economy. Come COVID, despite having a world-leading life sciences sector, Britain didn't have a UK-based manufacturer capable of mass-producing PPE or vaccines on home soil.

Chapter 6 focuses on the great financial crisis of 2007–08, when everything fell apart. The crash sucked in many countries, but the UK economy was hit particularly hard. The banking crisis revealed the larger problems of its Ponzi-scheme style economic model, built on growing private and public debt and reliant on an over-sized financial sector and fickle international investment. Although the Treasury was to appear the nation's saviour, the institution was also culpable for helping shape and then shore up such an unbalanced and unstable economic system.

The key question that occupies the chapter is why no substantial paradigm shift followed. Whatever version of capitalism that had been operating in the UK was no longer working. Even the super-rich of Davos, OECD and IMF technocrats, and the Queen of England could see that. Neoliberalism had hit its wall. Keynesians and other heterodox economists came out to cheer on the new economic revolution. And then ... nothing. But for a raft of new banking regulations, arranged by mild-mannered technocrats, it was back to the status quo. Governments everywhere absorbed their failing banks, loaded up their debt and flushed trillions in government-issue Monopoly money (QE) around the failed Ponzi-scheme system.

Chapter 7 reviews the post-financial crisis period and the Coalition government years, taking us up to 2016 and Brexit. In 2010, just as in 1979, Treasury orthodoxies and small-state politicians found a policy consensus on hacking back public expenditure. The only thing that mattered was eliminating the structural deficit. The trouble was that 2010 was not 1979. There was nothing to replace the impact of public-sector, local council and welfare cuts. There were no great state assets to sell off. The various forms of pseudo-Keynesianism in place stopped operating, as credit creation, big finance and the housing market ground to a halt. International investors (or Ponzi-scheme players) saw a busted economy and took their money elsewhere. When the mooted 'recovery' did come it was not U- but K-shaped.[13] The main government interventions – QE, ultra-low interest rates and housing market boosts – primarily benefited big corporate and wealthy asset owners. Rentier capitalism in Britain flourished.

In 2012–13, the Coalition, stuffed full of 'posh boy' asset owners, declared that the economy was recovering.

It clearly was for the bankers, property owners and big companies of London and the South-East. International investors were being tempted back too. The news media, as London-bound and small-state minded as the ministers and CEOs they reported on, were happy to agree that the nation had turned a corner. But all the while, salaries were not recovering, housing costs were shooting up, precarious working conditions were on the rise, and regional communities and economies were collapsing faster than ever. Then came the EU referendum. Unsurprisingly, the Remain camp's lead argument, that the economy would tank if the UK left the EU, provoked a general 'so what's new?' shrug of the shoulders. Anything the Treasury presented suddenly seemed no more or less plausible than any lie put out by the Leave side. The rest is Brexit.

The Chapter 8 postscript briefly explores the evident decline and recovery of the Exchequer. Brexit and the period after marks several things: the collapse of four decades of economic policy consensus, the breakdown of the British Establishment, and a direct hit to Treasury power. A political credit crunch paralysed the system for three and a half years and marginalized the Exchequer. The 2019 victory of Boris Johnson's reckless opportunists completed the delayed political and economic 'revolution'.

Ironically, the combination of Johnson's populism and a devastating pandemic have restored the Treasury. Both needed the institution's crisis-management and capital-raising abilities. And the Exchequer has obliged, finding hundreds of billions to hold up the economy, something we were told for ten years was impossible. Here we were back to government intervening in the economy in a way it hadn't done since the 1970s, and the Bank of England doing what it denied was possible before, creating hundreds of billions of pounds out of thin air (MMT[14] in all but name). What comes next – radical paradigm shift, return to an unworkable system, or decline into something worse – is anybody's guess.

The conclusion pulls together the varied findings from different chapters to give a long-view perspective on the changes and continuities over the period, as well as on the consequences that followed. It ends with some brief speculative proposals for change.

Two things to note before continuing. First, I'm not an economist. My perspective is that of a political/economic sociologist, something that will cause some mainstream economists to dismiss my findings. I can only answer that most chancellors and ministers in charge of the Treasury have not been economists either, and that the institution and its practices are as political and sociological as they are economic (as is the economics discipline itself). Second, I've realized while interviewing those who were there, reading historical accounts and having real economists review my chapters, that economic history is as open to wildly differing interpretations as any other kind of history. Whether 'right' or 'wrong', I try to present the personal accounts as they were relayed to me. The wider analysis and critique are, of course, my own.

2

Creative destruction and the road to nowhere: a microeconomists' story

The story of today's Treasury starts back in 1976. That was the year when the department suffered the humiliation of a forced IMF bailout. An institutional identity crisis followed. Shock treatment was doled out and changes begun. The arrival of the Thatcher government in 1979 then traumatized the department again and a system overhaul was pursued at several levels. A radically reconfigured Exchequer then played a big part in implementing the new ideas of the 1980s.

As this chapter argues, behind the big personalities, ideas and political battles of Thatcherism, the Treasury proved crucial to bringing actual, practical change. But at the same time, much of this change came to be directed by the Exchequer's own imperatives. The institution was more focused on asserting control over government departments and public expenditure and on forcing state withdrawal from national economic management of all kinds. This started with destroying older visions, alliances and practices rather than offering coherent alternatives. There was no grand economic vision of what would come next.

And it was all managed by a new generation of economists; people who were quietly effective at financial control and model-building but with limited wider economic experience or views. They proved to be perfect for re-establishing the Treasury as an enforcing finance department but little else. These rising econocrats then recast UK economic policy in far narrower terms. The application of fiscal levers, macroeconomics and grander national economic plans was out. Inflation targeting, microeconomics and technocracy were in. In the process, it wasn't just state economic intervention that was ditched, so was any notion of macroeconomic policymaking more generally. Henceforth, investment and business inspiration were to be sought from anywhere but the state.

Bankruptcy sets creative destruction in motion

By the early 1970s it was clear that the post-war political and economic consensus was breaking down. Both Labour and the Conservatives had operated within a paradigm that had emerged through the 1930s, the Second World War and the Attlee Labour government of 1945–51. This was built on the combination of a supportive welfare state, high taxes and regulations, and a mixed economy of private enterprise and nationalized industry. Governments, unions and corporate managers cooperated to manage the

UK economy. Keynesian demand-side management oversaw it all and had presided over a lengthy post-war boom period.

But come the late 1960s this formula began to break down. UK rates of growth and productivity slowed. The nationalized industries were increasingly uncompetitive and costly to government. Unions became more powerful and demanding. Inflation was an ever-present obstacle and the goal of full employment had become ever more difficult to achieve. Economic management became more complicated still with the breakdown of the Bretton Woods system (1971)[1] and the international oil crisis (1973). Both Labour and the Conservatives struggled to govern and to hold their fractured parties together while also managing economic shocks. The more the economy broke down the more governments tried to intervene to control prices, wages, the exchange rate and other values.

For the Conservatives in Margaret Thatcher's first cabinet, political failings were behind these economic problems. The state was doing too much and too badly, and all-powerful unions had too much influence. The 1970s highlighted these political failings: Edward Heath's loss to the National Union of Miners, the double election of 1974 and malfunctioning government, power cuts and commodity shortages, and then the Winter of Discontent of 1978.

In contrast, the view inside the Treasury was that economic policy was the bigger problem. Younger civil servants and advisors, who were there in the 1970s, framed the crisis in these terms. Two I spoke to, Lord Burns and Sir Alan Budd, helped lead the changes inside the Treasury. They had very different backgrounds but came together to become two of the leading authors of a UK version of monetarism in the 1970s. In different interviews, they explained their personal take on the intellectual breakdown that was taking place inside the Treasury.[2]

For each, it all came down to the outdated old Keynesians and policy practices that had come to dominate the department since the war. Alan Budd recalled the time he first worked in the Treasury for four years in the early 1970s. It was an era when ageing Keynesians were still firmly in control, despite rival economies having moved away from his ideas. They had expanded the use of fiscal macroeconomic policy well beyond its original remit:

> Those people and others around them had a profound belief in the effectiveness of fiscal policy. That basically, if unemployment's going to be too high you increase public spending … Keynes had been there during the war of course, and some of them had worked with him in Cambridge before the war, so Keynes had solved it. These were people who had lived through the Great Depression and seen the dole queues, and that was never to happen again, and this was the way to stop it … It was an aberration in some ways from the traditional Treasury view … If you take the long-term history, so to speak, the Treasury had been captured by the Keynesians.

In Budd's account, the Keynesians were never more than temporary interlopers in the larger history of the

Exchequer. They were tolerated by the Treasury against its natural instincts, but only as long as the economy was doing well. The broader goals were to balance high employment and low inflation using the Phillips Curve, while maintaining a positive balance of payments and healthy exchange rate. Fiscal levers were used to make the system work. Monetarist measures were a distant afterthought.

But by the end of the 1960s the theory was losing its predictive power. Come the early 1970s, despite various interventions, problems were growing. By the mid-1970s, as Terry Burns told it, classic Keynes could no longer explain the emerging problems, let alone remedy them:

> The fact is the whole post-war consensus had fallen apart. We had inflation at 25%, a huge balance of payments deficit, substantial government deficits and the IMF were here. The previous consensus of demand management through fiscal policy, incomes policy, devaluation when you've got the opportunity, as a way of trying to boost exports, had collapsed in a heap really by 1975/76 ... Because that standard Keynesian model could not explain what happened between 1971 and 1975.

For the Treasury, the turning point came in 1976. The key historical event of the decade, etched deep in its institutional memory, was when the Labour government ran out of money. It was forced to go to the IMF for a loan.[3] This signalled above anything else that the existing economic policy regime was untenable and that something else had to be put in place. As Sir Peter Middleton, a junior official at the time, recalled:

28

It all became very serious when in 1976 we effectively went bankrupt. We didn't default, but we couldn't borrow from anybody. We couldn't borrow internally. We couldn't borrow externally. The government credit was somewhere close to zero … It was a loss of confidence in UK economic management … talking to our various allies around the world, none of them were willing to lend us money unless we went to the IMF, which was code for saying 'unless economic policy is changed'.

In various insider accounts, it was the Treasury that was held most to blame for the loss of control over the public finances.[4] As Sir John Gieve, another junior at the time, explained: 'in my section of the Treasury, and indeed in the Treasury as a whole, the IMF episode, the loss of control of spending, was a traumatic event'. The 'old ways' of doing things, and the presiding layer of senior Whitehall mandarins, were heavily criticized. A series of reviews and restructuring took place. Several experienced figures were eased out.

It was during this protracted breakdown of Keynesianism that various UK-based monetarists began to get more of a public hearing. While public commentators such as Peter Jay and Samuel Brittan argued vociferously for a paradigm shift in *The Times*, Burns and Budd began working out the technical details. From their academic base in the London Business School, they developed alternative forecasting models of the British economy and the basic mechanisms for implementing monetarism. Their forecasts and critical analyses of government policy were published regularly in *The Sunday Times*. As Budd says: 'not only were we producing these articles, we were also rethinking our approach to economic policy. So, we became a UK-centre of monetarism of a sort.' Burns takes up the story:

> Jim Ball set up the Econometric Forecasting Unit, which then became the Centre for Economic Forecasting … and Alan and I started a publication called *Economic Outlook* in 1977. This was more or less at the time that the IMF were here, and we received quite a lot of publicity. We had a lot of attention in the latter part of the '70s, because we had spent a lot of time trying to integrate monetary policy and monetary factors.

Between them they had an increasing influence over both main political parties. They attended advisory meetings with Denis Healey, Labour's chancellor. They helped persuade him to take the first steps towards monetarist policy, in letting the exchange rate appreciate and attempting to control the money supply.[5] They wrote in detail about the need to control Treasury spending and the deficit as a means for controlling the money supply and inflation. Accordingly, they developed their 'medium-term financial strategy'. Keith Joseph, already interested in UK-based Friedmanite economists, was converted to their new thinking. He helped convince Thatcher and her inner circle.

In 1979, when the first Thatcher government was returned, larger steps were taken in putting the new thinking into practice. That required another shake-up of the Treasury. While political battles were being fought in the cabinet and across Parliament, similar confrontations were going on behind the scenes in the Exchequer.

For one junior official working in Keith Joseph's office at the time, the civil service generally, and the Treasury specifically, were being fundamentally challenged in their thinking: 'the radicalism of the Thatcher thinking was a very great shock to the department … the direction was set in those very early years by Sir Keith and Mrs Thatcher. If you didn't like that, that was pretty tough if you had a different view as an official.'

Just as Tory Party 'wets' were being eradicated from the cabinet, a parallel cull of officials was taking place in the Exchequer. John Gieve, having witnessed the institutional impact of the 1976 bailout, then observed the ejection of mandarins after 1979:

> There was a revolution in the Treasury … The top dogs in the Treasury were under suspicion when the Conservatives arrived as the people who piloted us into and not yet out of the disastrous decade … they [the Conservative government] did come in with a strong sense that this model had gone off the rails and that it needed to be radically changed, and they saw the senior civil servants as a potential barrier to doing that. And there were some big shifts in personnel in those years … a couple went very quickly and then two or three more went over the next two years, so that by sort of '81 you'd probably got most of your new team in place.

Reasserting control under cover of the monetarist experiment

We know that the economic failings of the 1970s led to the end of Keynesian, demand-side economic policy and larger state intervention in the UK. What is not so clear is what replaced it in terms of a national macro-economic policymaking framework. Of course, monetarist and supply-side economics is regarded as the alternative that was imposed. But what was that in practice? As presented here, it was never a practical or coherent system of economic management. Rather, it was an intellectual cover for other, more basic political and financial goals. For the Treasury, those were reasserting its political control across Whitehall and financial control over government spending. Thus, while the Thatcherites spoke monetarism, privatization and the rest, the Treasury mandarins were more preoccupied with balancing the books.

Historians link monetarism to the broader and vaguer catch-all of Thatcherism or to one of its close relatives, such as Reaganomics. Each advocated a reduced economic and social role for the state and a greater one for markets. That broke down in practice into a series of policy initiatives, such as smaller state institutions, privatization, less market regulation, lower taxes and so on. Many of these actions are as much about politics as about economics. In fact, none of them amount to an evidence-based, national economic plan for growth; that bit was just assumed to have followed the political steps.

Monetarism (money supply targets and interest rate policy) was the national economic plan bit of neoliberalism. It was assumed to be more empirically grounded. It had an intellectual rationale with some identifiable levers and mechanisms for delivery. And the UK Treasury became one of the first state institutions to experiment with putting the theory into practice. Enoch Powell, now more remembered for racist speeches, was also one of Thatcher's intellectual heavyweights. He declared that 'we invented monetarism too, there in the Treasury'.[6] Alan Budd patiently explained the details of British monetarism to me in a café at the bottom of leafy Highgate. It took half an hour. Fortunately for you dear reader, he also gave me the shorter summary espoused by chancellors of the time:

> The simple argument is fiscal expansion causes monetary expansion, which causes inflation, and actually, inflation means that there's no expansion of demand, you just get higher prices. Fiscal policy is ineffective. It doesn't work, only monetary policy works … And this had a number of implications. One was, if you want to control inflation, you have to control the growth of the money supply. Two, if you want to control the growth of the money supply, control fiscal policy, and three, if you want this to be effective in making inflation come down, you must let the exchange rate move freely.

As Budd and others viewed it, such a set of policies went against everything the 1970s Treasury mandarins believed. So they had to go, to be replaced by supporters of the new thinking. Geoffrey Howe, Thatcher's first chancellor, began implementing the new theory right away. First up was the phased release of exchange rate controls as a necessary step in embracing monetarist thinking. His 1981 Mais lecture[7] declared 'the fight against inflation' as the key policy goal. His budget of that year defied decades of Keynesian orthodoxy by increasing net taxes amid a recession and rising unemployment. Prominent economists wrote a letter to *The Times* to protest the economic illiteracy of his budget. As Budd recalled: 'That's not the sort of thing Donald MacDougall and Bryan Hopkin would have done. It's the reverse of what they would have done, and you get the letter from 364 economists and warfare breaks out and it's all very nasty.'

Later, Nigel Lawson famously spelled out UK monetarism in unequivocal detail in his Mais lecture of 1984. Here he made clear that the 'conventional post-war wisdom' that guided Keynesian macroeconomic policy was to be reversed. That had focused on achieving full employment by delivering economic growth by prioritising fiscal stimuli and leaving microeconomic policy to deal with inflation. However, to his mind, it should be the other way around: 'It is the conquest of inflation, and not the pursuit of growth and employment, which is or should be the objective of macroeconomic policy.'[8]

So, inflation targeting became the new primary goal of monetarist policy. This was to be achieved on the one hand by imposing sharp cuts in taxes and public expenditure while holding to a medium-term financial strategy. On the other hand, it aimed to control the growth and circulation of the various monetary aggregates that made up the money supply.

However, with hindsight, it's clear that basic monetarist policy in practice was a pale reflection of the theory. As critics of the time pointed out, there were large, gaping holes and contradictions in the thinking.[9] Many core aspects had to be abandoned relatively quickly.[10] For the Treasury men present at the time, the ones responsible for implementing the new policy, none of it really made much practical sense. Years later, Geoffrey Howe stated: 'I attach great importance to monetary policy ... [but] I do not believe in monetarism.'[11] Howe regarded the monetary aggregates part of the theory as a more extreme 'theology'.

Treasury officials who were there at the time all condemned it to me. Terry Burns, the least critical, admitted that his models were often not reproduced in the real economy. Alan Budd recognized that there were too many factors outside government control affecting the supply and circulation of money. As Budd put it: 'that didn't really work, because the relationship between the growth of the money supply and the growth of the economy was too loose ... No reasonable person would think that you can control the economy through monetary targets.'

Peter Middleton became the new Treasury permanent secretary in 1983, appointed after the purging of the Keynesian old guard and seen as sympathetic to the new monetarist thinking. Years later, he sounds scathing about the theory. He described the monetarist formulas encouraged by the IMF at the time as 'nuts' and 'myopic', and states that 'we never swung to a fully monetarist approach'. As he explained, any national economic policy would struggle to find such control in the real world, especcially when, at the same time, market and financial deregulation were doing the opposite:

I'd say that the big difference between theory and practice is in practice you actually have to do it. So when you think what you've got to do to put an effective monetary policy in place, you've got to control government expenditure, you've got to control government borrowing, you've got to keep an eye on the overseas position, which isn't entirely in your control, and you've got to look at credit expansion in some way or another, both domestically and imposed on you from the rest of the world. So, it doesn't matter what sort of monetary objectives you've got, achieving them is always going to be difficult, especially as we were trying to deregulate the banking system at the time and the economy. So, there were huge uncertainties.

The same problems applied to developing and enforcing the medium-term financial strategy. As Middleton put it: 'Medium-term financial strategies and the economic plan all had the same problem, you know, you became increasingly part of a linked-up world, and the models weren't very good at predicting the world.' In many accounts, the medium-term financial strategy was more 'rhetoric than reality' and could never be fully realized.[12] And for John Gieve: 'We had a whole series of medium-term financial strategies, and they all went disastrously off the rails. It was a sort of trial and error, it was an attempt to introduce and incorporate new thinking, but in very, very stormy waters.'

In effect, grander monetarist theory proved far too impractical to ever implement properly. Quite simply it was at odds with macroeconomic thinking more generally. The state's ability to control the money supply would only decline as the state itself withdrew from economic management and private enterprise was let loose. Just as the government was trying to control the money supply so, simultaneously, it was enabling the financial sector to create ever more credit and opening up the economy to large international flows of capital investment.

What was left was a notion of finding greater economic stability through attempts to manage inflation. The great replacement for Keynesian macroeconomic policy was ultimately reduced to something pretty limited: keeping inflation down. But they didn't get to that point until the 1990s. In the meantime, Thatcher's government and the Treasury focused on what they could control more directly, reducing taxation and public spending.

This takes us to the real, practical agenda of the Treasury in the 1980s, which was to restore control; control over government departments and control over public expenditure. For senior staff the overriding objective, both personally and institutionally, was to make sure that the IMF bailout humiliation would never be repeated. Everyone present at the time who I interviewed recalled how this event permeated the institutional psyche of the department. And everyone says how focused on regaining power over spending the Exchequer was. For Peter Middleton:

> So, the big change wasn't in macroeconomic policy … from '45 to '76 the long-term goal was pretty clearly a Keynesian-type goal. From '76 onwards it was a more controlling goal. And still is … You're the only department that's trying to do that. None of the others are.

They're all trying to find a way of spending more money.
It's how you make a political reputation.

Although the Treasury was held to blame for the IMF
loan debacle in 1976, the response was to give it more
power, not less. The loan rules laid down by the IMF
meant that government spending had to be brought
under tighter control. That required giving the Treasury
new powers to manage spending departments. Thus,
after years of waning influence, the Treasury-as-enforcer
role was boosted once again.[13] Thatcher herself saw the
Treasury as the institutional means by which she and
her allies could assert more control over ministers and
the civil service machine.[14] As Terry Burns explained:
'In none of this can you underestimate the role of Mrs
Thatcher as Prime Minister who, when it came to the
crunch, would support the Treasury in disputes about
public expenditure.'

The Treasury grip over the wider civil service was
strengthened in various ways. In 1981 the department
gained control over all senior civil service appointments
including permanent secretary positions. Both pay and
senior promotion in the civil service were set and
managed through the Exchequer itself. Increasingly,
permanent secretary positions were awarded to those
who had previously worked in the Treasury. The department also placed small staff 'expenditure divisions' in
each ministry to oversee its department's finances.

Tight financial control was also exerted organization-
ally and technically. A network of some 200 PFOs

(Principal Finance Officers), with an inner circle of 20, tied everything together. A 'Star Chamber' comprised of select officials and cabinet ministers was established to make final judgements on disputed spending plans. Beneath the political rhetoric of monetarist policy, M3 targets and the medium-term financial strategy, a whole new Whitehall machinery was being set up. Colin Thain and Maurice Wright extensively documented the evolving management accounting tools, rigid guidelines and practices of the Treasury in this period.[15]

It was by these means that the Treasury exerted its influence over all other departments and their ministers. Big spending departments with rival economic policymakers, such as the DTI and Transport, were cut down to size as budgets and staff numbers contracted.[16] The Exchequer also made sure to tap into their external incomes. Thus, those industries that remained in government hands found their profits being guided back to the Treasury rather than into new business investment. In fact, profitable ones such as gas and electricity had their prices repeatedly raised to increase their contributions.[17]

To these ends, many public policy rationales also had a Treasury economic reasoning: to raise revenues and get public spending under control, or at least seem to do so. For most of the 1980s, despite the numerous cuts imposed, such was the impact of the new economic shock treatment that public spending kept going up not down. This continued almost to the end of the Conservatives' second term in office.

So, officially the privatization programme was evolved for clear ideological reasons. The state needed to step back from economic control, thus enabling the private sector and market competition to take its place. During the Thatcher–Major years, there were 59 major public sales of state-owned businesses and 88 smaller, private ones.[18] For the Treasury, privatization was great for balancing the books. It took one source of costly public subsidies off its hands while also bringing in vital revenues. For many officials, a large number of state-owned industries were viewed as money-sucking liabilities that sat on the wrong side of their ledgers. Terry Burns explained the initial institutional logic:

> Some of the biggest financial problems of course were with the nationalized industries, who also were an open-ended problem ... If one looks over a ten-year period from the worst of 1975 say through to 1985 I think the extent to which the nationalized industries no longer required large subsidies was probably a major factor.

However, as privatizations proceeded, so the Treasury began to view the sell-offs as important sources of annual revenue in their own right. Civil servants were desperate to reduce the public sector borrowing requirement (PSBR) and were continually looking to other incomes to do so. As John Gieve recalled, different departments such as Energy or the DTI handled the actual privatizations, but it was always led by the Treasury, with the income quickly being routed back in the same direction. For one junior official at the time, who was involved in the early privatizations, ideological concerns were clearly secondary to financial ones:

> The Treasury were very exercised about getting these guarantees off the books. I know from talking to many colleagues, who dealt with the energy privatizations and telecoms, that the Treasury would be really, really driving for the receipts. I think for the people who worked on the privatizations, which were going to raise big money, there was much more of a sense that it was about getting the receipts in.

Council house sales were also very helpful for gaining the Treasury revenue. At the start of the programme, the Exchequer quickly blocked councils from retaining and reinvesting the profits. From an initial 50% take, the Treasury's share quickly rose to 75%. Sales in the 1980s in England alone reached £17.5 billion.[19]

By the early 1990s the income from privatizations and North Sea oil had dropped, but in the meantime public expenditure had been brought down once again. The civil service headcount had been cut by 19%. Some 600,000 jobs had been shifted from the public to the private sector. And the ratio of public expenditure to GDP had dropped from 44% in 1979 to 39.25% a decade later.[20]

Rise of the economists ... or the nerds shall inherit the Treasury

Those with a general interest in this period know something about the great political figures behind what became known as Thatcherism. But what of the new Treasury mandarins, the senior figures who worked behind the scenes to put Thatcherism into practice? I talked to several who were in or close to the Treasury then, each fairly junior civil servants in the 1970s: Sir Peter Middleton, Sir Alan Budd, Sir Steve Robson, Lord Burns, Sir John Gieve, Lord Turnbull and Lord O'Donnell. All were to become influential players through the 1980s and after.

None of them had much in common with the old Etonians and Establishment Oxbridge set of the Tory party. Only a couple had a public-school education. Several had closer links with the Labour Party. Terry Burns, brought up in County Durham, was the son of a coal mining union activist and studied at Manchester University. He did not come up through a conventional civil service pathway and was a clear 'outsider appointment'.[21] Peter Middleton went to a northern grammar school and Sheffield University and, according to Nigel Lawson, 'had never been fully accepted as a member of the establishment'.[22]

In some ways it's a mystery that it was these figures – less Establishment, more left-leaning – who were the ones responsible for creating the new regime. They were central to developing the institutional framework, thinking and practices of what was later to become known as Thatcherism, or the UK's version of neoliberalism. How to explain this?

One could say that, in true British civil service style, they were simply abiding by the demands of their political masters. I have had such an answer many times from officials. But although true to a degree, the Treasury and its officials have a lot more influence than that. I think there is another answer, and it comes down to the rise of economists with a very strong belief in market mechanisms coming to dominate the Treasury itself.

One of the most significant changes initiated in the Treasury in this period was the shift towards employing and promoting economists. Until the 1970s there were few economists to be found anywhere in government. More than that, those economists present rarely reached the higher civil service grades. 'Generalists', usually with a highbrow Oxbridge education in humanities subjects, ran things.[23] Anyone with something else, especially one of those specialist social science degrees such as economics, encountered an unofficial glass ceiling. This also applied to the Treasury. From today's vantage point, it looks quite bizarre; the beating heart of economic policymaking in Britain had hardly any actual economists.

There were signs that things were slowly beginning to change from the 1960s, when only a few dozen economists were employed across Whitehall. Both Cairncross and Theakston have noted a key shift then, with the establishment of the GES (Government Economic Services) in 1964. Numbers were growing in the 1970s and had reached almost 400 at the time of the IMF loan.[24] But despite this trend, the economists continued to be kept 'downstairs', serving more senior officials, the generalists, 'upstairs'. Gus O'Donnell recalled his experience as a junior economist there:

> This is still the era of gifted amateurs. There were still lots of 'generalists', that was the phrase that people used among themselves, who were not academic economists, who were writing wonderful prose for the chancellor ... when I arrived in '79, I was quite surprised at how many people there didn't know much economics at all. The economists sort of sat in the cellar, as it were, working on their model, and were kept slightly at arms-length.

Change was setting in as the Treasury attempted to modernize and become more professional after 1976. That shift continued after 1979. Peter Middleton had come in as a career civil servant rather than an 'economist' but had an economics degree and had had various economist roles in the Treasury. He was fast-tracked to the permanent secretary post in 1983. Almost all interviewees agreed that economics knowledge started to become more vital for progression within the Treasury in the 1980s (all except John Kingman, a history graduate). Terry Burns, who later succeeded Middleton in the permanent secretary role, made a point of promoting other economists in his wake. He looked back proudly at his legacy:

> By then, more and more crucial positions were filled by economists in the Treasury. Looking at the people who have recently filled the senior positions, many came in as economists as I had ... Jeremy Heywood came in as an economist ... Gus O'Donnell came in as an economist, Nick Macpherson came in as an economist. When I arrived as Chief Economic Advisor, no one in

the very top jobs came in as economists … it's now a
very different world to the way that it was.

These accounts also agree that the growth of economists
and their rise to the top took another leap forward with
the Labour government of 1997. In 2000 David Lipsey
wrote enthusiastically about the arrival of 'proper
economists' in the Treasury and their promotion to
top posts under Labour.[25] In 2001 there were 607 listed
'economists' in the civil service and by 2015 there were
1400,[26] all while civil service headcount was being cut
back significantly overall. Vicky Pryce, who came to
co-lead the GES in the 2000s, described the continuing
trends to me of economist numbers growing and being
increasingly appointed to more senior grades across
Whitehall.

Speaking to Gus O'Donnell on a hot July day in 2019
made things especially clear. He was looking back over
his thirty-plus years in Whitehall. Asked about the
biggest institutional changes that had taken place in
the Treasury, he remarked: 'I would say, basically, the
economists invaded the Treasury, and had their desire
to be involved in policy work. This was very much
led by Terry [Burns]. And, their desire to get involved
in all these things has, I think, professionalized the
Treasury quite a lot.' But O'Donnell's recollections
also highlighted for me two more important elements
of change that accompanied the rise of economists in
the Treasury. First, the new economists inheriting the
Treasury crown in the 1980s were not big thinkers
with grand theories to promote. Quite the opposite in

fact. They were ambitious but also narrowly focused, technical types, interested in models and econometrics. Second, other academic disciplines and alternative ways of thinking were steadily eased out. In effect, the professionalization of the Treasury also meant it pursuing a rather more technical economic policymaking pathway.

O'Donnell is regarded as one of the most able civil servants of the period. After three years as permanent secretary to the Treasury (2002–05) he went on to lead the entire civil service until 2011. His nickname was GOD, and this was not simply a play on his initials. But prior to his impressive rise, he describes his younger self as a bit of an economics geek, then excited by the potential of the discipline to fix all. Economics begins to sound like Isaac Asimov's *Foundation Series*[27] where the future pathways of whole civilizations can be calculated mathematically, thousands of years into the future:

> We were the techies with our jumpers and elbow patches and corduroys ... I was quite a technical economist at that point. I was teaching econometrics and stuff like that. So, I was very much into the modelling side of it ... But those days were also days of great hope in economics. If only we built the models big enough, we would be able to predict the world and then we would sort of work out the right policies for it and it would all be straight-forward. Looking back on it now ... I think 'how naïve' those models were.

The young O'Donnell was not the only economist nerd on the block with great faith in models. Several of those who became the leading lights of the new-look

Treasury were similarly interested in the narrower 'techy' elements of the discipline. Peter Middleton told me he had no great interest in economic theory. Nigel Lawson, in his biography, describes him much more as an able civil servant and technician rather than economist.[28] Sir Dave Ramsden, who later took over the GES in the New Labour years, constantly refers to himself as a technocrat, driven by a 'love of numbers', by way of excusing his perspective on everything. Great economic events of recent history, such as the banking crisis or austerity, are explained excitedly with reference to models, scenarios and obscure acronyms.

Both Alan Budd and Terry Burns, despite their grander ideas, were brought together by a shared interest in mathematics and models. Burns told me he was inspired by his tutor at Manchester University, James Ball, 'an economist-cum-mathematician-cum-model-builder'. Burns then followed Ball to the London Business School where they endeavoured to create the perfect forecasting model for the UK. In the early 1970s Alan Budd was an econometrician, doing something similar in the Treasury. He was then invited to join Burns and Ball to do the same at the London Business School.

When I met Burns, much of the conversation was about … yes, models: 'I have a bit of a spreadsheet mind where I can think in terms of simultaneous systems and feedback loops and things … because I'd spent all this time building this simultaneous econometric model, I had to learn to think as a system.' He proudly stated that Geoffrey Howe and Nigel Lawson hired him because they needed someone who could take on and dismantle the Treasury's own failing model. Burns fought model with model. He comes across still as one of those hopeful economist types described by Gus O'Donnell; the type who thinks perfect models exist and can be made to predict anything:

> Alan and I were trying to integrate these various ideas into the model ... And we were trying to relate fiscal policy and monetary policy. We were trying to extend the horizon away from sort of a short-term demand management approach to it ... And so, it was a question of pulling the thing apart and saying 'where are the weaknesses in this, what is it that we are missing, what are the bits that we have not been able to explain?' ... the Treasury model had had to adapt to some extent, although they'd done it by having more or less two models. And what I made sure of when I got there was that this became one model.

In effect, for better or worse, the young officials who usurped the old Keynesians in the Treasury were largely technical economists. In many ways this was an undoubted improvement on having genteel generalists in charge. But it also narrowed the horizons of the Exchequer, perhaps meaning it was not necessarily equipped to look outside the box or deal with larger economic trends.

The increasing dominance of technical economists in the Treasury can be seen as problematic for other reasons. Every chancellor I interviewed expressed a degree of scepticism about the application of pure economic theory to actual politics and policy in government. This was a point made in the talks by all six chancellors in Howard Davies' edited collection.[29] As O'Donnell also reflected, the triumph of Treasury technical economists also meant the displacement of other professions and ways of thinking. To his mind, the profession, as classically taught, had several blind spots and limitations, best explained by other social science disciplines. However, in conquering the institutional summit, the Treasury also got rid of those important alternative perspectives:

> I suppose part of the disappointing thing is the absence of other professions. So, when we talk about the micro stuff, psychologists? Zero in the Treasury. Social researchers no ... I wish it were more multi-disciplinary. I wish we had got more scientists, more social researchers, more psychologists. That would have been really useful.

We're on a path to nowhere ... or the end of macroeconomic management

In some ways, the two previous sections help explain another big shift in the Treasury: the slow abandonment of macroeconomic policy. The department's primary goals were to gain financial control of government spending and to professionalize itself by employing more technical economists in senior roles. Those institutional trends, combined with the new political consensus on state withdrawal from the economy, meant that macroeconomic policy became a secondary sideline.

Of course, the downgrading of macroeconomics was an obvious consequence of the new politics. A number of policy levers for national economic regulation were rapidly abolished in the first Thatcher government: prices and incomes, international exchange and bank lending limits. Through the 1980s the national industries were sold off and systems of subsidies and investment perks abandoned. Fiscal measures were entirely rejected as a means of managing the economy.

But inside the Treasury too, the long-term trend since the early 1980s has been for the department to both marginalize macroeconomic policy and give away its tools of management. In many people's minds Keynes had inadvertently elevated macroeconomic policy to a place in government that it should never have had.[30] A return to 'normal' meant the Exchequer having more modest goals. Theoretically, that meant the state getting out of the way while also creating stable conditions within which competitive markets could thrive. Stability was to be achieved with balanced budgets, fiscal rectitude and a strong currency with low inflation and a steady exchange rate.

Attaining the steady currency and low inflation was the complicated bit. Different measures were tried following the rejection of big fiscal levers alone: the monetarist experiment, shadowing the Deutsche Mark, then joining the ERM (European Exchange Rate Mechanism) in 1992. All failed. Following this last dramatic and costly failure, Norman Lamont put in place a new regime of setting interest rates to control inflation. Henceforth, regular inflation reports would be produced and the Treasury, in conjunction with the Bank of England, would set interest rates. Ken Clarke then established this routine and publicized the event, so creating the 'Ken and Eddie Show'.[31] In 1997 virtually the first major policy enacted by Blair and Brown was to take the next step in handing the whole responsibility to the Bank of England and its new Monetary Policy Committee (thus preventing prime ministers from manipulating rates for political advantage).[32] As Gordon Brown explains, this was more a Labour than a Treasury decision: 'To plan for long-term stability, we chose to make the Bank of England operationally independent for meeting the inflation target. We set entirely new fiscal rules, including the "golden rule". This was not the Treasury view. It was our view that Britain under-invested for the long-term.'

In effect, through various steps, Treasury macroeconomic policy was reduced to setting interest rates to keep inflation under control. That policy tool was then handed over to the Bank of England. One senior official looks back now, noting that this step marked the end of the Exchequer's role in macroeconomic policymaking:

> In '97 Mervyn went to see Gus and said: 'It's all over for you as a macro institution now. What you need to do is build yourself up as absolutely world class in microeconomics, because that's what most of government is now … no longer monetary economics but welfare and microeconomics.'

In 2010 another key Treasury function was given up with the Coalition government's creation of the OBR (Office for Budget Responsibility). This handed over economic and fiscal forecasting to a new, independent body. If rate setting had been handed to the Bank of England to restrict prime ministerial political interference, forecasting was given to the OBR to prevent chancellors doing the same.

Ultimately, over time, a quiet, barely noticed revolution has taken place in government. Macroeconomic policy has been outsourced to less politically accountable technocrats in arm's-length institutions. John Gieve summed up the historical policy arc to me:

> Up until the '70s fiscal policy was seen as the main regulator of the economy ... by the time you get to '97, really, managing the economic cycle is seen as a function of monetary policy, i.e., interest rates. And interest rates are going to be set by the Bank of England on the basis of a formal explicit target. And that is seen as the heart of economic policy. Fiscal policy, by that stage, is sort of put on an autopilot. It's not seen as a way of managing the economy. The best thing you can do about it is to sort of obey the golden rule, which is famously what Gordon Brown came up with. In other words ... you just basically try and keep it on a medium-term sustainable course, and you leave the Bank of England to keep the economy stable.

If the institutional changes didn't convince me that the Treasury had given up macroeconomic policy, talking to officials and advisors did. Peter Middleton confessed: 'until I joined the Treasury, I can't say I was all that interested in macroeconomics'. A senior official, who drove many a privatization programme, told me: 'I was always a microeconomist really, not a macroeconomist.' Terry Burns was focused on his theoretical models. Alan

Budd was clear that the Treasury should never have been engaged in macroeconomics in the first place and was instrumental in setting up both the MPC and OBR systems.

When New Labour arrived in 1997, they had accepted the central tenets of Thatcherism with regard to state withdrawal from economic management (privatization, no industrial intervention, cut fiscal levers, etc.).[33] That included the rejection of traditional macroeconomic policy. Talking to Ed Balls and Gus O'Donnell, all this was accepted from day one. Both believed that New Labour still intervened in the economy in multiple ways. But this was through what Balls referred to as 'the micro foundations of the economy' and what O'Donnell called 'smart microeconomic activism'. As Balls explained it to me, the days of traditional macro intervention were over. Micro was the new macro:

> I was very influenced by what you would call new Keynesianism … very much about imperfections in the way the micro foundations of the economy worked and what you did about that … So, in that sense we tried to make the Treasury more worried about the micro foundations, because I think that's where I thought the intellectual energy was at that time. You know, it wasn't old-style Keynesian or old-style monetarists, the new Keynesian synthesis … And I would call that the prevailing view at the time. I think it's probably still the prevailing view really, other than in Unite.

Talking to those in charge of the Treasury over the 2010s, it was clear that macroeconomics was part of a past era (see Chapter 8). I was quite struck at the lack of broader thinking about economics generally from the officials and minister of the Coalition government. Nicholas Macpherson and Tom Scholar, the Treasury's permanent secretaries since 2005, were entirely in step with this narrower remit. Neither George Osborne nor Philip Hammond had any interest in economic theory of any kind. Rupert Harrison, Osborne's chief economic advisor for a decade, is described by himself and others as a microeconomist. As with the New Labour years, supply-side measures were the main means of economic intervention. John Kingman, another senior Treasury mandarin through the New Labour and Coalition years, confirms the same in his long view of institutional change:

> I think the bigger change over the time I've been in the Treasury has been a much greater emphasis on micro-economic policy. The intellectual seeds of which were probably sown by Nigel Lawson, who argued famously in his Mais lecture that the Treasury should focus much more on microeconomic policy ... and over the last twenty years the Treasury has taken much more interest in microeconomic policy, and I think it's a good thing.

Conclusion

By the time John Major became prime minister, greater Exchequer control had been truly re-established. This power grab was facilitated in several ways. The department's institutional influence was consolidated across Whitehall. The Treasury now resembled a large spider at the centre of an extensive financial and procedural web. Chancellors became more closely aligned to prime ministers and further elevated within cabinets. The Treasury itself became a powerful enforcing institution used to keep rival ministers in their place.

Ultimately, the Exchequer became one of the most powerful departments of its kind in the world.[34] In Simon Jenkins' estimation: 'It is by far the most potent finance ministry in the free world.'[35] This influence also meant that spending power was pulled back from the regions and consolidated in Number 11.

But also by the 1990s the new path had been set. Successive UK governments had released themselves from most aspects of national economic management. They were no longer going to regulate prices, wage levels, international capital flows or bank credit. Neither were they going to manage companies, push for full employment, invest in new industrial sectors or use fiscal levers to stimulate growth. Macroeconomic management had been reduced to setting interest rates and maintaining low inflation. Those, along with other research and analytical functions, were then outsourced to the Bank of England, OBR and other bodies.

Of course, chancellors and Treasury officials wanted the economy to be managed, to be stimulated, grow and thrive, but henceforth that was to be left to others. Who these others were and how they were going to step in was all rather hazy. Who took on these roles and what did happen, as well as the part played by the Exchequer in facilitating this, is the subject of the next three chapters.

3

Financialization not neoliberalism: the City's Trojan Horse enters the Treasury

For historians, the 1980s was the decade when neoliberalism took off as a political project, although its thinkers and think tanks had been around a lot longer.[1] But the arrival of the Reagan (1980) and Thatcher (1979) governments was when the ideas were really put into practice.[2] So began the new era of free markets, smaller states, lower taxes and everything else we associate with the dominant creed of neoliberalism. Whether admiring or critical of what transpired, historians agree that free-market thinking came to trump all. I'm not so sure.

As this chapter explains, what took place in the 1980s could be more accurately termed financialization than neoliberalism.[3] Much of the transformation was not initiated by free-flowing private enterprise but in the corridors of the Treasury. Many of the central figures of the Thatcher revolution came not out of business but from the City. They didn't read Friedman or Hayek at bedtime but scoured the *Financial Times* over breakfast.

Such people first took over the Treasury and then the Department of Trade and Industry (DTI). Other parts of government were to follow. Ministerial changes of personnel were followed by bureaucratic ones. In effect, a political coup took place without anyone noticing. City and banking perspectives became a powerful influence in government economic policymaking and institutional management.

This distinction matters because financial market and free-market thinking are not the same. Financiers and neoliberals agree on several broad ideals. But their experience of markets, money, employment and a host of other things can be very different. And their notions of how to make markets work better are different too. What benefits the rise of big finance is not necessarily advantageous to business generally. Thus, it matters that the Thatcherites were guided by financial-market thinkers when navigating their way to the new world of small states and free markets.

Being Nigel Lawson ... or City-think infiltrates the Treasury

The first time I began to wonder about the conventional historical critique of neoliberalism was when I met Nigel Lawson. If you had to pick just one mastermind behind the implementation of the Thatcher project, it would likely be Baron Lawson of Blaby. In past accounts he is one of the biggest beasts in a political era chock-full of 'big beasts', head and shoulders above today's weakling Tory ministers.

Many frontline politicians write fairly dull and easily discarded memoirs. Lawson produced a door-stop of an autobiography that still sells well three decades later.[4] For years, it was compulsory reading for Treasury ministers and officials; 'the best textbook on economic policy', Lord Turnbull informed me. Others reverently recall the impact of his 1984 Mais lecture.[5] He turned watery market rhetoric into full-blooded neoliberalism.

As a junior minister in the Treasury (1979–81) Lawson guided Geoffrey Howe towards abandoning exchange controls and implementing monetarism. When leading the Department of Energy (1981–83), he did the ground-work for utilities privatization. As Chancellor of the Exchequer (1983–89) he then relentlessly cut taxes, privatized and deregulated.

I was frequently reminded of his prior standing when I interviewed him. When we met, in the House of Lords, he was holding court in a large red leather chair in the corner of one of the tea rooms. As we talked, various barons and baronesses couldn't help but sidle up to pay their respects. It's not often that you witness the ennobled doffing their caps (some lords and ladies are more equal than others). During our oft-interrupted exchanges, it was clear that Lawson was always attracted to the free-market approach. He lavished praise on those economies that had embraced such principles:

> I was always aware that the United States economy was the most successful economy in the world, and it was also, of the major economies, the freest, the most wedded to the market economy and I didn't think that this was the case here. And, equally I had visited Hong Kong which ... had reinvented itself on free-market principles and had done extremely well.

However, it was when I asked him about his intellectual inspirations that something more interesting started to emerge. Lawson took relatively little notice of expert economic opinion of any denomination. Back in the 1980s he was one of a small group going against mainstream economic opinion. He ignored the frequent attacks on him by eminent economists in the same way he now swats aside the views of 99% of climate scientists on global warming. His self-belief, then and now, remains solid.

Asked about his sources of intellectual inspiration he referred back to himself. No Chicago School economists, no publications from the Institute of Economic Affairs, Bow Group or Adam Smith Institute. Instead, he harked back to his many years as a financial journalist:

> I had a regular column in the *FT* for a time in the '60s and even further back you will find my ideas on what had gone wrong and where we should go during my time as City Editor of the *Sunday Telegraph* from 1961 to '63, and I wrote a weekly economic column there in the early '60s, and then wrote a weekly column for the *Financial Times* ... getting to know the City well and also getting to know the political scene well were both educative processes.

As we discussed one radical policy shift or another, he explained how this prior experience had informed his approach. When talking about problems with industry, he was clear that national ownership was to blame: 'Everybody realized there was a problem but nobody really could see any solution and it seemed to be fairly obvious that if state ownership had failed then the answer must be to get rid of state ownership.' As he then explained, his City experience had shown him the answers that others could not see:

> I had the advantage I suppose, initially, of a particular financial dimension. In 1959, '60, I was the senior writer of the Lex column on the *Financial Times* and therefore I got to know the City of London very well and I got to know how companies report to the marketplace, how new issues worked and all that practical stuff. And so, I think that was helpful in trying to think how you would set about getting rid of state ownership.

This was a key reason why most nationalized industries weren't simply sold off to the private sector but floated on the London Stock Exchange. To be clear, companies were not just de-nationalized, they were transferred into the hands of City investors (something I will return to later).

Similar responses were given when Lawson was asked about the release of exchange controls, changes in corporation taxes, stamp duty, dividend payment controls and so on. Whether or not he referred back to his City experiences, he applied a financial market logic to his decisions. One of his great concerns on a budget day was 'what is the financial market reaction going to be?' And here he prided himself on understanding investors rather more than 'any Treasury official could possibly have known, however clever'.

Nigel Lawson was not the only one with such a background. As I looked through the biographies of other chancellors and junior Treasury ministers of the period, all too often there appeared a strong link to the Square Mile. Geoffrey Howe, Thatcher's first chancellor, was a lawyer but told me he was very much guided by City-linked Lawson and Sir Keith Joseph. John Major, the next chancellor after Lawson, spent many years as a senior executive at the Standard Chartered Bank. Norman Lamont, the chancellor after Major, spent over eleven years at the investment bank NM Rothschild and Sons, becoming director of Rothschild Asset Management.

I interviewed Lord Lamont at the offices of one of the many financial companies he has become a director of since leaving politics. Like Lawson, Lamont was an ardent free-marketeer: 'I think a low-tax, small public sector economy is the way of the future.' Like Lawson, he had studied economics at an Oxbridge college, but he admitted that the subject was of limited use at Westminster: 'It's useful as a way of thinking but it isn't really a practical tool for politics.' More important to him were those visionary figures around him. He modelled himself on Lawson, telling me that his philosophy 'was very similar to Nigel Lawson's, probably identical'. He also mentioned the financial journalist

Samuel Brittan and Keith Joseph as sources of inspiration. Joseph, a leading intellectual figure for the Thatcher inner circle, also had established City links. His father had been a Mayor of the City of London. He himself had been an Alderman of the City of London as well as an underwriter at Lloyds of London.[6] Lamont also explained how useful his stock exchange experience had been to him:

> My time in the City did inform my disillusionment with the policies pursued by Heath because I worked as an investment manager and I could see the problems that were building up and the harm that was being done, and the distortions that were being created by the policies. So, I suppose in that sense, my time in Rothschild's did have a big impact.

Go down the ranks of more junior ministers in the Treasury in these years and they are dotted with people with financial experience and networks. Cecil Parkinson had fifteen years as a chartered accountant in the City. Peter Lilley had been an analyst at the stockbroker W. Greenwell and Co. John Moore worked at a Chicago investment bank and then the London offices of international stockbroker Dean Witter. John MacGregor and George Young were both at Hill Samuel, the bank and financial services firm. Others, such as Lord Cockfield, Leon Brittan, John Biffen and Nicholas Ridley, while not having extended City careers, had held positions there and still retained their social networks.

The period of Conservative government, from 1979 to 1997, was unique in this respect. Figures from the world of finance had entered government and the Treasury before, but never to this extent. Going back through the post-war period no Chancellor of the Exchequer had had a previous career in the City. Barely any had studied economics since Hugh Dalton and Hugh Gaitskell in the Attlee Labour government of 1945–51.

The infiltration of City-linked personnel also took place at the highest levels of the Treasury bureaucracy. Peter Middleton, who became the Treasury permanent secretary in 1983, had been an economist and had financial experience. After stepping down in 1991, he joined Barclays as group deputy chairman and has held a number of top banking jobs since. Terry Burns, who took over as permanent secretary in 1991, also had financial links. After leaving in 1998, he took on a number of financial board roles, eventually ending up as chairman of Santander UK.

Being Cecil Parkinson ... or City-think infiltrates the Department of Trade and Industry

City influence via the Exchequer spread to other departments too. A resurgent Treasury, with its control of appointments and personnel across the civil service, meant that finance-based thinking spread. And the department the Treasury had most interest in reshaping was the Department of Trade and Industry.

In the post-war period, the various incarnations of the Department of Trade and Industry had become fairly strong in government.[7] It had a major input into economic policy and industrial management and had maintained a degree of autonomy from the Treasury. The department had become fundamental to the tripartite politics and state economic interventions of the time. The nationalized industries were run by it. Heavyweight politicians such as Harold Wilson and Edward Heath had managed it. Union and business leaders, from across the regions, converged on its premises.

In other words, the DTI was everything that the Treasury and City were not: outward-facing, industry-oriented and nationally connected. In City–Treasury thinking the DTI lay at the heart of everything that was wrong with the British economy. So it was the DTI that was first on the Treasury list for re-education. The DTI suffered some of the harshest cuts of any Whitehall department under the Conservatives. It lost half its staff over the course of the Thatcher and Major governments. The DTI's own budget dropped pretty continuously from 1.35% of GDP in 1979 down to 0.7% by 1987.[8]

As with the Treasury itself, changes were pushed through by the appointment of ministers with a similar world view. During Thatcher's time in office there were 12 Secretaries of State for the DTI. Of those, half had spent part or all of their pre-politics career in the financial sector. Eight of the 12 had been junior Treasury ministers before being appointed to lead the DTI. People such as John Nott, Lord Cockfield, Cecil Parkinson and Peter Lilley had both City and Treasury experience. Only one of the 12, Paul Channon, a bit of a fifth Beatle, had neither background.

None of these figures stayed very long or supported their own department. Keith Joseph, the first in post in 1979, had spent several years arguing that a department of industry should not even exist. David Young, another in charge, publicly referred to it as the 'department of disasters'.[9] Several others showed clear disdain and talked openly about closing it down. Most willingly colluded in the break-up of the department: the privatizations, the brutal budget cuts, the closures of regional branches and the regular culls of staff. Like many of their cabinet peers, they were at one with the free-market plan. To that end, the nationalized industries, trade union bosses and bloated state institutions were all fair game. They exchanged these views publicly across the department and cabinet. And many drew on their shared City experiences to develop their alternative visions.

In this respect, Cecil Parkinson typified those who had taken on the DTI Secretary of State role. He was effortlessly charming, smartly dressed, 'shaken not stirred'. The qualities that had beguiled Thatcher were still very much in evidence on the two occasions we met at Westminster (once in 2007 and once in 2013). But there was also iron beneath the velvet. At the mere mention of unions or the nationalized industries he snarled angrily.

Parkinson, as chairman of the Conservative Party and in various departments, loyally supported Thatcher's project.[10] He was widely thought of as a likely successor to her until an affair with his secretary brought him down. He fixed me with a strong stare as he explained the free-market views he held at the time: 'We were ideologues. I don't deny that. We were determined that the socialists had had their way with Britain from '46, really, to '79 and we were going to have a different Britain.' But, as with Lawson and Lamont, Parkinson drew no inspiration from any of the big thinkers of the 'neoliberal thought collective':[11]

> I followed my instincts more than I followed ideas which I read or picked up. Somebody once asked me 'was Margaret Thatcher much affected by Hayek' and I said 'No, I don't think so, but she was very happy that he agreed with her' ... I responded in a similar way to the Institute of Economic Affairs, and so on. They struck a bell with me. I mean that was just the way I was going.

His brief tenure in charge of the DTI lasted only four months, being cut short by the scandal of his affair. But it was here that he made his biggest contribution to the reshaping of the British economy: Big Bang, delivered in 1985–86 but negotiated in 1983. This event broke open the London Stock Exchange, leading to its sudden explosive growth. It hasn't looked back since.

Parkinson's actions did as much for the rise of financialization as those of any of his peers. At that point it was the DTI which oversaw the financial sector, then seen as another wing of industry. That Parkinson took this on and succeeded was down to his own personal experience of the Square Mile. In effect, it took a City man to do what previous ministers wouldn't or couldn't do when it came to reforming the financial markets:

> I came into Parliament after sort of fifteen years in the City as a chartered accountant, ten years as a partner in the firm. So I had views about a number of things, quite strong views, and to my surprise, they became subjects that I had to take decisions about. For instance, I had quite strong views about the autocratic nature of the City and the need to open it up.

His personal experience of the London Stock Exchange was of a clique of firms that controlled trading activities. This 'closed shop' of members not only benefited elite insiders over others, it was holding back the expansion of the City itself. Parkinson's conflicting motivations were part outsider seeking revenge, and part insider seeking to elevate his professional alma mater to future glories:

> We had a central securities market which was a slightly grander version of the Manchester Stock Exchange. They were all partnerships, they were all under-capitalised, they couldn't handle really big transactions and the world's top players were all excluded, they couldn't be party to it. And so we set out to open the thing up, it wasn't an accident, because we felt that the London Stock Exchange would wither on the vine if it stayed in the state it was.

As in the Treasury, the senior ranks of the DTI bureaucracy were similarly realigned to the thinking of the Treasury–City nexus. For many junior officials who worked there in the 1980s, it was abundantly clear that the DTI was regarded as a pariah department. It had to either transform or be wound up. As one DTI official, a junior at the time, explained:

I was in Keith Joseph's office '81, '82. That was an absolutely seminal time in that everything around industrial policy, or the work of the DTI, was being rethought from absolutely first principles ... the radicalism of the Thatcher thinking was a very great shock to the department, so I can remember as a junior private secretary putting the papers in the box for the minister and they would come out with 'Don't they know there's been an election?' written over some of them.

On the one hand, eager junior staff were inspired by the new ideas and radical overhaul. On the other, there was also a very real sense of unease and forced conformity. DTI civil servants who wanted to advance, or even retain their jobs, had to buy into the new philosophy:

If you were working on the big privatizations there was complete alignment. That was really pointing the way between Number 10, the Treasury and DTI in that territory. So that was a very tight relationship in terms of looking in the same direction, thinking the same things, very tight at ministerial level, tight at official level ... so long as the DTI was driving the big privatizations on energy, telecoms, Rover, the sort of innate tensions between a DTI view of industrial policy and a Treasury let-the-market-go view was perhaps more subdued in that period.

As officials recalled, various policies were managed across different departments but actually originated in the then City-oriented Treasury. For John Gieve, the Treasury acted as both policy general and chief strategist when it came to things such as privatization:

There was for a while a minister for privatization, a minister in the Treasury who saw it as a key role to promote privatizations. But most privatizations were fronted by the relevant ministry ... looking back on it, this was a Treasury-led programme, even though the Department of Energy, the Department of Industry and so on fronted these things, it was a consistent Treasury-led programme.

As the Treasury and DTI became more City-oriented, so they also absorbed the ideas, personnel and practices of the financial sector. There was an increased two-way exchange of economists moving between the Treasury and the Square Mile.[12] City 'experts' were frequently invited in to consult on privatizations, taxation matters and New Public Management practices.[13]

Financialization in the shadow of neoliberalism

Looking back, for both Thatcherites and critics, the 1980s was the decade when neoliberalism truly took hold and free markets expanded. The history of the time focuses on things such as crushing the unions, particular the miners, selling off the nationalized industries, monetarist policy, tax cuts, deindustrialization, and so on. Each resulted in social upheaval and unrest. All these things are true. Each contributed to the reorganization of the economy along free-market lines.

However, what is less clear is the extent to which much of the reconfiguration was influenced by the re-energised financial sector. London's financial sector had been a significant force in the UK economy up until the early part of the twentieth century (see Chapter

5).[14] It had been much subdued by the rolling back of Empire and the policies of national economic management. But it remained a strong force and retained strong professional and other links to the Treasury and the Bank of England. Thus, come the Thatcherite overhaul of the UK economy in the 1980s, it was well placed to step into the void left by the state's rapid withdrawal from economic intervention.

So, privatization and deindustrialization were not simply an outcome of state withdrawal and the general embrace of free markets. They were also guided more practically by two key policy shifts that largely went undocumented in economic histories of Britain. First, much of UK industry was not simply privatized; it was handed over to the City to manage. Second, the financial sector was actively favoured in various ways.

Most larger sales of nationalized industries, such as British Telecom, British Aerospace and British Gas, were done very specifically through floating them on the London Stock Exchange (LSE). Such deals raised £65 billion. The many private sales of smaller entities, such as Sealink or the National Bus Company, in total raised a tenth as much (£6.7 billion).[15] A large proportion of shares went to small investors but, within a few years, the great majority fell into the hands of big financial institutions.

Throughout, City personnel were there guiding the process from the start. One senior Treasury official, who was engaged in multiple privatizations, described how the Exchequer managed this liaison between government and the LSE: 'There was a small team in the Treasury which dealt with all the privatizations … they would organize beauty contests to select a team of City advisors, they had an investment bank. In the early days you selected a merchant bank and a stockbroker and accountants.' As Parkinson explained in relation to the preparation of energy company privatizations:

> When I got there, we appointed bankers, brokers, engineers, accountants, regulatory advisors, you name it, we got the lot. I said this is the team that's going to take the privatization from now, a set of ideas and thoughts, to companies which have been floated, and I didn't want brokers coming along at the last minute … They were going to be in it from the start, so you would have nobody to blame if the thing isn't marketable.

In effect, this significantly increased the role of the LSE and professional investors in the management of the UK economy. For those who work in the financial sector, capital markets, rather than governments or retail banking, are the best way to allocate investment in a national economy. When Lawson, Parkinson and Co. were in charge, that finance-centric thinking became standard practice. For Stephen Haddrill, a senior official in the Department of Energy in the 1980s, getting outsiders in was vital to making privatization work for both the Exchequer and the City:

> The Treasury had to work with the underwriters as well as departments. It needed a lot of financial expertise, which perhaps it hadn't really needed before in quite the same way. The privatizations drove a very close relationship with the City. And Thatcher was very

determined that the privatizations would succeed. I remember Nigel Lawson when he was Secretary of State for Energy, one of the oil ones had not gone so well in the sense that an awful lot of the shares had been left with the underwriters because the City thought it was overpriced. But he was cock-a-hoop because he got all his money. And she gave him a real roasting because she said: 'That's all very well you've got your money, but are we ever going to be able to sell anything in the City again?'

Just as importantly, regulatory changes gave further control of public companies to the financial sector. After 1979 DTI Secretaries of State, from Norman Tebbit to Labour's Patricia Hewitt, oversaw a relaxing of takeover rules. They also reduced the grounds on which governments could intervene to stop them. Apart from a few key exceptions, takeovers could only be prevented on 'competition grounds'. Takeover activity flourished in the period. Accordingly, Britain became the easiest of all the major economies in which to do them, and it had the highest success rate of hostile takeovers. Between 1991 and 2005, relative to GDP, they far outstripped the levels of any other G7 nation including the US.[16]

Regulatory changes also increasingly emphasized the key goal of 'shareholder value'; that is, that companies should be managed in a way that produced healthy returns for investors. From the 1970s, financiers seeking corporate governance reforms promoted this principle. Through the 1980s and 1990s the DTI duly obliged. Where the 'fiduciary duties' of company directors were spelled out, it was made clear that these were primarily to investors. Other stakeholders, from employees to customers and even the company itself, were of secondary importance.

Each time committees looked at the issue, usually following a corporate scandal, panels were dominated by large City institutions. Each of these – Cadbury, 1992, Greenbury, 1995 and Hampel, 1998 – then further emphasized the importance of shareholders above all else. These were then reinforced by boards at the LSE and Financial Reporting Council, both of which again were dominated by Square Mile representatives.

For critics, this is a major reason why British companies came to consistently lag behind the OECD average spend on research and development, and why dividend payments to shareholders have been significantly higher than the norm.[17] It's also a reason why the average time a company share is held in the UK is generally lower. Thus, in the 1980s, investment in manufacturing rose 2% per annum, but profits by 6% and dividends by 12% per annum. In 1994 the world average spend on research and development was 4.85%. The UK's leading companies, by R&D investment, spent only 2.29%.[18]

In addition to handing more direct control of UK industry to the City, the financial sector itself was boosted in multiple ways. These often gave finance a distinct advantage over manufacturing and other sectors of the economy. One important change came with the release of strict controls on bank lending that had been in place since 1945. In 1981 the bank 'corset', which required banks to keep a high level of capital reserves with the Bank of England, was unwound. The following year banks were allowed to enter the mortgage market alongside building societies. Between 1980 and 1982 the banking sector share of mortgage lending leapt from 5% to 35%.[19]

The Square Mile was also aided by a series of hard regulatory and fiscal measures which removed perceived restrictions on financial activity. Classic financial market thinking, of the kind taught in textbooks, dictates that capital markets operate best when trading is as frictionless as possible. As regulations and taxes are considered a drag, the impetus is on removing these. Under Geoffrey Howe, exchange and credit controls were removed. Stamp duty on share and bond sales was slowly cut from 2% to 0.5%. Dividend payment controls were ended in 1982. For Nigel Lawson, these decisions came back to his world view that reducing financial market transaction costs was the best way forward:

> Transaction taxes do a particular harm because you need to have transactions, that's how markets work. If there are no transactions there's no market, so you don't want to put barriers in the way of transactions ... What happened with the reduction in stamp duty was not only many more transactions but, as a result, the revenues increased despite the rate being reduced. So that was very satisfactory.

Lawson's fiscal boost for finance often came at a direct cost to industry. For example, capital investment allowances for factories and machinery were removed, primarily hitting manufacturing. These savings then helped fund cuts in finance and corporation tax more generally. He explained his logic for cutting capital investment reliefs: 'That was entirely my own thinking. Obviously having decided that I wanted to reform, right at the beginning, corporation tax, and to have a lower rate of tax on profits, offset by a gradual winding down of all these reliefs, which had no economic rationale.'

This financial-market thinking was maintained through the Major and Lamont years and continued to benefit finance over manufacturing. Major defended finance and government support for it in his 1990 budget.[20] He axed stamp duty on securities as well as stamp duty reserve tax. There were regular increases of VAT on goods and services which added costs to industry but affected finance relatively little. At the same time, financial and insurance services were made VAT-exempt.

From 1979 onwards UK industry and UK finance went in opposite directions. The trends, although repeated to a degree in many mature economies, were far starker and more pronounced than almost anywhere else. Repeatedly favouring finance and financial market thinking while ruthlessly cutting ties with manufacturing had a lot to do with this. Between 1979 and 1989, financial services investment grew 320% while that in manufacturing increased by only 12.8%.[21] In the same period, manufacturing's share of GDP dropped from 28.4% to 22.2%, while the share of the financial sector went from 11.6% to 19.8%.[22]

New Labour picks up the financialization baton

By the time New Labour came to power in 1997 the financialization pathway had been set. Far from questioning this, the new government embraced it.[23] There was no repeat of the 1980s when multiple City people took on key ministerial posts. But several of Gordon Brown's key economic advisors came from the City too.

Chris Wales, who came in in 1997 as a tax specialist from Arthur Anderson, had been a City accountant. After 2003 he went on to work for PwC and Goldman Sachs. Shriti Vadera joined the Brown team in 1999 following a 14-year career as an investment banker at UBS Warburg. After a decade of government roles she too moved back to the City. Ed Balls, the most influential economic visionary for Blair's Labour Party, joined Brown in 1994. He then became chief economic advisor to the Treasury after 1999.[24] Like Lawson, he had studied PPE at Oxford and, like Lawson, his main work experience was as a leader writer for the *Financial Times*.

At that point, a dearth of ex-finance types in New Labour's ministerial ranks was not that important. By 1997 the City infiltration of the Treasury had already been completed. The Exchequer took on a number of seasoned investment bankers such as James Sassoon and Adrian Montague (see Chapter 4). Mandarins increasingly moved between the institution and the financial sector as it became department practice for upwardly mobile officials to have a secondment in such institutions during their career. The list of Treasury permanent secretaries to succeed Terry Burns over the New Labour years reads Andrew Turnbull, Gus O'Donnell and Nicholas Macpherson. Each had experience before, during or after their Treasury years (or all three) of working in international finance and banking. This covered both private investment banks and international organizations such as the IMF or World Bank.

The interactions between the City and the Treasury, and government more generally, became more normalized. Those present in these years talked of the steady exchange of financial consultants and officials. City experts continued to advise on privatizations, government investments and capital-raising exercises. As Dan Corry, a long-term Labour economic advisor, recounted:

> The real issue was the City and getting financial advice ... the people you'd employ there were clearly people who understood the City and financial markets. They became quite useful in all sorts of things around government ... the big bank leaders were much more into the Treasury and into Number 10. And I was aware in Number 10 that the banks had a strong line into the place, not only to the prime minister, but to Jeremy Heywood [head of the civil service] for instance.

The main reason that Labour and the Treasury began to embrace the City more was the realization that the sector was so lucrative. It didn't just bring jobs, it offered up large quantities of tax and contributed significantly to Britain's balance of payments. Some of those interviewed describe a period in the early 2000s when the Treasury had an epiphany. After a few years of poor relations, ministers and officials woke up to the fact that the City had huge income-generating capacity. As Lord Sassoon explained it: 'Gordon Brown and the Treasury came to realize the tax revenue generating importance of the financial services sector ... And that it seemed to me had a certain amount of influence on the way that the Treasury and the financial sector interrelated in those years.'

Just as with earlier Conservative governments, Brown's fiscal policy kept favouring finance. In 1998 he reduced capital gains tax for investments in non-business assets from 40% to 24%. In 2000 he altered the tax regime on bonds to boost London-based bond markets. As Stephen Byers, first a Labour Treasury minister and then in charge of the DTI, explained:

> It became very clear that London was going to be the sort of financial capital of Europe and a major global financial player. So, I think we got the benefits of that, and it became a very attractive destination ... and we didn't want to do anything that would kind of cross that.

And just as before, they did what was required to set it free and watched it grow. Ed Balls, like Nigel Lawson before him, drew on his City knowledge and contacts to help facilitate the new 'light touch' approach. As Geoffrey Robinson observed, certain Treasury officials put aside their distaste for the sector on this basis: 'They didn't like the City much, you know. They came to like the City because of the bonuses and the tremendous [tax] contribution ... Ed [Balls] became Minister of the City and he went round preaching "Deregulation, light touch, light touch" everywhere he went.'

The UK financial sector continued to grow rapidly in the New Labour years. From 1970 to 2008 the sector grew at twice the rate of national income in the UK. Up until 1989, finance was responsible for 1.5% of total UK economic profits. By 2007 it was 15%.[25] Even after the financial crash, Labour figures still regarded it as a potential golden goose for funding worthy projects. As Dan Corry put it:

> The financial sector will be an important part of the British economy, it will be an important wealth generator for those on the left who want to get some revenue, to get some tax, to do some good things on public services, you know, you're going to have to have the big public financial services sector.

There were some experienced figures who wanted to challenge the new direction of travel and to help manufacturing in the same way. People such as Margaret Beckett, an ever-present figure in Labour's cabinets, both in opposition and government for almost a quarter of a century. She had a degree in metallurgy from Manchester and experience in industry and industrial policy. She was first to take on the DTI in 1997. She was all too aware of the divide between financiers and industrialists and it was clear which side she favoured when we talked. But all her experience and political clout counted for little when she arrived. She found a dysfunctional, imploding department, more or less resigned to its own self-destruction:

> People were demoralised. We had a huge generation gap in the middle of the department where they'd had to

get rid of lots of people and they hadn't been replaced in the Thatcher cuts. And the department had got lots of different bits in it that had never been brought together.

Come 1997, Beckett and her advisors found themselves pitted against the now reified policy orthodoxy of Treasury and DTI officials. The department had cut many of its long-standing ties to industry and was fiercely opposed to schemes offering industry support of any kind. She had numerous arguments. When she tried the 'don't they know there's been an election' line officials simply ignored it and Number 10 offered no support: 'The Treasury had always been paranoid about economic intervention … Tony [Blair] had got too many people around him who clung to the old economic orthodoxies.' As she, among others, explained, interventionism sounded just too 'Old Labour'. Whether or not Blair and Brown had Old Labour sympathies, they were never going to express them in public or lend the required political support. She lasted little more than a year.

New Labour didn't have much left to privatize but they disposed of what they could. The DTI continued to be cut and restructured until its replacement by the rather smaller Department of Business, Innovation and Skills in 2007. At the same time, the one business sector that did get backing was finance. As Vicky Pryce, a former chief economic advisor to the Treasury and joint head of the Government Economic Services, admitted:

> The industrial policy that developed was one that basically said there's very little money for business support … everyone was under the influence of the financial

> sector though, I think, probably including the DTI …
> we were probably all of us far too impressed by how
> well the financial sector was doing and how competitive
> it was internationally.

New Labour also continued the earlier policies of handing greater control of corporations to the LSE. The 2000 Financial Services Act and 2006 Companies Act, produced by the DTI, officially recognized the Financial Reporting Council and LSE as having legal jurisdiction in the areas of corporate governance and takeovers. The 2002 Enterprise Act made it even harder for ministers to intervene and block takeovers.[26]

Thus, in the New Labour years, the rise of finance and decline of manufacturing continued apace. Just looking at the UK's industrial sector, the downward trend had obviously begun back in the 1950s, but the rate of decline increased markedly in the Thatcher and New Labour years. In the UK in the 1970s, 30% of GDP and 35% of employment were in manufacturing.[27] By 2010, 13% of GDP and 10% of employment were.[28] The UK, which had been responsible for 25.4% of world manufacturing exports in 1952, was producing just 2.9% of them by the end of New Labour's tenure. In the 1970s trade surpluses in manufactured goods were running at 4–6% annually.[29] By 2010 these had turned to trade deficits averaging 2–4% annually.[30] The drops were as pronounced in the Labour years as they had been the Conservative ones. From 1979 to 1987, 29% of manufacturing employment, or 2 million jobs, were lost.[31] Under Blair's Labour, between 1997 and 2010 there was a further 42% drop, from 4.3 million jobs to 2.5 million. In 1997 manufacturing contributed 20% to the economy, but that figure was only 12% by 2007.[32]

Of course, all developed economies have experienced a marked decline in their manufacturing sectors over the same period, when production moved abroad to countries with cheap labour costs. But by many measures, Britain's retreat was far quicker and more encompassing than almost anywhere else.[33] In the 1970s UK and German manufacturing were on a par in relation to their economies. By 2011 three times as many German workers were employed in manufacturing as in the UK. German manufacturers' share of GDP was twice that of the UK.

In contrast, UK finance simply exploded. In the mid-1970s UK bank assets were equal to roughly half the UK's annual GDP (as they had been throughout the twentieth century). By the mid-2000s they had expanded to five times the UK's annual GDP.[34] In that same period, the value of the London Stock Market went from two-fifths of government income and expenditure to more than three times it. Evidently, the biggest winners of the neoliberal experiment were those working in finance.

Conclusion

As documented here, the UK's economic transformation of the 1980s was not simply a radical push into free markets. Neoliberalism, like capitalism, comes in many varieties. The one adopted in Britain was very much influenced by people with financial market backgrounds. They knew a lot about the City and capital markets but relatively little about manufacturing and regional industries. Markets to them were all about transactions, not about production, labour or materials. Industry was part of an ageing, foreign space for them. Finance was their new world.

And it was finance, rather than the Chicago School, that gave them their direction. For them, everything we now associate with neoliberalism was a bright but hazy image. It lay there, tantalizing but blurry. Financialization shared many of these vague, abstract but inspiring elements. But it also contained a ready-made set of market practices, institutions and tools for achieving its goals. So, a large part of the UK pathway to its free-market future was constructed with those practices and tools.

This meant that British industry was not simply marketized; it was financialized. Manufacturing withered as quickly in the UK as it did almost anywhere. Likewise, finance grew as quickly in the UK as almost anywhere else too.

Perhaps the greatest indicator that the Treasury has become well and truly intermeshed with big finance comes from looking at the career trajectories of recent officials and ministers. Looking at the Coalition government (2010–16), every senior figure who managed Treasury economic policy – George Osborne, Danny Alexander, David Cameron, Rupert Harrison, John Kingman and Nicholas Macpherson – later gained positions in investment banking. So too, the last two chancellors Sajid Javid and Rishi Sunak have come from the sector. Prior to becoming an MP, Javid had an 18-year career working for Chase Manhattan and Deutsche Bank. Sunak had a 14-year career in high finance, first working for Goldman Sachs and then a series of hedge funds. Few seem to have noted this shift. Just as it had been normal to have chancellors without economics or business experience for decades, now it seems normal to put investment bankers in charge.

4

Pseudo-Keynesianism, debt and magic money trees: the financial fixers come to town

One thing that historians are clear on is that Thatcherism marked the end of large-scale state intervention in the economy. Public spending was reined in. Fiscal levers were no longer deployed to boost employment and economic activity. Instead, supply-side measures, such as lower taxes and deregulation, were rolled out to encourage private market activities. Markets and corporations then stepped into the large space left by government.

However, this is a partial telling of the story. Yes, both Conservative and Labour governments kept privatizing, deregulating and lowering taxes. But up until 2010 neither substantially reduced their spending nor stopped trying to stimulate economic activity. They instead found alternative revenue sources and attempted to achieve economic stimuli through other more covert means. In effect, pseudo-forms of Keynesian-style demand management continued behind the scenes.

Tory and Labour configurations of pseudo-Keynesianism took different forms. They emerged out of compromises between Treasury restrictions and party-political goals. On the one side was a tougher, more enforcing Treasury, focused on reining in spending departments and ambitious ministers. On the other were political leaders determined to keep taxes down but also growth on track, public spending stable and floating middle-class voters onside. This meant that politicians and Treasury officials had to look for creative financial solutions to fill the growing gap.

So came the era of government fixers, intermediaries and magic money trees: the high-level accountants, the business consultants and financiers. They offered multiple ways of generating alternative forms of Treasury income while also encouraging wider economic activity. Almost all of these initiatives found ways of creating capital or capital equivalents to flush around the economy, many of which usually resulted in an accumulation of long-term public and private debt. The models of pseudo-Keynesianism used different forms of financial wheeling and dealing but the results were the same: short-term stimuli, long-term debts and a select group of super-rich beneficiaries.

Squaring the accounting circle under Thatcher

On the face of it, the Conservatives set out to greatly reduce state economic intervention. The 1980s are remembered as an era of spending cuts, public sell-offs and withdrawal from state economic management. Demand-side thinking and government forms of economic stimulation were roundly rejected.

However, behind the big political vision of state economic withdrawal there were two important practical policy considerations. First was a need to maintain public and welfare service provision to a level consistent with citizen expectations at a time of high unemployment. That required the Treasury to keep securing a healthy level of income at the same time as it was cutting taxes and getting spending under control. Second was to ensure that the economy was being stimulated by other, private means. Something or things had to make up the gap as the state stopped throwing money at industries and services. So successive governments tried to do both of these things, with a variety of methods, sleights of hand and consequences.

The most obvious way of making things add up for the Thatcher governments of the 1980s was by selling off numerous state assets, usually on the cheap. They were desperate for income as, with a tanking economy and high unemployment, public spending could not be reduced for several years. This meant selling off council housing and North Sea oil reserves as well as the big, nationalized industries. Each of these was done with a clear political and ideological logic. But behind the rhetoric, these actions helped the Treasury balance its books while also giving a wide-ranging stimulus to the economy.

Privatization had various economic and political rationales. The economic ones were about market and private enterprise being able to do things cheaper, better and more efficiently. Politically, the line was about Thatcher's 'popular capitalism' drive and the goal of a shareholding democracy. Share offerings were made easily accessible to the wider public. On both counts, the policy was seen as a success. In 1980 there were some three million individual shareholders in the UK. This rose to 11 million by 1991.[1]

Council house sales were the same. Publicly they were all about enabling home ownership for the poorer members of society. The 1980 legislation to support this was called 'Right-to-Buy'. By 1989 some 1.5 million council homes had been sold off. As Michael Heseltine explained, the policy had a clear justification: 'Council house sales was part of the wealth redistribution, the privatisation process ... and it became one of the most popular policies of the '79 election campaign.' Home ownership went up and by 1989 some 67% of dwellings were owner-occupied.[2]

What was played down in delivering both policies was the extent to which they also kept the Treasury accounts looking respectable, and helped government to pretend it was reducing public spending. Between 1979 and 1996 privatization raised some £72 billion for Conservative governments.[3] Sales of council houses, along with other government land and property sell-offs across England, Scotland and Wales, made £30.6 billion in the 1980s alone.[4] North Sea oil revenues also found their way back to the Treasury and helped to significantly reduce official public sector borrowing.[5]

To aid the official line of reducing state spending, receipts from sales were officially reclassified as 'negative expenditure'. Leo Pliatzky, who was fairly critical of changes in Whitehall after his departure, details this accounting ruse in his 1989 book on the Treasury.[6] Geoffrey Robinson similarly pointed out to me what had taken place: 'Thatcher got away with it, she privatized the industries and pretended these capital gains, the capital income, was treated as revenue. It wasn't, it was capital sale, you know, it should have gone on the capital account not the revenue account. She got away with it.'

Something similar was done with North Sea oil income. Thus, in 1984, the official PSBR ratio to GDP read as 3%. But without privatization proceeds it should have read 12.2%. Without the revenues from North Sea oil, the ratio would have reached 24.2%.[7] As council house sales proceeded, they also contributed to keeping the official PSBR ratio down. In 1987 Nigel Lawson publicly declared his success in bringing the PSBR in £1 billion below target, without acknowledging the year's income from £2 billion of right-to-buy receipts.

What was also significant was the extent to which these sales helped stimulate the wider economy, by making equally useful contributions to individual bank balances. Most share sales in the nationalized industries were offered to the public at reduced rates. They immediately rose in value and were then sold off for a quick profit. Council houses were also sold at a discount on current market values. This began at 33% for those who had rented their homes for three years and gradually went up to 60% for those who had occupied for thirty years. As with shares, many were sold off to third parties fairly rapidly.

In this respect, the privatization process gave its own economic stimuli to the wider economy. Thus, while manufacturing and public-sector jobs were being shed in the hundreds of thousands, and real wage rises slowed, money was still being circulated through the economy in other ways. As well as direct tax cuts, share offerings and council house sales all gave individuals additional spending power. The middle classes expanded accordingly, as did their consumer spending.

Of course, there were also big losers, most obviously and immediately local councils and anyone who lost out from the wider sale of public industries and other assets. Over the course of the 1980s, councils went from building a third of all new housing to virtually nothing by 1991.[8] Over time, those sales were to affect future generations and institutions, and generate debt. The winners of the time were also obvious: a Tory Party that went on to enjoy four election victories, and the Treasury itself.

The thing is, governments ever since have continued to try and achieve this multi-plate-spinning trick: of balancing budgets while also reducing headline taxes and also maintaining public services and stimulating the economy. But they've had to do it without the abundance of state assets to sell off.

After 1997 New Labour had a lot fewer things to flog. Councils, understandably, stopped building council houses. There were few large industries left to privatize, although they sold several smaller things. They also made one-off tax raids on the privatized utilities and bankers' bonuses. The one-off sale of radio spectrum licences to mobile phone companies proved even more lucrative. After 2010 the Coalition government managed to sell the Royal Mail, some smaller things (excluding the resale of banks that had had to be temporarily nationalized in the financial crisis), and more spectrum sales.

All these sales and tax raids proved very useful for filling spending gaps and financing new initiatives. But they didn't come close to the incomes achieved by the big sell-offs of the Thatcher era. Neither did they help stimulate the wider economy more generally nor directly contribute to personal finances and consumer spending (sometimes the reverse). This meant that subsequent governments would have to come up with other creative ideas to generate Treasury income and stimulate the wider economy. So began the era of debt-driven accumulation. This came to be funded by a series of private-sector sources, from high street banks to the City to non-financial firms. Each provided new sources of private credit to fund everything from the expanding mortgage market and personal finance to long-term government infrastructure projects. The beauty was that this was all set in motion without the Treasury itself having to spend anything at all (at least not initially).

The UK was not alone in this shift. Ann Pettifor, in 2006, was the first to notice the larger pattern of debt-driven free-market economics in the US, UK and other supposedly wealthy, stable economies.[9] She had noticed a steady rise in personal, household debt levels, as individuals increased their mortgages, credit card borrowing and other loans. For Pettifor, the growing ranks of 'debtor-spenders' were stimulating economic growth through a cycle of borrowing, consumption and house buying. Her dire warnings of an imminent 'first world debt crisis' were ignored by mainstream economists, legislators and bureaucrats.

This is an account that has been explored by several authors in the US and UK since. All of these see a post-Keynesian demand management economic model being replaced from the 1980s onwards with a private, debt-based one.[10] 'Debt-fuelled consumption' increased as growth rates slowed and wages stagnated, coming to take the place of corporate and state investment in the economy. For Colin Crouch, 'privatized Keynesianism' meant that individuals rather than governments took on more debt as a way of stimulating the economy.

However, this is only half of the story. The other half is that UK governments started doing the same with their own finances, that is, covertly drawing heavily on sources of credit, first private then public (the Bank of England), to cover the annual budget gap, while also attempting to stimulate wider economic activity. Thus,

I use the term 'pseudo-Keynesianism', encompassing both privatized and covert government forms of economic stimulation. Without both of these the UK neoliberal economic paradigm would have shuddered to an early halt. As time went on, such activities became increasingly incorporated into public policymaking. But they also led to ever-growing private and public debt mountains.

To achieve all this required clever accounting and private-sector knowhow from outside the Treasury. Which takes us to the financial intermediaries and fixers who increasingly came to occupy senior positions in the Treasury over the period.

Rise of the financial fixers

In order to generate new revenues and stimulate the economy in alternative ways, the Treasury had to look beyond Whitehall for talent. As several people recount, real-world experience in finance and business was in short supply. Brilliant Oxbridge graduates, yes. Laser-focused microeconomists, tick. Capable civil service administrators, present. Actual private industry experience? Nope. As Geoffrey Robinson concluded: 'There's an other-worldliness about some of the officials in the Treasury – they never got out of there. They didn't know about industry, and they didn't know about the City.'

Thus, neither innovative ideas nor actual sources of revenue were likely to come out of 1 Horse Guards Road. That meant that, as each new government from Thatcher onwards tried to either radically alter economic policy or modernize Treasury practices, they found themselves inviting outside 'experts' in from across the private sector. Such individuals helped with everything from privatization and bank deregulation to generating new forms of taxation and capital. So began a limited but steady trickle of financial fixers into the Treasury.

Cecil Parkinson talked proudly of the teams he assembled from the LSE and elsewhere as he readied national industries for public sale. Sir Steve Robson, who worked on multiple privatizations, recounts his development of more enduring specialist teams in the Treasury, to work with other departments on the government's sales and private-sector contracts. Nicholas Macpherson watched this evolving trend, from Conservative through to New Labour:

> If you were in the business of doing large-scale privatiza-
> tion, it probably helped to have a few corporate financiers
> on secondment at the Treasury. You'd bring in expertise
> to deal with issues … I can remember in the 1990s there
> was a new fad under Ken Clarke for private finance, the
> Private Finance Initiative, which then got further
> momentum when Labour got in in '97 under Geoffrey
> Robinson, so you'd bring in people who would be good
> at doing private finance deals.

I talked to several such intermediaries who worked under both the Conservatives and Labour. They had substantial careers in both government and the private sector, usually working for an elite investment bank, one of the big four accountancy firms or top business consultancies. Often they moved back and forth between the two several times. They are typical of what Janine Wedel refers to as 'flexians'; elite power players who glide effortlessly between mobile, fluid private and public 'flex nets',[11] leveraging their knowledge and networks as they go. They have proved vital two-way players. On the one hand, they generated new sources of capital for governments and economies, and on the other, they enabled big business and finance to gain useful access lines to government.

One category of flexians are true believer civil servants, with pre-civil service careers in the private sector, who slowly gained senior positions in the Treasury. Here there are people like the late Jeremy Heywood. Between being principal private secretary to three chancellors (Lamont, Clarke and Brown), and becoming cabinet secretary in 2012, he had a four-year stint as a managing director at the investment bank Morgan Stanley. Heywood's name comes up periodically, usually in relation to how financiers got access to the top tiers of government. In 2021 news reports suggested he had done the same with the now collapsed Greensill Capital and supply chain finance.

The figures mentioned most to me were Sir Steve Robson and Sir John Kingman. Robson came to be known as 'Mr Privatization' for his work on public sales in the 1980s and 1990s. Those who mention him describe him as a free market true believer, convinced that public management was always inferior. 'I promise you it's ten times better than it ever was in public ownership', was his reported refrain whenever Geoffrey Robinson questioned how a privatization had gone. After leaving the civil service in the early 2000s he went on to sit on the boards of RBS and KPMG. Before becoming a senior Treasury stalwart, John Kingman had worked at Lazard investment bank and as a writer on the *FT*'s Lex column. In the middle of his Treasury career, he spent two years at Rothschilds and, upon leaving in 2016, became chairman of Legal and General. Both men not only zealously pushed privatization, PFI and other public–private initiatives, they acted as crucial linkmen to the City.

There were other, lesser-known intermediaries who, nonetheless, provided vital expertise on the private sector. Edward Troup and Chris Wales, expert accountants, came from Simmons and Simmons and Arthur Anderson respectively, and went on to advise Ken Clarke and Gordon Brown. These poachers-turned-gamekeepers brought their tax knowledge to the Treasury, helping both Clarke and Brown to create new taxes and counteract various tax-avoidance schemes. Both also continued to flit between private and public during their careers.

For the Conservatives, seconding private-sector experts was rather easier, as they already had wide corporate and financial networks to draw upon. For New Labour, things were more complicated. In advance of taking power in 1997, the shadow Treasury team had begun making City contacts with their 'prawn cocktail offensive'. Once in power, Brown and Balls began recruiting their private-sector fixers. Like a Hollywood heist movie, they gathered a diverse crew of expert advisors and personalities, all with varied skillsets and networks. United by an adherence to New Labour values, they came from accounting, business consultancy and the City itself.

Among those I met was Geoffrey Robinson (a suave Robert Vaughn). He was a valuable networker and talent recruiter to the cause. Robinson had had a lengthy business-cum-politics career in which he had floated between the Labour Party and industry executive positions, taking on a financial role in both. He was Brown's 'inside man' and 'fixer' and, fittingly, New Labour's first Paymaster General.

It was Robinson who helped persuade the senior Treasury official Sir Steve Robson to stay on with Labour after 1997. Robson, the institutional expert on privatization, was the seasoned 'safe-cracker' in the team, persuaded to stay on for one last job. He set Labour on their way to privatizing what they could at the start before retiring. Labour did manage to flog off NATS and BNFL,[12] as well as $3.5 billion of gold reserves. And Robinson was there to help pull in Chris Wales ('the fiscal fence'). He was one of three from the now defunct international accountancy firm Arthur Anderson. His key initial contribution was working out how to apply a one-off windfall tax on utilities companies according to sound accounting and legal principles.[13] He went on to develop a wider range of taxes to aid Labour spending.

In 1998 Robinson was caught bang to rights for secretly lending Peter Mandelson the money to buy a house. Upon his resignation, Shriti Vadera was lured from the investment bank Warburg to take on the talent-spotting and financial-networking roles. Shriti (now Baroness) Vadera comes up often in conversation. Vadera, who was more an enforcer than a charmer (more Jason Statham than Robert Vaughn), became one of Brown's core trusted advisors, later being appointed as a minister in the Brown government. She terrified the stiff upper lips at the Treasury while bringing in the knowhow and contacts of the City. In Dan Corry's estimation:

> Shriti, unlike most of us and most of the civil service, understood the City. I worked with her quite a lot on the Railtrack thing and she was very good because we had lots of officials that knew everything about trains … but the real issue was the City, and getting financial advice, and Shriti was very, very good on dealing with the City.

Vadera created the Shareholder Executive for managing government shares in private companies, and its sister body UKFI (UK Financial Investments), to deal with the nationalized banks after the banking collapse in 2007–08. These were later merged into UK Government Investments.

Others were to follow the City–Treasury pathway, often by bypassing usual Treasury recruitment procedures. Sir Adrian Montague came from the investment bank Dresdner Kleinwort and worked on the PFI taskforce of the Treasury. James Sassoon followed Vadera from Warburg where, among other things, he had worked with the Major government on a number of privatizations. Both helped set up bodies such as Partnerships UK, to manage PFI projects. Both, along with Vadera herself, were to eventually end up in the banking world once again.

I talked to most of these figures along with others there at the time. All strongly believed in private-sector supremacy when compared with plodding, inexperienced officialdom. The downsides of their activities, like the build-up of huge long-term government debt or the collapse of outsourced public services, were things they barely acknowledged. Each instead gave me a sense that they were there to bring necessary expertise and street sense into the Treasury. They developed financial management units that operated in ways more akin to their private-sector counterparts, thus producing contracts and practices that benefited both sides. The Treasury produced more robust contracts and reduced its risks while the private side could walk away with respectable profits.

However, downsides apart, the influx of private-sector expertise also had unforeseen consequences. Such figures helped build stronger links between the Treasury and the big investment bankers, business consultancies and accountants. They thus contributed to the revolving employment doors that spun ever more quickly between the Treasury and the private sector. Consequently, they were another means by which the UK government itself became subject to a form of privatization from the inside, whereby policies and practices changed the Treasury mindset to embrace commercial norms of public management.[14]

Labour's pseudo-Keynesianism

Part of Labour's metamorphosis into New Labour required its own very public rejection of the earlier Keynesian economic consensus. Blair, Brown and others had spent years trying to persuade business and financial leaders that they could be trusted with the economy. Doing so meant jettisoning established party commitments to public ownership, full employment, high levels of taxation, strong union rights and industrial intervention.

Before his death, John Smith had initiated this makeover with various overtures to the City. Tony Blair rebranded New Labour with his Clause 4 moment. Gordon Brown and his inner circle continued to make great efforts to work the business leader crowd. Prior to the 1997 election they declared they would stick to Tory tax and spending restrictions. Once in power, Brown continued to reduce tax rates for individuals and corporations, in much the same way the Conservatives had. His prudent and austere tendencies proved to be a natural match for the Treasury.[15] Various interviews made clear to me that Brown quietly harboured Old Labour proclivities but, in public, he rejected anything that could be construed as such. As Geoffrey Robinson put it: 'That was the thing, Gordon didn't want to be seen to be Old Labour in any way, but he was essentially Old Labour at heart, as we all were, except Ed [Balls].'

And yet Brown had larger ambitions. New Labour had grand plans for restoring public services and national infrastructure, alleviating poverty and developing a dynamic new economy. They too wanted to stimulate the economy towards growth without resorting to state ownership or active economic intervention. And, behind the scenes, Keynesian thinking was still seen as an intellectual source of inspiration. 'We were pretty Keynesian, although we were always worried about inflation ... I always wanted us to be much more interventionist', said Dan Corry.

Labour's ambitious spending plans, as well as needing to stimulate the economy in new ways, required capital. With few assets to sell off, and greater public borrowing and debt rejected, Labour was going to have to adapt. Chris Wales and his Arthur Anderson team proved useful for implementing Labour's windfall tax on the privatized utilities, and for generating innovative new taxes. By such means, Brown was able to lower headline personal income and corporation taxes while still increasing the tax take as a proportion of GDP overall. But rather more was needed to restore struggling public services, invest in new schools, hospitals and transport, and kick start the new UK twenty-first-century economy.

Which is where private finance initiatives (PFI) came in. PFI, private investment with government guarantees but no up-front costs, seemed the magic formula. The idea originated in Norman Lamont's time. Ken Clarke wanted to get it going but told me that few PFI-style projects were enacted under him, for lack of investor buy-in to the crumbling Major government, and a lack of faith that a Labour government would see the projects through. But investor scepticism proved wrong as Brown jumped on the idea. As Geoffrey Robinson recounts in his autobiography, despite criticism from across the political spectrum, Labour put their 'fingers in the PFI'.[16] And New Labour's band of financial fixers were key to operationalizing the PFI initiative. Lord Sassoon explains the logic:

> The basic strategy and approach were that infrastructure and other big public investments could be better, in the sense of more cheaply and efficiently, procured in the private sector. The actual additional funding costs in the private sector were more than outweighed by the gains in efficient procurement of the asset. That was the underlying philosophy, one that incidentally Steve Robson aided by Adrian Montague had done much to put in place … with concentrated pools of outside specialists who were working on the implementation of a range of public private partnerships.

For another flexian fixer who drove developments inside the Treasury, it was all about creating a professionalized operation within the Exchequer, one that could direct activities across government departments and public entities up and down Britain. Thus was born Partnerships UK, a new unit designed to upscale PFI initiatives. That former official recounts intentions at the time:

> We created something called Partnerships UK, which professionalized the role of advising across the whole of government, in particular local authorities, who were the main clients, who were mainly the people doing the PFI, because hospitals and schools, etc. being built, … So, we increased some of the standardization and we also provided some experts, a combination of

people that came from the Treasury and some private-sector people ... made up of 30, 40 people at various points.

Such was the thinking of those setting up Partnerships UK that it was decided it should become an independent Plc, half owned by the Treasury and half by private investors; in other words, a private consultancy run for profit by the Treasury and its private partners. As one official, central to creating the new organization, explained:

> We adopted a privatization model of having a unit in the Treasury which would be a centre of expertise and support for the people in departments doing these projects ... initially in the public sector and then it was spun out of the public sector and into a life of its own, as a company that was jointly owned by the Treasury ... the feeling was that it really wasn't the Treasury's job to provide free consultancy to other departments forever. So, let's change it into a paid for thing, let's make it very much private sector in its manning ... So, it gradually became much more private sector in its staffing and became paid for.

In 2012 the Treasury released the details of PFI projects dating back to 1992, but mostly initiated under New Labour. 719 projects with a capital value of £54.7 billion had been completed or were in process. They included 118 NHS building projects with a capital value of £11.6 billion.[17]

I asked several who were there about PFI. Balls, Kingman, Robson and all the financial intermediaries who came in to organize its development put a rather positive spin on it: 'more efficient procurement'; 'vital for generating new investment for infrastructure'; 'professionalized government operations, delivering projects far cheaper'; 'moving government risks to private providers'. However, what some admitted with a bit of prompting was that the main reason PFI was extended was because of how it looked on the Treasury's books. With each year, more of them came to be set up as 'off balance sheet', meaning they didn't show up as conventional government spending or debt.

Many long-standing Treasury mandarins had a very different view of what had happened, largely against their advice. Two former Treasury permanent secretaries, Lord Turnbull and Lord O'Donnell, did not hold back in their criticisms to me of what had transpired and why. It was something cooked up by advisors, keen to give Gordon Brown what he wanted. According to one senior official:

> I was opposed to it. I had rows with people like Steve Robson and Shriti Vadera, a whole range of people ... their arguments for it were we need more investment. We need more public sector investment, so we want to build more hospitals and schools and all the rest of it. We can't do it the traditional way because that'll show up as debt and debt is bad, so we need to do it this way. Total crap! ... at the time these things were classified off balance sheet, which meant that they were, quotes, 'free', you know. So, when you're an activist person like Gordon and you worry that you're going to be attacked from the right for putting debt up too much, when someone comes to you and says, 'don't worry, you can spend a lot more money and it won't show up as debt',

it's like wow this is really clever. And I'm afraid I lost every single argument on that ... I regard that as a personal failure.

What everyone really knew but wanted to ignore was that PFI would leave growing future liabilities. The same 2012 Treasury release also revealed that the £54.7 billion of capital value projects would eventually cost £301 billion in repayments over 30–40 years. In many cases, repayments would rise slowly, only peaking several years hence. A number of NHS and other projects would end up saddled with huge annual debt repayments and very expensive service contracts, making some institutions financially unviable.[18] In effect, if privatization involved 'selling off the family silver', PFI was about selling any future silver, as well as the future dining table and dinnerware too.

PFI had been widely condemned by the Conservatives, officials and public accounts committees during Labour's tenure. But the disturbing reality is that after 2010 it never went away. It just metamorphosed into different forms. George Osborne was highly critical of the practice as shadow chancellor. But as chancellor in the Coalition years (2010–15), he signed off on 61 new PFI projects worth £6.9 billion within a year.[19] He then devised a new version called PF2. As one recent senior official put it with a great sense of frustration:

Things like PFI were extraordinary, I just didn't understand why the Treasury promoted PFI. George Osborne said PFI was a discredited Gordon Brown policy and then replaced it with something that was basically identical, called PF2 … because he had such strict PSND[20] targets he wanted to find a way to keep things off balance sheet if he could. So likewise, Hinkley Point had to be done off balance sheet which is why it's so extremely expensive. If we'd done it on balance sheet it would have been a whole lot cheaper.

The student tuition fees system, which came into being under the Coalition, was another off-balance-sheet scheme. Loans did not register as expenditure and would only be declared thirty years into the future when bad debts would be written off. Estimates were that up to 45% of all such loans, running to several billion pounds each year, would not be paid back.[21] 'Ridiculous. It was actually very bad policy for a number of reasons', says that same official. 'But under public sector accounting it was free because you didn't actually pay for it until the end of the loan's life.' Unless checked, the scheme threatens to be more costly to the Exchequer than all the PFI projects combined. By December 2021 the value of outstanding loans was calculated to be £160 billion and, if this continues, the figure is expected to reach £560 billion by the mid-century (at 2019–20 prices).[22]

PFI was officially abandoned by Philip Hammond only in 2018, not because of the debts and other problems highlighted in endless reports, but because it came to be reclassified once more as on-balance-sheet debt. So, as several officials admitted, 'what would be the point of it?' Even then, as Hammond explained to me, a core part of the PFI logic was still in place and ready to be exploited during and post COVID. Governments that wanted the private sector to be more involved in funding chosen schemes were already making use of what he called 'contingent liability':

> I had already discovered, and my successor would have easily spotted the joys of contingent liabilities in public accounting. You can offer any number of guarantees but don't use public money. Let the private sector do things and underwrite them with a guarantee that doesn't show up anywhere as a contingent liability. It only shows up if it crystallizes in our public finances. We're talking about eye-wateringly large sums of money being pumped into the economy. But actually doing it through the banks, with sovereign guarantees underpinning, is a very neat way by the Treasury. And I predict that tool will not be abandoned ... That will be PFI mark 3.

And then there was quantitative easing (QE). This was introduced in the aftermath of the financial crisis in 2007–08, when private finance initiatives were never going to fund the massive financial and economic fallout. So the Bank of England worked with the Treasury to create electronic money to buy back government bonds from companies. This emergency and temporary action gave the government much-needed funds. But it was also meant to stimulate the economy by increasing investment and capital flows at a time when banks were in survival mode and not lending. In 2009 £200 billion was created.

However, what was temporary has now become the norm. There have been five more rounds of QE since then. By the end of 2020, £895 billion of such funds had been generated with no account of how they would be returned in the future. There is also evidence to show that they did more to inflate asset prices (property, shares) than they did to stimulate real-world economic activity.[23] In Norman Lamont's and Peter Middleton's views (they were not the only ones), QE was yet another sleight of hand economic stimulus with problematic side-effects:

> There is not much money around in the public sector. It's usually short of money. It's usually running a deficit of some sort. So quantitative easing is funded, not by the Bank of England, but by Treasury loans, which are never going to be repaid ... but what you do is stimulate more and more consumption, so you get a completely unbalanced economy.

Through PFI, QE and smaller schemes, New Labour found a pseudo-Keynesian formula for increasing income and spending significantly while also reducing headline taxes. Once again, for the Treasury the main objective was to keep the budget and borrowing under control. At the same time, new capital flows continued to be flushed around the economy as a result of policies and off-balance-sheet public spending. Both public-sector PFI projects and financial-sector growth brought jobs, taxable income, sustained employment and a general feel-good effect in the wider economy. The Conservatives of the last decade adopted these approaches too and added their own-brand versions to the mix. But in all cases, the short- and medium-term fixes were storing up large amounts of future debt and potential instabilities.

The great housing market bubble

One important form of pseudo-Keynesianism, promoted by both Conservative and Labour administrations, has been the continued growth of the housing market. Political leaders of both left and right saw the value of a buoyant real-estate market to job creation and middle-class homeowners. Likewise, both the financial sector and the Treasury saw property development and the housing market as important sources of revenue. Thus, politicians, bankers and officials did what they could to keep it all going. Rather conveniently, all those in charge also ignored the long-term implications of these policies and the unpleasant side-effects that would follow.

In the 1980s Thatcher's ministers not only enacted 'Right-to-Buy' and liberated bank mortgage lending, they also encouraged the private housing market to bloom in multiple other ways. In 1975 Labour had introduced a land development tax of 80%. That was cut down in stages and then abolished altogether in the 1985 budget. The Tories also introduced mortgage interest relief (MIR) to encourage continued activity when interest rates were high. MIR, the 'sacred cow of Mrs Thatcher's housing policy', grew and was maintained in spite of Treasury objections and declining inflation through the decade. The 1988 Housing Act abolished rent controls and liberalized the private rental sector. This in conjunction with buy-to-let schemes encouraged more house buying and selling.[24] But, as Peter Middleton explained, successive Tory governments were loath to intervene to slow the boom:

> Let's say you get a housing bubble, which is the one governments have wrestled with during the whole of my time. You then put the lid on it and then you come under huge pressure because house prices aren't going up, which is regarded as a sign of a difficult economy ... a stagnant housing market is never very good for your economy. It's one of the places where people put their money.

Nothing much changed under Blair and Brown. Right-to-buy continued. Previous Labour leaderships had pledged to introduce land development taxes, and to maintain or raise capital gains taxes on property. Neither happened after 1997. Instead, capital gains continued to drop. In 2003 they further removed planning restrictions on developers. They had their own tax incentive schemes for house buyers. As lending levels and house values rose, so did credit-debt. In the decade up to 2007–08, private credit creation increased by 10% a year, well above the general growth rates of 2–3%.[25] Between 1995 and 2005 household debt as a percentage of disposable income increased by 53%.[26] For Gus O'Donnell, New Labour was as reluctant to change things as the Conservatives:

> The housing market has been a big issue for many, virtually all my time in the Treasury. When I started working for Nigel Lawson, I remember doing something ... that was a theme throughout the whole of my time there ... the Treasury trying to get a more sensible

taxation system on housing, and ministers being very reluctant to move on it.

But, of course, the Treasury also benefited from an ever-rising housing market with a large turnover of properties. Every sale bought capital gains. As with the financial sector, housing, pure and simple, was a regular form of revenue. In Edward Troup's estimation, 'to a certain extent the booming housing market has been milked at the upper end by ramping up stamp duty rates'. As Chris Wales acknowledged, taxable housing income was in the forefront of officials' minds:

> It wasn't that people weren't aware that house prices were going up. Obviously, it was a big driver of stamp duty revenues, so we were inevitably conscious that the buoyancy in the house market was leading to better revenues in that area … It provided room to pull some other levers and reduce some of the burdens of taxation in areas where it needed it. So, growth in the housing market, if it helped me to do something that was quite valuable in terms of relieving the tax burden somewhere else, then I was quite happy.

The housing market also contributed to the expanding financial sector which itself brought generous tax revenues and aided Treasury objectives (see Chapter 3). In fact, for several authors, the two sectors were mutually reinforcing developments, feeding off each other.[27] After the 1970s, a virtuous circle was set in motion. Vince Cable explained the system that was still in place in the 2010s: 'We had an economy increasingly reliant on domestic credit, borrowing, property markets and other factors, which were reinforcing each other. The banks lend on property, so when property increases in price, banks lend more to them.' Thus, homeowners could borrow more for further consumption or property investment. And all the while personal mortgage debt continued to rise. Between 1987 and 2014, outstanding mortgage debt increased by 781%.

Finance continued to expand itself on the back of this cycle. Securitization, whereby loans were transformed into mortgage-backed securities (MBSs) for trading on financial markets, smoothed this growth. By 2007 an estimated €531 billion of outstanding mortgage loans were being traded in EU financial markets as MBSs.[28]

What became disturbingly clear during my interviews with former ministers and officials from the New Labour era was how abstract a phenomenon the housing market was to them. Promoting it was a stated political and economic objective that encouraged economic activity and pleased middle-class voters as their homes increased in value. It was also a great source of taxable revenue. But as Chris Wales also explained, there was no expert knowledge of the housing market in the Treasury. Neither was there any attempt to think through how the cumulative impacts of different property-related taxes might impact upon individuals:

> There wasn't necessarily enough appetite to address things in a kind of holistic way. Property has so many interfaces with the tax system … it's about the whole

spectrum of tax issues from council tax through to stamp duties on purchase, to capital gains tax and inheritance tax issues, and the VAT treatment of real estate ... but there wasn't really a suitable framework in the Treasury through which to work together. There was no team at the Treasury for whom property was at the centre ... but from a taxpayer's perspective, actually they're dealing with all of these things simultaneously.

More than that, housing itself was excluded from wider economic planning and thinking altogether in the Treasury. Housing costs figured relatively little in wider macroeconomic calculations. In 2003 they were removed altogether in the switch from the RPI to CPI[29] method of calculating inflation.[30] So, although the largest annual expenditure by most individuals was on either rent or mortgage repayments, changes to these were excluded.

In fact, housing, like financial activity itself, was bracketed out from the mainstream economic thinking and macroeconomic models being deployed in the Treasury.[31] For several observers, these omissions lay at the heart of government and regulatory failures in the lead-up to the financial crash (see Chapter 6). As Steve Keen writes, the DSGE models[32] that came to dominate macroeconomic theory in treasuries and central banks everywhere conveniently omitted these as well as other forms of private debt. Ever-mounting debts, housing and financial bubbles were all disregarded as potential threats to the economy. Looking back, some years after his retirement, Lord Turnbull sees just how this self-serving institutional groupthink developed prior to 2007–08:

> What was going on here was the Government was a beneficiary of taxes, through capital gains tax, stamp duty, VAT, receipts were buoyant, bankers' bonuses, usually a lot of tax. So somehow or other, why should they rock the boat, because it looked as though our financial position was actually rather good. But it turned out that there was a lot of self-delusion in that, we had misjudged what the real underlying growth rate was … Asset prices didn't really feature at all, because we made the silly move from the RPI to the CPI … that meant we were looking at a basket of consumer goods excluding housing. Virtually everything you looked at in all these things here, all made in the Far East, were coming in at a very, very low prices.

The Coalition government after 2010 showed that few lessons had been learned. George Osborne and his team launched their own schemes to get the ailing housing market going again in 2012 and 2013. Such schemes used the 'contingent liability' method of encouraging banks to lend again to house buyers by offering them cheap credit and guarantees. In a senior advisor's words: 'it wasn't the government spending more money directly through fiscal policy … we were using the government balance sheet in other ways to stimulate the economy'. All involved then denied that they might have been contributing to another housing bubble. According to one official, Osborne responded to such concerns at the time saying: 'if it drives up house prices that would be a high-quality problem'.

Ultimately, the Treasury as an institution developed a sort of split personality when it came to thinking and policy with regard to both finance and housing. On the one hand, officials and ministers were acutely aware of the fundamental importance of those sectors to the economy and the Treasury itself. Apart from drawing in hefty revenues, they also stimulated activity and employment in the wider economy. They seemed like magical, natural resources. Helping them continue could only be good. On the other hand, the same Treasury managed to disregard them; to treat them as organic, self-correcting markets and to bracket them out of its macroeconomic models. This ability to exploit both yet, intellectually, remove all responsibility for their development now seems a truly grand act of self-deception.

Conclusion

In June 2017 Theresa May, in response to questions about restricted public spending, repeatedly stated that there was no 'magic money tree'. Governments couldn't just tax and spend as they wanted indefinitely. The phrase and the thinking behind it are contested. However, the main point made throughout this chapter is that there have indeed been multiple magic money trees identified and exploited by the Treasury since 1979.

For Thatcher's chancellors the first was the annual windfall that came with selling off state-owned industries and the large stock of council houses. The second came from the deregulation of the financial sector, started by the Conservatives, and further pushed by New Labour (see Chapter 3). This facilitated widespread private credit creation, hugely expanding bank capital levels, and provided a large source of taxable income to the Treasury. The third, linked to the second, was the pumped-up housing market, again both spurring economic activity and bringing in Exchequer revenue. Labour developed two more of their own: PFI and quantitative easing.

The great thing about all these sources of capital was that they didn't seem to cost the Treasury anything at the time (apart from the costs incurred by all those advisors, fixers and financial intermediaries). They either didn't show up on the balance sheet or appeared to be natural forms of capital, drawn from external sources. Each, in their own way, appeared to stimulate activity in the wider economy without direct state intervention. Each could be presented in market terms, thus adding to the idea that old-style Keynesian forms of demand management remained part of the past. Keynesianism but not Keynesianism.

Unfortunately, big costs were incurred. But these usually came much later, with the bill falling to later administrations. So, as council houses came to be sold off, and the private rental sector expanded, the Thatcher government eventually found itself paying out more in housing benefit than it had received from the sales themselves. The debts incurred by PFI were eventually forced back on to the Treasury's balance sheets as the statisticians reclassified them. The direct costs of the bank bailouts after 2007–08 were larger than the tax receipts gathered from the financial sector going back to Big Bang. Government deficits were to spiral upwards as both the housing and financial markets collapsed, and the economy entered recession and an extended period of stagnation.

In addition to government debt there was corporate debt, extensive public institutional debts (from PFI) and ballooning personal debt. In the late 1970s the private debt to GDP ratio was 60%. That rose to 127% in 1991 and to 197% by 2009.[33] Total UK household debt reached £1.5 trillion by 2014 and individual student debt had increased to £54 billion. Some 9 million people, or 18% of the population, were classified as 'over-indebted'.

5

Visions of empire and globalization: the rise of the internationalists

In 2022 there appear to be a number of competing visions of Britain's place in the international economic system. One of those, espoused by Boris Johnson and his varied supporters, is nationalist and expansionist, and is linked to a past age of empire. Like other such governments, there is a push to strengthen borders and cast aside international institutions and cooperative agreements. By such means lies the possibility of 'taking back control', including control of the UK's position in the global economy. Brexit means that Britain is once again able to roam freely across the world, able to establish its own international operations and to restore its earlier 'greatness'.[1]

This vision stands in stark contrast to two alternative but overlapping internationalist views. One of these is deeply enshrined in the Exchequer. A strong part of the Treasury orthodoxy, going back to William Gladstone's time, is manifested in its support for free trade and anti-mercantilism. It is not that the Treasury is opposed to empire per se. In fact, the Treasury and the British Empire share a long history of mutual support and profit. Rather, the Treasury sees other, modern forms of internationalism as being more beneficial to its own and the nation's economic interests.

The third position, which has become increasingly strong across the political and professional classes over recent decades, espouses a modern liberal ideal of globalization, cooperation and cosmopolitanism. Leading figures in UK governments, from Margaret Thatcher to David Cameron, believed all forward-thinking leaders had no choice but to embrace the new reality and guide the British economy accordingly.

The first vision I believe to be rather fanciful and outdated. But, as I argue here, the latter forms of internationalism, contrary to Treasury and political thinking, have been fairly fanciful too. They have brought many positives but have also thrown up long-term negatives for the UK. If anything, their policies have had the effect of hollowing out Britain's economy, an almost reversal of imperial expansion. In recent decades the Exchequer and successive chancellors have reshaped the UK economy from a nation that secures economic advantage through foreign exploitation, to a country that attempts to profit by selling its assets, services and people to others.

How did this come about? As this chapter explains, following the dismantling of state economic management and controls in the early Thatcher years, the Treasury strongly embraced the older free-trade Gladstonian philosophy that had once served the empire-based model of the British economy so well. Similarly, successive governments focused, not on supporting home-grown industries, but on gaining international competitive advantage by luring foreign multinationals, investment, ideas and innovation to UK shores.

However, the reality did not always match the ideals of the Treasury and leading politicians. There were many unforeseen outcomes. The opening up of UK Plc also meant handing over the economy to the fickle management of foreign-owned investment banks, mobile multinationals, super-rich expats and international investors. Their priorities were no more aligned to the interests of UK citizens than those of former British imperialists had been to the foreign nationals of the Empire.

The Treasury, empire and open economy

The Treasury and the British Empire share a long and varied history. It stands to reason that the oldest and most powerful department of state would always support the national economic interest. And so it has. It just hasn't always been clear on whether that's best achieved by having a more open or closed economy.

The first major overhaul of the Treasury was driven by Charles II's need to fund his wars with European rivals in 1668. A more powerful Exchequer enhanced the ability of monarchs to successfully finance military actions.[2] In various historical accounts the British state also worked hand in hand with industrialists and merchants to expand its formal (and informal) empire.[3] As Britain's industrial revolution made it the 'workshop' of the world, so the Treasury funded expansion overseas and profited accordingly. As well as contributing financially to the military and administrative infrastructure of empire, the Treasury advocated the imperialist doctrine of mercantilism. This nationalist economic policy, common across Europe in the sixteenth to eighteenth centuries, supported home-grown industries and exports, and restricted imports with high tariffs.

In various accounts, Gladstone's ascendancy in the nineteenth century marks the period when an alternative Treasury doctrine became firmly established. William Gladstone's four decades of parliamentary dominance included four stints as Chancellor of the Exchequer. There he overhauled civil service practices and changed the Exchequer's philosophy forever. Gladstonian liberalism advocated free trade, laissez-faire economics, low taxes, small states and balanced budgets.

According to revisionist historical accounts, such policies aided expansion of the British Empire in some fundamental ways. For Ingham, and Cain and Hopkins, 'gentlemanly capitalism' provided the real thrust of Britain's imperial success in the nineteenth century.[4] They argue that the biggest overseas push was led, not by industrialists, but by a combination of the wealthy landed gentry and emerging City elites. Right at the centre of 'gentlemanly capitalism' lay the triangle of the Treasury, the Bank of England and the City of

London. Each of these institutions shared and profited from the combination of imperialist expansion and the Gladstonian philosophy of an open economy. Between them they enabled the City's banking and financial services sector to multiply in all directions, while making London the 'clearing house' of the world. The Square Mile slowly made itself integral to multiple elements of global trade and finance. The profits from these activities also made an invaluable contribution to Exchequer coffers and to the national balance of payments. And this success story was maintained by a strict institutional adherence to free trade, free markets and the sterling–gold standard.

All this worked exceptionally well for Britain until the First World War. Two world wars, the depression, the decline of empire, and the new managed, Keynesian economic policies each obstructed the previous, free-flowing regime. The gold standard broke down and sterling ceased to be the world's reserve currency. Consequently, the Treasury and the financial sector lost political influence and global economic hegemony. Keynesianism meant that the British economy had become not only more state-managed, but also far more inward-looking and self-contained. As Alan Budd explained:

> The world in which these Keynesians had grown up with, was this post-war world in which international capital market movements were very controlled, there was a fixed exchange rate, there were exchange controls, there was rationing. At the end of the war we reverted to being a fairly closed economy. So, these international

forces, although they're still important, were nothing
like what they became.

Circumstances changed once again in the ten years
that followed the 1976 IMF bailout. In many ways the
period marks the point when the UK economy went
back to the future; back to being international, returning
in various respects to its pre-1914 incarnation. As
Keynesianism and industrial intervention were dropped,
the older, Gladstonian Treasury philosophy resurfaced.[5]
Fundamental to this was the opening up of the UK to
the global economy once again.

Just how internationalist and Gladstonian the Treasury
default position now is became clear to me when talking
to several of its former permanent secretaries. Foremost
among these in recent decades is Lord Macpherson. I
met Macpherson at the offices of C. Hoare & Co. in
Fleet Street. This is Britain's oldest privately owned
bank, and he has been chairman there since leaving
the Treasury in 2016. It looks like a Hollywood reimagin-
ing of a nineteenth-century London bank (think Gringotts
in *Harry Potter* but without the goblins). Meeting
Macpherson here in some ways brought to mind those
elements of a previous era of wealth, internationalism
and Treasury–City networks.

Macpherson spent thirty-one years at the Treasury
and was its longest-serving post-war permanent secretary.
He oversaw regimes as diverse as Brown's big public
spending years and Osborne's imposed austerity ones.
Yet through these quite different political regimes,

Macpherson maintains that there was a long-standing 'Treasury view' and has conveyed this in various talks. His 2014 Mile End speech makes everything very clear.[6] Ten core elements are sketched out. The first of these, taking up most space, is 'a belief in free trade'. As he states, 'the Treasury has always been opposed to protectionism and mercantilism'.

These core ideas came through again during our conversation. Repeated throughout was the idea that free trade sits centrally in the broader philosophy of free markets and non-intervention. Their combination is what economies thrive on. Nations should embrace them accordingly:

> If you stay at the Treasury long enough, I think there is a tendency to realize that there are limits to what the government can do to support economic activity ... there's quite a strong antipathy towards trying to rig markets, which is one of the reasons why I think historically it's been attracted to free trade ... The Treasury, I think it's fair to say has always favoured multilateralism ... it's better not to discriminate when it comes to trade policy in terms of tariffs and so on.

It was clear, talking to Macpherson and others, that after 1979, renewing the British economy would involve opening it up once again. Britain was a small island nation. Its open economy and expansionist trading history had been essential elements underpinning its past economic success. So, it was hoped, they would again in the future.

Opening up the UK again in the 1980s was marked in various ways. Three particular areas are worth noting.

The first of these was the decision taken by the new Thatcher government to end currency exchange controls. This took place in stages between 1979 and 1981. According to Geoffrey Howe, Thatcher's first chancellor, such moves preceded domestic policy shifts towards a more market-led economy. As Howe admitted, no one was quite sure what would happen next: 'I told Margaret then that I'd decided we really had to get rid of exchange controls completely. And her reaction was slightly light-hearted. She said "Well, on your own head be it Geoffrey." Because one didn't know exactly what the consequences would be.'

In Howe's account things worked out and he kept going.[7] For others looking back, this change, not widely debated at the time, proved very significant for the wider policy shift. Macpherson, in his Mile End speech, said: 'The abolition of exchange controls in 1979 was one of its [the Treasury's] greatest triumphs.' Nigel Lawson explained to me that: 'Freedom of capital movement is, if anything, more contributing to the change in the nature of the world economy than free trade.'

A second key step towards internationalization came with the deregulation of the City of London. The talks for this began in 1983 when the financial sector was regulated by the DTI. A long-running court case had been challenging the restrictive practices of the Square Mile. The case was expected to run on for years with no clear outcome. For Cecil Parkinson, Nigel Lawson and others, ending the City's cosy monopolies would be a way of restoring it to its former position in the global economy. For Alan Budd, 'The world of international finance was changing dramatically, and if London wished to be part of it, it had to change.'

Both Parkinson and Lawson believed that if the City agreed to open itself up, this would better achieve their aims than resolving the outstanding legal case. Returning London's financial sector to its previous international prominence was the larger goal. As Parkinson explained:

> We wanted the big players to come into our market. If we were going to compete with Wall Street, if we were going to have a role as a world class financial centre, then you couldn't have a little local centre and securities market. You had to have a market where all the big players were there and so it wasn't an accident that they came. It was opened up so that they would.

The 1986 Financial Services Act ('Big Bang'), which ultimately followed, did everything hoped for. As well as modernizing the trading technology, it ended the exclusive, insider networks of the City and allowed entry to international players. Big foreign banks, capital and knowhow flowed into London.

The third step was the move towards economic integration within the European single market. Ironically, from today's post-Brexit vantage point, Britain took the lead. In Philip Hammond's view: 'The European Union today would look incredibly different from what it does if the UK had never been in the single market. It was a British invention.' Arthur Cockfield, a former Treasury minister, led Britain's delegation to Europe. The Thatcher government saw developments here as a way to promote

its free-market and anti-protectionist ideals.[8] In John
Gieve's recollection:

> Arthur Cockfield … was perhaps the most important
> forger of the concept of the single market in Europe.
> On that front we had great success in the Thatcher
> years, in spreading the idea of free and open markets
> through this concept of the single market with mutual
> recognition of standards, which Cockfield had been quite
> an important generator of.

This resulted in the 1986 Single European Act, pushing
the principles of free movement in goods, services,
capital and people. It also tied the British economy
more to the EU rather than to its former colonies of
the Commonwealth.

By these and other means, Britain's economy was
once again forced open and pushed to integrate with
an additional set of forces and organizations. However,
the British and world economies of the late twentieth
century were very different from those of the immediate
post-war period and even more different than those of
the late nineteenth century. In 1945 Britain was still a
world power; 25% of all world trade in manufacturing
came from the UK and half the world's trade was
conducted in sterling.[9] In 1979 Britain had far fewer of
the international advantages it had had before: no reserve
currency, no sprawling set of colonies to exploit, no
world-leading industrial base, and relatively smaller
concentrations of wealth on home soil. Opening up to
the global economy was going be different this time.
This form of internationalization was not likely to

benefit the British economy in the same ways it did in the years of empire.

Internationalism not national ownership and identity

My first understanding of why things were different this time came when talking to Lord Turnbull. We met at his office in the House of Lords. This involved climbing doggedly up a long staircase to reach the top of what he called the 'Gormenghast Tower'.[10] Like Macpherson, Turnbull had a long, distinguished career in the civil service, with roles that included being Mrs Thatcher's principal private secretary, the Treasury permanent secretary and the head of the civil service.

Turnbull spoke with a gruff but grand authority. Our interview was more of a monologue, delivered with the forcefulness of an articulate sergeant major. With barely a word from me, Turnbull worked his way through some of the questions I had sent him beforehand. From time to time, I managed to squeeze in a follow-up query.

It was when I asked about the decline of British industry in the 1980s that I got a particular, jolting insight. 'What do you mean by industry?', he demanded. 'Manufacturing, particularly in the regions', I answered. 'Oh right. That had been declining since about the 1880s', he boomed. I plucked up courage and interrupted again: 'but it declined a lot faster than Germany or other European countries at the time. What happened to our industrial strategy?' I then felt the full force of his Windsor Davies. His tone suggested he was having to explain something basic to someone who should know better:

> Well the Treasury is an anti-mercantilist place. It doesn't believe that there is something magic about the production of goods. It believes what matters is value added … the great charge against Thatcher is that she destroyed coal, steel, shipbuilding, where I think the right observation is that she put them out of their misery! … But what matters is you're generating employment and value added and tax revenues out of something that is sustainable, and I don't think it matters whether it's car production or financial services.

I was expecting the 'so what?' response to my decline of UK industry question. For many interviewees and commentators this had been a historical inevitability. Cheaper, skilled labour from emerging economies came to undercut the wealthy economies of the West.

What I wasn't quite ready for was the idea that it didn't matter whether or not we even had UK-based companies or manufacturing. When Turnbull said 'anti-mercantilist' he didn't just mean opposition to tariffs. He also meant opposition to any measures that protected national industries. Such supports were regarded as an impediment to producing competitive, innovative companies and efficient markets in the UK. Thus, any concern for British industry was misplaced romanticism.

If I had any doubts about that, talking to other top Treasury officials and chancellors confirmed this broader interpretation. Norman Lamont, John Major's chancellor for three years, stated: 'What matters is economic activity and prosperity, not [national] ownership ... I don't think a product really has a nationality.' Terry Burns, permanent secretary for most of the 1990s, focused very much on the national economic benefits of free trade. As he explained, protectionism was the easier short-term political choice but was always bad economically in the long run, and the Treasury had to resist it:

> One of the fundamental issues of economics is that long-term protection works against the interests of the country, and that you are better off with competition and having new entries. It is tough when people say 'Well look, all these jobs are being destroyed' ... It's one that the Treasury's had to face up to throughout. But by and large the people who have been chancellors have supported that ... I think the UK is probably less protectionist than almost any of the major countries.

These same figures had overseen the winding down of state support for UK-based industry across the country in the 1980s and early 1990s. In addition to hacking the DTI back (see Chapter 3), big infrastructure programmes that supported regional industry were cut drastically. They went from 4.07% of public expenditure in 1974 to just 0.92% by 1988.[11] One by one, the National Enterprise Board, the National Economic Development Council and its various offices were all closed down across the regions.

This almost anti-nationalist philosophy was similarly reproduced in relation to citizenship and national identity. Whenever I brought up the topic of immigration with former Treasury officials and chancellors, it became clear that a long-standing policy of the department was to strongly support this on purely economic grounds. Alistair Darling, chancellor in the Brown years, explained the thinking more broadly:

> The Treasury view is, and always has been, that immigration is essential for the future prosperity of this country … Most immigrants are hardworking. They contribute rather than the opposite. And that's the dominant view … The Treasury ethos generally speaking is that anything that stimulates economic activity is a good thing. And they are blind in a nice sort of way, not a pejorative way, to people's nationality and all the rest of it.

Speaking to David Cameron some years later, it was clear that he had struggled with this enduring blunt economic logic with its politically costly blind spots: 'The Treasury just believed that immigration was a good thing, it increased GDP, not necessarily GDP per capita, but there was an economic benefit that was worth capturing.' For Nicholas Macpherson, little had changed even in the anti-immigrant, post-Brexit years: 'Even now, and I saw it under George Osborne and I'm sure it's happening under Philip Hammond, it will be the Treasury which is arguing for the least restrictions on, say, skilled migration.'

From this perspective, those at the Treasury have thought relatively little about national identity and how that has evolved over centuries across the communities and regions of Britain. Citizens, like capital flows and corporations, are mobile entities. The most able of them gravitate to the countries with the best political and economic systems. Any sense of national character is of secondary importance next to individual economic rationality. People are more attracted to economic opportunity than to place and culture.

For each of these top officials, national ownership and identity really do not seem to matter very much. If anything, the subtext is that British ownership, on account of its molly-coddled, state-owned past, is probably substandard. Similarly, national place of birth is less important than an ability to contribute positively to a national economy. Whichever government has been in charge, the 'Treasury view' remains consistent. Officials prioritize 'economic thinking' in the service of the nation, over what they see as misguided nationalist sentiment about the economy and its citizenry.

This view has had various consequences for the nature of the British economy and wider society. These were to become painfully clear in the 2016 EU referendum (see Chapter 7).

The political classes embrace globalization

If the 1980s were about opening up again to the international economy, the 1990s had a new term: globalization. Pretty much every senior politician I spoke to for this book, from the 1990s until the end of the Cameron government, positively embraced the ideals of globalization. They did so far more than the public perceived. Prime ministers and chancellors tend to play down their positive engagement here, preferring to be reported in the media as standing up for Britain's interests on the world stage.

It's only when you read their autobiographies or speak to them in person that you realize just how much several generations had adopted the liberal internationalist and cosmopolitan values of the new creed. Ken Clarke truly embraced the emerging philosophy before the term existed. He speaks warmly and enthusiastically about his engagements at ECOFIN,[12] the G7, Washington meetings and the Clinton administration when chancellor. He also supported EU membership to the bitter end:

> I was in favour of the international order. I spent an astonishing amount of my time at meetings with my international colleagues. At ECOFIN, I got very close to my European colleagues, and we were doing a lot of work preparing for the single currency which we were all in favour of … The G7 were seriously good in normal meetings. We used to meet at various places around the world and I got to know and coincided with three [US] Treasury Secretaries … and they were all trying to go together, what got called the Great Normality, applying these rules, applying the principles of free trade, trying to move towards developing the globalized economy … it was a time in which tremendous laws and reforms were being initiated.

Nicholas Macpherson sees an internationalist line running through from Ken Clarke up to Philip Hammond.[13] The same sense of enthusiasm for liberal internationalism is as clear in the autobiographies/biographies of Clarke and Brown as it is in those of Cameron and Osborne.[14] As Macpherson reflects:

> All these governments were very internationalist, outward looking … I happened to be Ken Clarke's private secretary and therefore experienced the transition directly at first-hand from Ken to Gordon Brown in '97. The rhetoric changed hugely, but in terms of their view of the global economy they were all remarkably similar … globalization, the world is becoming more integrated, and there's no choice but to engage with it.

The globalization philosophy became more developed in the New Labour years. In between dining on the ideas of Clintonite Democrats and Third Way centrists, they also binged on all things global. Upwardly mobile policy wonks no longer talked about opening up to the international economy. Now it was a matter of how the British economy could become best placed to take advantage of global business shifts.

The man who signally represented New Labour's emerging internationalist economic philosophy was Ed Balls. References to the 'global' pepper the personal accounts of his earlier self. In a 2006 *New Statesman* interview he stated: 'When I was at college … We didn't have to ask the question of whether we should adopt a globally integrated, market-based model.'[15] His autobiography talks of the need to embrace 'globalisation and the dynamic market economy'.[16] He sounded very much the cosmopolitan when we talked about his experiences and economic influences. All this fed into New Labour economic thinking, aimed at putting the

UK in the best position possible to benefit from a globalizing world economy:

> I wrote a paper, which is actually in one of the Treasury books we edited, called 'Open Macroeconomics in an Open Economy',[17] which was in the autumn of 1997. This was about how could you behave in a global capital market without cutting yourself off from the world? … We were absolutely managing the globalization of capital markets, which we thought was a given. We were absolutely managing the globalization of product markets, which was actually working in complicated ways … I would call myself somebody who was pro-open economics and pro the advantages of globalization.

Others in the New Labour economic policy loop talked in similar ways about the global. While Tony Blair was showing off his Franglais and invading distant countries, they were engaged in serious debates about the international economy. For Stephen Byers, who had senior ministerial posts in both the Treasury and the DTI in the Blair years, 'we were beginning to think about what is the role of government in relation to industry, in a sort of global economy'. Dan Corry, an ever-present economic advisor, sketched out the backdrop to his policy work: 'I tried to interpret what we were trying to do on the economy as being within a kind of market system with open markets, mobile global capital and all the rest of it.'

Global integration was achieved by promoting the development of a new, dynamic economy that was ready to take on its international competitors. That meant an educated and flexible workforce, developed infrastructure, efficient markets and competitive companies. Everyone was adamant that there would be no going back to Old Labour thinking. No going back to nationalization or powerful unions. No Keynesian dashes for growth. And no handouts for UK companies, failing or otherwise. They would be left to sink or swim on their own. Even non-specific policy supports such as 'regional selective assistance' or 'industry sponsorship' were frowned upon.

In this respect, the Treasury was also highly critical of the 'trade' as well as the 'industry' parts of the DTI. If regional support distorted natural markets at the local level, then government attempts to aid exporters distorted them at the international end. This was explained by Vicky Pryce, a former chief economic advisor at the DTI:

> Quite a large part of the fight was to ensure that export promotion remained a substantial part of what UKTI did, because there was a move for a while to say: 'Right, we don't need to push exports.' This is the very free market thinking in the Treasury: 'They find their own level. They go wherever. Why do we want to do it? Do we have any proof that any help we give leads to additional exports?' Of course, we did have rather a lot of proof.

While successive governments, from Thatcher's onwards, took away a range of supports for UK industries, quite the opposite happened in relation to successful foreign multinationals. Governments did what they could to encourage these to set up in the UK. International investors, skilled labour and innovative CEOs would be lured with lower taxes, favourable regulations and other incentives. As Chris Wales, Gordon Brown's chief advisor on tax measures, explained it, in stark contrast to the attitude against supporting UK companies, policy often aimed at incentivizing successful foreign companies to move to Britain:

> We used to have a little mantra about making the UK the best place in which and from which to do business … because we wanted to see the UK as a centre for ownership of international business … We changed the rules for the treatment of overseas holdings, both treatment of capital gains and treatment of dividend income. So it became much easier to have your headquarters or your parent company in the UK and to invest outwards. So that was a big part of the idea that you should make it easier and more tax efficient for companies to have their ownership structure with the UK at the centre.

Sir Brian Bender, a civil servant who began and ended his career in the DTI, saw policy continuity from Thatcher onwards. Whatever it was called, the policy vision was the same. Although the country may have stopped producing the George Stephensons and Henry Royces of the past, they were going to persuade the Steve Jobses and Jeff Bezoses of the future to set up in Blighty:

> Largely Blair continued the Thatcher economic policy but put a more social face on it. So it was that philosophy, combined with a philosophy that as a trading nation it was in Britain's interest to be open, and get what various people called the 'Wimbledon Effect'. You know, we may not win Wimbledon at all, we have now, but we have stars who play there.

There is no greater example of the 'Wimbledon Effect' than the UK's automobile sector. Whenever I asked someone at the Treasury or former DTI about the decline of British manufacturing, I always got an instant rejoinder: 'Look at the success of the car sector.' Back in 1955 the UK was the second largest car manufacturer in the world.[18] Five companies made 90% of the output and four of them were British. But by the mid-1970s the industry was in decline and the UK had dropped to sixth in the world. Car production peaked at around three and a half million units per year and then began dropping off. Government interventions and attempts to restructure seemed to do little to stop the downward trend. In 1982 a new low was reached with production dropping below 900,000 units.

The response of the Thatcher government, apart from trying to crush the unions, was to invite successful foreign firms to set up in Britain. At the same time that support for UK industry was being wound down, a series of 'sweeteners' were being dangled in front of expanding multinationals. US and Japanese firms had an added incentive to come to Britain: to use it as a base for gaining access to Europe's new single market. The most significant corporation to jump was Nissan in 1986, lured to Britain with millions of pounds in grants. Honda and Toyota followed. Tens of millions of sweeteners and guarantees were turned into billions of foreign investment in British-based car plants. For Brian Bender the policy of foreign investment bore the richest rewards in the car industry:

There were a number of instruments of intervention. When I did the regional policy job, I was the budget holder for the regional development assistance grant ... If they invested in an assisted area, we were legally permitted to offer regional development assistance ... the most successful one and most game changing one was Nissan, because it changed the face of the British motor industry ... the combination of inward investment and technology and so on means we now produce at least as many cars in Britain as we did in the 1970s. [sadly not true]

The pattern continued through the Thatcher, Major and Blair governments. British car makers continued either to go bust or be taken over by overseas multinationals. In 1994 Rover, the last British-owned volume car maker, was sold to BMW. But outputs continued to go up. By the mid-1990s peak, car production had added another million annual units since its 1982 low point. In the early 2000s Stephen Byers, as Labour DTI Secretary of State, recalled that he maintained the pattern of incentivizing and assisting foreign car companies.

Nissan had quite a small car plant in Sunderland to begin with, and they were about to take a key decision, which was about whether to expand the Sunderland plant, almost double it in size, or whether to go somewhere in Eastern Europe. We were desperate to get it to Sunderland ... I was on a trade visit to India, and I said to Carlos Ghosn, who was the chief executive of Nissan in Tokyo, 'I want to come and see you' ... That for him was the thing that swayed it. It was our commitment, and that the environment would be a good one for Nissan.

Many interviewees, from Byers and Bender in the New Labour years back to Lawson and Lamont in the Conservative years, spoke proudly of the reborn British car industry. Britain's dominance of the sector was never restored, nor could it hope to be. But a fairly stable and competitive industry base was developed. That meant large numbers of workers employed, local economies boosted and millions of units exported each year. Thus, Norman Lamont enthused about Tata's success (no longer true):

> If you take foreign ownership of the motorcar industry today, I would argue that's been beneficial to the country, rather than struggling on with the government pumping money into it and never succeeding in turning it round. I think Tata Jaguar is a spectacular example of that. What does it matter if he's Indian or British?

Investing in Britain or hollowing it out?

For many of my interviewees, as they looked back over their time, there was usually something nagging at them. That something was the question of British ownership (or lack of it). Behind the spiel, the success of foreign investment, the embracing of globalization, there was the ongoing worry about the implications of the shift. For John Gieve, those concerns never went away but were always buried under the Treasury free trade and free markets mantra:

> On ownership, right from the '80s, from Big Bang onwards, and indeed before, there's been a running worry in government and in commentary about are we wise

> to let foreigners buy everything? ... but in fact, there's been a longstanding policy, successive governments have decided not to do anything about it ... And, you know, of course most other countries think this is mad, and that ownership does matter.

No one quite predicted how fast and to what extent ownership would be transferred to overseas entities and what the consequences might be. The moves towards internationalization in the 1980s completely transformed the shape and nature of London's financial centre. Within a year of the City's 'Big Bang', almost all of London's broking houses and other intermediary firms had been taken over by foreign, primarily US, investment banks. By the end of the century, the LSE had the biggest overseas investment presence of any of the world's large financial centres.[19]

At the same time, not only did the British lead the drive towards the European single market in the 1980s, they very much practised what they preached. Many other states agreed to liberalize their trade policies, but most of them maintained rather more in the way of protections and backing for their key industries.[20] The combination of an open economy and a deregulated stock market left UK companies more open to international takeovers than in any other rival economy. Foreign ownership of British companies since the 1980s has leapt. For Terry Burns, a dominant Treasury presence in the 1980s and 1990s, Britain had gone way further than any of its rivals, perhaps a bit too far:

There was a very conscious programme of removing obstacles, and several aspects were very unpopular like, for example, not favouring British institutions over American or European institutions ... what happened of course was that lots of what were British institutions became swallowed up by international institutions. I think very few countries probably would have tolerated that, but again there was quite a long tradition of London being a relatively open system.

Speaking to Lord Burns in 2014, I realized that even he was not aware of how far things had gone. Back in 1981 overseas investors owned just 4% of LSE shares traded. UK-based individuals held 28% of shares and UK-based institutions, such as insurance and pension funds, managed 47%. By 2014 things had changed entirely. UK pension and insurance funds held 9% and individuals a further 12%. Overseas investors now owned 54%.[21]

Contrary to expectations, the doctrines of internationalization and globalization have not always benefited Britain's industrial sector particularly. By some indicators, the reverse is true. Yes, innovation and new investment in industries old and new was very positive. But that investment has also been erratic, with profits and capital often flowing abroad rather than into research and development in the UK. For Nicholas Comfort, who has documented the long-term decline of British industry, the problems of too much foreign ownership are clear: 'when a British plant is doing well, the profits flow overseas – and when it does badly, there is nothing to stop the owners closing it down or transferring production somewhere cheaper'.[22]

British companies have also been undermined by the combination of an aggressive takeover system and a relative lack of state protections. By 2010 many of Britain's once world-leading companies had been either wiped out, taken over by foreign multinationals, broken up and sold off for parts for easy profits, or shrunk beyond recognition. The marked gravestones include GEC, ICI, Pilkington, Corus, BOC, BAA, Cadbury, Redland, Tarmac, Blue Circle, RMC, British Plasterboard, Aggregate Industries and Hansen. Just 23 of the original FTSE 100 companies of 1979 survived to see the 2010s. Along with these also went numerous UK-based supply chains of small and medium-sized firms, each providing parts, tools and raw materials.[23]

There have been many inquiries and post-mortems into the British industrial collapse. Some causes were frequently identified well before the 1980s upheaval: poor management, lack of investment, industrial relations problems, a strong pound and not having to rebuild from scratch after the war. Since the 1980s two more have been added to the list: an all-powerful financial sector and foreign ownership.[24] Many studies link a number of UK industrial ills to this combination.

The 2016 EU referendum result was a devastating blow to four decades of open and internationalist economic policy. A big pull for overseas multinationals, whether they offered services, food supplies or manufacturing, was Britain's unfettered access to European supply chains and markets. Leaving the single market quite simply confounded that. Multinationals began to withdraw accordingly. Big finance was one of the first to get moving, as over a trillion pounds worth of funds and operations were relocated to better investment opportunities abroad.[25] Philip Hammond, who tried to manage the fallout, explained just what it really means when a company or product doesn't 'have a nationality':

> A lot of people in financial services in London are not necessarily looking at the world from the point of view of the UK economy … Goldman Sachs would say something like 'We're not overly worried any more about Brexit' … What Goldman Sachs meant was 'We, Goldman Sachs are going to be fine because we've put in place arrangements that mean we can just abandon stuff in London, and we've built ourselves a place inside the EU, and if we need to, we'll switch our trading there' … But of course, from the UK point of view that decline in activity in London in favour of growth in activity somewhere else, from a chancellor's point of view, that is a nightmare.

As for Britain's car industry, it was already in decline before Brexit. Apart from high-end specialist manufacturing, it has been on a downward trajectory again since the mid-2000s. The accession of Eastern European countries to the EU in 2004 presented new opportunities to multinational car-makers. They offered the same access as Britain to the EU, but their skilled labour came more cheaply. By 2017 the UK had dropped from being the sixth to the thirteenth largest car manufacturer in the world (fourth in Europe). 1.67 million cars were built, and only 44% of the content of those vehicles was produced in the UK itself.[26] All in all, unit production had fallen below the 1990s revival peak and was half the 1970s peak. If content percentage is included, not to mention factoring in a population increase of almost 30%, even pre-Brexit the revival was looking decidedly peaky.

The spectre of Brexit has been hovering over the sector ever since the vote. In 2015 inward investment in the UK car industry was over £2.5 billion. That has dropped substantially in every year following. In the first six months of 2019 it was a mere £90 million. In early 2019 all the major car producers – Nissan, Toyota, Honda PSA, Ford and BMW – were threatening to pull out of Britain. In mid-2019 Tata-owned Jaguar Land Rover announced an annual loss of £3.6 billion (sorry Lord Lamont). One by one, Honda, Nissan and Ford each announced the closures of plants, in Swindon, Sunderland and Bridgend respectively. By January 2021 the combination of Brexit and COVID had contributed to the lowest levels of production and export since the early 1980s. Over the previous year, production, sales and exports all dropped by a third, with just 921,000 units being built, barely above the low point recorded in 1982.[27]

Both Brexit and COVID, in different ways, have revealed just how degraded the UK manufacturing base has become – its broken supply chains, its skills gaps, its low levels of productivity and lack of long-term investment even in sectors where Britain has advanced capabilities. One senior official in the Treasury explained just how clear this became when the pandemic hit:

We didn't have a single manufacturing plant for vaccines, not a single one. We have, by common consent, the second-best life sciences research base in the world, we have world-class research and development capability in our universities and in our big pharmaceutical companies in the UK, but we have very little manufacturing capacity because although the drug companies do a lot of their research here, they built their manufacturing plants overseas. So, initially, we had no vaccine manufacturing in the UK, literally none. This had to change.

Having a globally oriented and open economy has been detrimental to Britain in other ways too. It is not only British companies, banking and finance that have passed into distanced and temporary overseas hands. So have essential utilities, energy generation, social and economic infrastructure, land and property. In 2012, 60% of top-end homes were foreign-owned, with many lying empty for much of the year; 90% of such properties were bought and sold anonymously through tax havens.[28] Globalization has also enabled large companies and the super-rich to reduce their tax contributions.[29] Corporation tax, as part of the global 'race to the bottom', has been reduced steadily since 1979, when it was 52%, to 19% in 2022. By 2010, 98% of FTSE 100 companies had subsidiaries of joint ventures registered in tax havens; 83% of large companies had offshore accounts and an estimated $21 trillion was held in such havens.[30] In the tax year 2020/21, HMRC estimated that it had lost £35 billion in non-payment, including £7 billion in tax avoidance and evasion schemes.[31] The Tax Justice Network, which designates the UK as 'the global leader in tax avoidance', put the figure rather higher for avoidance and evasion, at £160 billion.[32]

And in early 2022, with growing Russian and Chinese expansionist tendencies and militarization, it's becoming clear that encouraging reliance on energy supply and investment from those countries was perhaps not such a good idea.

Conclusion: it all comes back to empire

Ultimately, it all comes back to these competing visions of Britain's place in the global economy and recollections of empire. For critical historians, the Empire did most for a select British elite and caused untold harm to millions of people in the colonies. For the Brexiteers it made Britain 'great' and can do so again, led by Churchill's modern incarnation, Boris 'Biggles' Johnson. For one former chancellor, who watched the Brexiteers close-up, it is a 'view of the world rooted in the last days of Empire, the late 1950s when there were all these English-speaking people who looked to us as the mother country ... resolutely rooted in the past, no real sense'.

For the keepers of the 'Treasury view' and the globalizing politicians, the physical Empire may be gone, but the embrace of liberal internationalism did much to replicate its economic benefits. They dragged Britain's outdated economy and what was left of its manufacturing into the modern era and a new age of growth and prosperity.

To my mind, however, both these perspectives are starry-eyed in their own ways and mistaken. The first has as much credibility as a boy's-own comic book fantasy. The second has had a lot more going for it but has also tended to emphasize the gains while ignoring the losses, losses that have become all too evident for many parts of the nation.

In 2013 I interviewed Lord Heseltine, a former Tory DTI head, about the state of the British economy and its industrial base. Heseltine was a towering figure of the Thatcher and Major years. He still was when I spoke to him: tall, forceful and with his distinctive, now grey mane of hair. Heseltine's views on industry, the economy and Europe are almost diametrically opposed to many of those in his party, most especially the hard Brexiteers. He is regarded as one of only two heads of the DTI since 1979 to have actively supported UK industry and taken a more interventionist approach (the other being Labour's Peter Mandelson). He is also a pro-European 'Remainer' whose continued criticism of Brexit led to his suspension from the Conservative Party in 2019.

In 2013, three years before the Brexit vote, he ranted to me about the folly of decades of internationalist economic policy. He railed with the same sense of forced frustration that Andrew Turnbull had expressed just a few weeks earlier; only making the exact opposite argument. Like all Tories, he was very much a free-market man. Unlike the internationalists he was rather more critical about the accompanying, purist free trade bit. In his view, the national economic interest had been terribly damaged by the extent of Britain's openness and its lack of protections:

> By and large if you look at the people who own Britain's largest companies, they're not British. They're international investment operations ... The long-term interests of this country, the industrial base, the scientific elements, the research and development facilities, the supply chains, all these things have no consequence at all. Well that is unlike any other capitalist economy, unlike any other, starting with America. And we parade it as a virtue.

Heseltine, like the Brexiteers, linked empire and economic decline too, only in very different ways. Unlike those pushing to leave, he did not pine for the days of empire. Internationalism had worked well for the UK economy when Britain had an empire. Unfortunately, modern policymakers could not see that internationalism did the reverse when the Empire no longer existed:

> What people cannot get round their minds is that actually we had the first mover advantage of the industrial revolution and the most protected market in the world, called the British Empire. And because it was a world market, the Empire was worldwide. We called it free trade, but it wasn't free trade at all ... What we didn't realise was that this actually was imperial preference of one sort or another, a hidden preference. And we turned it into an economic theory. Now I'm perfectly supportive of fair trade, but free trade in which we open every opportunity to somebody else despite what they open to us? That sounds to me a bit naïve.

6

The great financial crash and the great failed paradigm shift: a technocrats' tale

September 2007 was when the UK's seemingly healthy economy collided with hard reality. That was when the Northern Rock bank suffered a very public collapse. This preceded the wider implosion of the global financial system and worldwide recession. It painfully revealed Britain's exposure to international finance but also the corroded foundations of its economic model.

But perhaps almost as shocking is that nothing substantial changed thereafter. Once the immediate crisis was dealt with and a 1930s-style depression had been avoided, it was almost business as usual. No political, economic or intellectual paradigm shift emerged. And, arguably, the UK economy has been floundering ever since.

The real question driving this chapter is why did nothing really change? What accounted for 'the strange non-death of neoliberalism' and everything associated with an economy driven by financial markets, internationalization and debt?[1] One part of the answer supplied here is that much of the result came down to the technocrats in charge and their inability to challenge wider Establishment interests.

Genteel technocrats, armed with 'expertise' and a public service ethos, took on forceful political and financial self-interest, and lost. It was never a fair fight. Thus, technocrats backed off from major confrontation with the power nexus of political and banking elites. Technocrats gave public cover to that same nexus. They were central to a shifting crisis narrative that went from government and banker mismanagement to technical explanations of economic failure. Once the crisis was reframed as a technical debacle, more limited technical responses became the answer. 'The great moderation'[2] and great financial crash was followed by the great elite consolidation and greater failure to achieve a paradigm shift.

The great financial crash: 'They all did it'

I'm starting with one prominent overview of the crisis that prevailed during the financial crash and in the immediate years that followed. In this history, the Treasury was a relatively innocent bystander that was left to deal with the consequences of a large-scale financial pile-up.

Enough accounts have now been published about the crash to fill the shiny new wing of an elite business school library. None single out one factor or set of culprits alone, but they do emphasize a few over others.

Some focus on the dangerous and self-serving activities of the bankers and traders who pushed the wider financial system into unsustainable dysfunctionality.[3] Others elaborate on the global system imbalances and mounting risks that had developed in the years prior to the crash.[4] Others still look more at the failings of economic policymakers in national finance departments and international institutions.[5] They all share certain parts of the tale though.

Ostensibly, the crisis trigger was the sudden collapse of the overinflated subprime mortgage market in the US. For years, mortgages were thrust at impoverished buyers who had minimal understanding of what was happening or ability to service their debts in the long term. Similar housing bubbles were taking place in many countries including the UK where, from 1995 to 2007, house prices doubled in relation to average earnings.[6]

Although subprime was the trigger, a mix of financial deregulation and opaque wheeling and dealing in financial markets made things many times worse. An increasing proportion of bank financing was taking place in the unregulated shadow banking sector. At the time of the collapse, this sector was worth $16 trillion in the US, $4 trillion more than in the regulated sector.[7] This allowed banks to leverage up their debt levels and lend out far beyond their reserves. In 2007 Northern Rock had assets of £1.5 billion but loans amounting to over £100 billion, over 80% of which came from global money markets.[8]

The growing risks of all this debt – both personal and in banking – were hidden by new types of derivatives and other opaque forms of financial engineering. Mortgage-backed securities (MBSs) packaged up tranches of highly risky subprime mortgages, then mixed them up with more secure mortgages using collateralized debt obligations (CDOs). The resulting outputs were given a AAA risk rating and sold on to trusting banks and pension funds across the world (half of subprime debt was owned by European institutions). Between 1998 and 2008, the total derivatives market of CDOs and other complex assets rose from $15 trillion to $600 trillion, equivalent to twelve times total world output.[9]

All this trading created impossibly large amounts of virtual capital to be repeatedly invested across the system. When the bubbles finally began to burst, the complex networks of investors and IOUs began to fall apart. Banks stopped lending as no one knew who owed what to whom. A credit crunch followed as lending stopped and debts were called in. Banks began to fold. Lehman Brothers in the US was the most high-profile casualty in September 2008, a year after Northern Rock's forced rescue in the UK. Financial institutions and governments were sucked in from all over the world.

All accounts of the crisis convey a story of devastating financial meltdown on a par with the 1929 Wall Street Crash. This threatened to bring down the global banking system and deliver a deep depression and social chaos. The impending crash is presented in Hollywood blockbuster disaster terms. But instead of a rogue terrorist group with nuclear weapons, it is a rogue banking system and derivatives of mass destruction threatening to wipe out all of humanity. Alistair Darling, appointed chancellor less than three months before Northern Rock went down, relayed to me in measured tones just how terrifying the whole episode felt at the time:

> From November 2007 most of my time in the Treasury, until 2009, say two years, was focused on stopping the entire system from collapsing. It was crisis management for about two years. And that obviously involved the banks. But from the end of 2008, 2009 onwards, when it was obvious that we were heading into the economic abyss, then public spending and the control of it was a concern. But the biggest concern was how did you stop a recession going into a depression.

Consequently, finance ministers and technocrats everywhere were forced to take radical courses of action that they would never previously have admitted were possible. Banks and other institutions had to be bailed out or nationalized. Four large US investment banks (Merrill Lynch, Citigroup, Bear Stearns and Morgan Stanley) each had to borrow $1.5 to $2 trillion to avoid bankruptcy. Governments everywhere introduced ultra-low interest rates and created trillions in quantitative easing. Government debt shot up. US national debt went up 50%. The UK's external debt rose from 22.5 % of GDP in 2007 to 66.5% in 2009. Others, such as Japan, Greece, Italy and Portugal, soared above 100%. In 2008–09 governments together offered a total of $15 trillion in a mix of loans, guarantees and bank bailouts. By 2012 the total cost to the UK alone of such measures had reached £1.2 trillion.[10] Meanwhile individuals and non-financial businesses experienced mounting debts, bankruptcy, job losses and repossessions. Arguably, many parts of the global economy have not recovered since (although certain companies and individuals have thrived).

By almost all accounts, the crash and its magnitude took everyone in authority by surprise. There were a few people who warned of the growing problems and potential for disaster. But those who did, by definition, lacked credibility or were marginalized for speaking out.[11] Andy Haldane has held many senior positions in the Bank of England over three decades, including being its chief economist. He was one of the few to ask difficult questions prior to the collapse, but he believes nobody saw the size and scope of what was to come:

> I don't think anyone called the crisis. A lot of people have exhibited supernatural powers of hindsight after the fact … Some people got some bits of it right and we were among those actually. But no one, without exceptions, put together the pieces and got the scale of this right.

In the post-mortems that followed, multiple culprits were singled out as being to blame for the crash: poor financial regulation, blind adherence to free-market thinking and faith in the self-correcting properties of financial markets, opaque and highly risky trading of complex financial products, inept credit rating agencies, ignorant and dishonest politicians, large international trading imbalances and free-flowing Chinese capital and, of course, greedy reckless bankers.[12]

What became clear in the plethora of media commentary and longer accounts was that no one was really to blame because everyone was to blame. Even the venal, self-serving financiers who caused it all weren't really to blame because they were ignorant too. Gus O'Donnell, head of the civil service and Cabinet Office at the time, says:

> I was truly appalled by the state of knowledge in the individual banks as to their positions. I remember the senior members of various banks coming together and being asked 'Are you going to be able to open on Monday?' And the chairmen saying: 'We don't know' and being told to go away and come back and tell us.

Everyone was unaware and unprepared for what came. For Adair Turner, the technocrat's technocrat, institutions of all kinds and nationalities shared the same misguided belief in the system. As Turner, who had multiple vantage points from which to view the crisis, put it:

> There was a very deep conventional wisdom and intellectual delusion held by powerful institutions across the world … It's believed by the Federal Reserve, it's believed by the US Treasury, it's believed by the IMF … it had invaded the UK Treasury, the UK FSA, the Bank of England, the Basel Committee. It was very deep. People believed that we had created such sophisticated forms of risk management that the risks that would previously have been created by excessive leverage were no longer there … this is Murder on the

Orient Express, they all did it. Because, you know, had I been there at the time I might have done it as well.

In this respect, the Treasury and the Labour government, like everyone else, were largely innocent victims of a perfect storm of problems, hidden from view and created in faraway places. Most people I spoke to, when pushed, admitted that the Treasury made mistakes. However, quite simply, like everyone else, the institution was justified in taking the collective *force majeure* line.

Although taken unaware, the Treasury and its sister institutions did respond well. If anything, the debacle was to become the Treasury's and Gordon Brown's finest hour. At the time, Brown was one of the few world leaders with a wider grasp of international finance and stepped forward very quickly. Just before he became prime minister, he and Ed Balls had war-gamed the possibility of a major bank collapse with Mervyn King and the Bank of England.[13] Having managed Northern Rock's demise a year earlier, they were more prepared than most for dealing with the global financial meltdown.

Initially, as the crisis grew, the Treasury, the Bank of England and the Financial Services Authority (FSA) could not agree on whether to let banks fail *à la* Lehman Brothers. There were debates about what combination of measures and tools to apply to restore the system. However, in time, the three institutions began operating smoothly together. RBS and Lloyds TSB were effectively nationalized, joining Northern Rock and Bradford and Bingley on the nation's books. A mix of central bank liquidity, bank guarantees and capital injections were developed and implemented to quickly halt the crisis.[14] Adair Turner took over as chairman of the FSA just a few days after Lehman collapsed. He recalls how quickly and efficiently it was dealt with:

> By the time I arrived there that machinery was working very effectively. I just walked into a system which was completely structured, sensible, calm, hardworking. The effective way was to say: 'Where are we in this crisis, what are we going to do?' Meetings between me, Alistair and Mervyn, then the next layer down there as well, and then instructions: 'OK, Hector [Sants], Tom Scholar, John Gieve, Paul Tucker, get the machinery producing papers and the options for the next time round.' So, I think that bit was quite impressive … I walked in the door on Saturday, September the 20th of 2008 and there was then just I guess two weeks and a couple of days and we were through to October the 5th and we were sitting down with the banks explaining the need for a financial rescue package.

The blueprint constructed by the Treasury and its fellow institutions was then exported and adopted by other nations. The global financial system was stabilized and economic Armageddon was staved off. Gordon Brown, the self-styled Bruce Willis of the crisis, was both praised for taking an international lead and ribbed for suggesting that he had saved the world.[15] Yippee-Ki-Yay bankers!

Ultimately, this larger history came to be rewritten in the Coalition years (see Chapter 7). But even so, although New Labour was held more to blame for its pre-crisis profligacy, the Treasury avoided much of the public criticism. Against the odds, it had rescued the British economy after all.

However, I believe that the Treasury and other institutions were rather more implicated in what happened. Before explaining why, let's just be clear on one thing: the bankers did it. The financiers made huge fortunes out of the system in the lead-up to the crash. They caused the pile-up. They walked away with their reputations sullied but their fortunes largely intact. And in most countries no one who profited was held accountable or prosecuted. As Matt Taibi of *Rolling Stone* magazine concluded: 'Nobody goes to jail.'[16] There was no real-life Yippee-Ki-Yay moment for those awaiting the meting out of Willis-style retribution to the financial terrorists behind it all (although a few bankers were publicly humiliated). A big reason for this was that the bankers and financiers didn't act alone. They had multiple accomplices and enablers, each of whom saw benefit in letting international finance rip and then, after the crash, leaving the system relatively unscathed. In the case of the UK, the Treasury and the Bank of England were enablers as much as they were victims and saviours.

More broadly, the Treasury, the Bank of England and politicians of both parties were implicated because the UK had taken one of the lead roles in shaping a global financial system that was to implode. After 1979 they had refashioned the UK economy, letting go of macro-economic levers and withdrawing state interventions.

Instead, they actively ushered much of the economy into the controlling arms of big finance (Chapter 3) and global companies and investors (Chapter 5). They had turbo-boosted their financial and property markets over many years, watching huge debt levels mount up (Chapter 4).

By the late 1990s this mix had helped to create a new operating model for UK Plc: Ponzi-scheme capitalism. Together, light-touch regulation, low interest rates, free-flowing global capital and internationalism combined to cause a series of volatile asset bubbles. Companies and citizens, their properties and assets, were steadily sucked into these financial networks through securitized and traded debt. Markets in company shares, property, commodities and complex financial instruments all began to resemble a series of Ponzi-scheme bubbles. Economic value and profits became increasingly derived through debt trading, financial market activity and rentier behaviour.[17] Meanwhile, real, productive investment declined, while private, corporate and government debt continued to rise.[18] The UK was not alone in this but, along with the US and a couple of others, it was a global market leader.

There were warning signs about where all this could be leading and how national economies might be brought down. Various countries in Latin America and Asia had seen their economies powerfully destabilized as international finance had come, created a bubble and then deserted. Then in 2000 there was the dot.com boom and bust. UK and US stock market values had doubled or tripled over a few years on wild speculation, and then collapsed entirely, wiping out trillions of dollars (much of it from public institutions and pension funds).[19] There were more concerning financial trends in the 2000s.

However, the response of the UK and US governments to these crises was to drastically lower interest rates and push other fiscal stimuli to keep all the financial plates spinning. They chose to keep the 'great moderation' operating rather than question its dangerous flaws or show any interest in making it safer.

Institutional ideology and political expediency

Setting aside the broader picture, the UK Treasury, the Bank of England and the Labour government were implicated in a more specific story of institutional failure in relation to its financial sector. How were they and what was the nature of the failure?

The tale, or rather various versions of the tale, was told to me by the technocrats there. Pretty much everyone I talked to in relation to the crash was first and foremost a technocrat. Even Alistair Darling, the chancellor at the time, looks and sounds like a technocrat: well-spoken and well-mannered, academic, thoughtful and expert-oriented. They all adhered to the New Labour mantra of the day, 'evidence-based policy'. Each had years of experience in a range of public and private financial institutions. Lurking beneath a visage of polite reflection, and more than willing to admit to institutional mea culpas, they are all also well versed in the art of subtle deflection. Common phrases, which invariably come before criticism of others, are: 'He's a good friend of mine so I can say this' or 'I love him but'.

There are various explanations and accompanying narratives of what went wrong. One of these is a story of institutional culpability based on ideological blinkeredness and political and financial expediency. Senior civil servants and ministers were not simply impartial and rational. They were too accepting of mainstream economic theory and financial market thinking because they were also great beneficiaries of the system that the theory advocated. They were all too willing to accede to the views of the professionals of the banking lobby, and encouraged a see-no-evil, hear-no-evil approach to the City and growing incongruities.

Asked about what went wrong and how the key state institutions of economic management might have done better, several explanations are repeated. One of these is that, across the Treasury and the Bank of England, there had come to exist a blind faith in mainstream economics. From the 1980s onwards there was a steady growth in the number of economists employed at the Treasury and across the civil service (see Chapter 2).[20] As Andy Haldane observed, although institutions were professionalized, intellectual horizons had become narrowed: 'For a while pre-crisis we were very largely an economics factory ... with a very heavy reluctance to move away from the bog-standard off-the-shelf models.'

The belief in free-market economics was compounded by a particular faith in financial markets, particularly from some central figures at the time. Both Ed Balls, Brown's chief economic advisor, and Mervyn King, governor of the Bank of England since 2003 (and deputy since 1998), had prior professional and academic interests in financial markets. Both had been at Harvard and had interacted with the same financial market economists who became influential in the US Treasury and Federal Reserve. Accordingly, the Bank of England and the Treasury were intellectually predisposed to taking a hands-off approach to financial regulation to the point of almost ignoring it altogether.

In 1997, when financial regulation was being rede-signed, a new Financial Services Authority came into being. Although overall regulatory authority was sup-posed to be shared between the three institutions, it was an excuse for the Bank of England and the Treasury to concentrate on other policy priorities. For the Bank of England that meant focusing on its new remit of monetary policy. Those working on the financial stability side noted the resource consequences of this downgrade. As John Gieve remembered: 'We had four or five people working on Barclays whereas collectively the Americans may have had 400 working on Bank of America.' As the 2000s wore on, reports expressing concerns about the risks connected to asset bubbles or bank leverage tended to be all too easily filed away and forgotten. For James Sassoon, who chaired the monthly financial stability standing committee: 'It was very noticeable in that period that ... it was not a priority of the Bank, that appeared to see itself with a single purpose of setting interest rates, in order to meet the inflation target.'

In fact, several interviewees questioned the personal role of Mervyn King, both before the crisis and during it. He is often described as leading the embrace of the Bank's new monetarist remit with all the verve of an ivory-tower academic given a huge grant to play with. It was he who was enthralled by the Greenspan doctrine in the US of self-correcting financial markets and who then ignored the Bank's regulatory duties.[21] Yet in the various post-inquiry investigations, he claimed that this had never been the Bank's responsibility, something that incensed various officials. One ranted at me:

> He managed to spin a narrative over the next few years that the Bank of England lacked the tools and powers to do anything about it ... I call him the Keyser Soze of the financial crisis. The greatest trick he ever pulled was persuading everyone that his responsibility for the financial crisis didn't exist ... Mervyn, can you point to where you said that prior to the financial crisis? Why did you cut the financial stability stuff? You were obsessed with monetary policy, weren't you?

It also became clear that the Treasury was similarly inclined to give the City what it wanted, supported by key Labour figures. It was becoming increasingly clear just how profitable the financial sector was to their administration (see Chapter 3). One official recalled a speech made by Tony Blair at the IPPR in 2006, in which he lauded the City and criticized the inhibiting activities of the FSA. Others talked of Balls's 'light touch' financial regulation speeches. 'There was a general ethos of deregulation', shrugged Lord Macpherson, 'which you can argue ended up going too far and helped trigger the financial crisis.' Adair Turner explained just how in thrall the Treasury was to financial market thinking:

> I do think the Treasury had probably been bought off in the 1990s and early 2000s with this sort of free financial markets rhetoric ... Gordon [Brown] invited the absolute high priest of that philosophy, Alan Greenspan, to give a lecture at the Treasury about that in 2005, '06 ... a big element of it was Nigel Lawson. The whole of the Treasury was the centre of the belief that a larger and more sophisticated financial sector was ipso facto a good thing.

Ed Balls got very defensive when I asked him about his public advocacy of 'light touch' regulation: 'Don't forget I wasn't there in the financial crisis ... The truth is I only ever said light touch once as far as I remember. Yeah, in my first week, and I got told off by Callum McCarthy.' He went on to explain that much more intrusive regulatory regimes, such as in the US, had also missed the crisis. It was all about understanding the risks.

Others challenge Balls's account and the positions of the Treasury and Labour government. Dominic Lindley probably knows as much about institutional failings as anyone. He was an economic advisor to the Treasury Select Committee in the 2000s and managed the first Banking Commission review of what went wrong in 2009.[22] He says that the speeches by Balls and Blair are the only public, documented accounts of Labour's push for deregulation. But he is clear from the verbal evidence that this was an institution-wide view that was clearly disseminated downwards:

> The impression was the Treasury officials and ministers wanted light-touch regulation, so you gave them light-touch regulation … There was a specific objective on the regulators to promote innovation, and also to maintain the position of the City of London as an attractive location for financial businesses … the regulators will say they were responding to political imperatives.

For many who were present at the time, no one at the top of either the Treasury, the Bank of England or the City wanted to countenance flaws in this increasingly lucrative system. Things were not adding up, but no one had an interest in calling this out. Edward Troup, a senior advisor on tax in the Treasury, admitted that things did not make sense but no one saw value in questioning the pattern:

> The tax from the financial sector seemed to be growing at a significantly greater rate … in hindsight I think that's because the financial sector was pretending to make profits which in reality it wasn't … we were puzzled by it, but it was good news because it all turned into tax revenues … the incentive, at least from my bit of the woods, to say 'what the hell's going on here, this cannot be right', wasn't there.

When the economic data didn't fit the models or forecasts, they preferred to change the assumptions and parameters rather than question the models. Andrew

Turnbull disdainfully remarks: 'The Brown/Balls mantra was balance across the cycle. But you kept redefining the cycle in ways that were beneficial to you.' Lindley, from his vantage point on the Treasury Select Committee, watched the ever-more dubious intellectual twists and turns used to sustain the positive economic narrative:

> They started to make over-optimistic tax forecasts based on the fact that financial sector profitability was growing faster than GDP ... then as the economy took a bit of a downturn in 2003, they kind of adjusted up the end of the forecast period to balance it over time. And then, Gordon appeared one day in the Treasury Committee, and basically said our economists now think that the economic cycle, which we thought started in 1999 now started in 1997. And of course, '97–99 was when we had some surpluses in the current budget ... that was the time when people started to realize that the golden rule was just a totemic thing.

Something similar happened with regard to the booming housing market. For Dan Corry: 'Everyone knew that house prices were way above what they could be, should be ... but I don't think anybody saw it crashing like it did ... you look back on that and you think blimey that was risky.' Those present in the Treasury Select Committee said that the housing bubble was frequently discussed. But, according to Lindley, the Exchequer response was that interest levels were low and serviceable, and it didn't want to impede business growth with higher rates. Just as with the dot.com bust of 2000, there was always a reason to explain the bubble.

Officials involved in monitoring financial stability at the FSA or the Bank of England also said there existed more serious questions and doubts. Internal reports had been registering concerns for two years leading up to the crash. These included the leverage accumulating on bank balance sheets and debts rising for households and non-financial corporations. But such reports and meeting minutes were too easily disregarded. As Andy Haldane recalls:

> I oversaw our publication on this, the Financial Stability Report. And we did try with words to highlight some of the risks that we felt were building up in the system. Indeed, we carried out stress testing ... We're talking '05/'06 and early part of '07, basically before the crisis broke ... but words don't necessarily matter that much if everyone is still having the party. In the words of Chuck Prince, as long as the music's still going everyone's still dancing. And everyone was still dancing during that time and us trying to say things to drown out the party music wasn't very effective.

Ultimately, the Treasury and the Bank of England put finance and housing out of sight in their management of the economy. Like many others, they had bought into the faulty mainstream economic and financial market thinking that made it all possible. They ignored the growing anomalies and risks, choosing instead to keep collecting the tax. New Labour got to invest in new schools and hospitals, the Treasury balanced its books, and bankers' bonuses kept flowing. What wasn't to like?

Solving the crisis: from paradigm shift to technical solutions

In theory, after everything that happened, it would have been logical to fundamentally interrogate what had gone wrong from every perspective. If there was an obvious moment for a paradigm shift it was now. And yet that didn't happen. Why?

Two important developments dictated how the crisis came to be framed and managed behind the scenes, and thus determined the shape of future solutions. On the one hand, political, institutional and financial elites combined to close down debate about the economic system that they had co-created. On the other, a more technocratic and banking-oriented framing of the crisis developed. This then dictated that technocratic solutions would be enough to fix things. There was no opportunity for the kind of open discussion that might have produced a meaningful paradigm shift.

The closing down of debate began as the nexus of Treasury and financial-sector leaders, of necessity, moved closer together to deal with the crisis. While politicians and unions publicly chastised bankers, the Exchequer had to work with them. It had a dearth of financial expertise in the institutions and needed outside help to advise on what was wrong and how to fix it. It also now had the nationalized banks to manage. Conse-quently, it turned to the prime source of expertise it could access: the banks themselves. As Alistair Darling recounts:

> When Northern Rock happened, there was a man and a dog in that department, because it had been so run down … We had to completely re-staff the financial stability part of the Treasury, and we had to get outside help from various banks and things, you know, the non-troubled banks, Goldman Sachs and people like that, to start with.

Several officials described to me how bank leaders and seconded financiers became regular visitors to both the Treasury and 10 Downing Street. Nicholas Macpherson says, 'As a result of the financial crisis the Treasury got far more involved in the banking system than it ever had before.' The irony wasn't lost on some critical observers. Bankers caused the crisis and bankers were now telling the Treasury how to fix it. As Lord McFall, then chair of the Treasury Select Committee, put it:

> You got people drafted in from the City to help sort out the financial crisis, which they made … Politicians were captured by the banks. You know, the bankers are the only ones that as an industry could get to the government and engage with them and they were very strong.

There are several signs that the banking lobby clearly ratcheted up its activities in the period. While the crisis was still raging, various self-aggrandizing reports were published by the City and the Treasury itself, pointing out the vital contribution of the Square Mile to the UK economy.[23] Alistair Darling and Boris Johnson, then Mayor of London, joined top banking leaders to support this case. By 2010 some 129 organizations were recorded as lobbying on behalf of the UK financiers. At that point, the sector was also responsible for over half of all party donations to the Conservatives, now in government.[24]

What was equally concerning was the refusal to have a proper, public inquiry into what happened. The biggest financial crisis in living memory had just occurred, throwing the country into recession. Government had used hundreds of billions of pounds of taxpayers' money to bail out the banking system. However, the Labour government refused to hold an investigation. Lord McFall, as chair of the Treasury Select Committee, was one of those demanding such a review but was ignored:

> It's a matter of record in the Chamber, I was calling for a Royal Commission on banking and they didn't want to know … I was pushing to get change in the financial services industry. But to be honest with you, there was nothing elsewhere, there was nothing from government on that.

In the end, McFall, with the financial and organizational support of the consumer group Which?, set up his own all-party review, chaired by David Davis. Published in 2010, it called a wide range of witnesses and was highly critical. It demanded 'significant reform' of the financial sector.[25] Its headline recommendation was to split up the banks as well as calling for other stringent regulatory measures.

It was only then that the government responded with an 'independent commission' on banking, eventually producing the Vickers Report of 2011. The remit here was rather narrower, the tone less critical and the recommendations more moderate.[26] For the

Manchester Business School's CRESC centre, it was anything but independent. According to them, 'the IBC final report marks the burial, for the moment, of any radical structural reform of the financial system'.[27] Vince Cable, who sat on the earlier review, acknowledged that by then the political moment had passed:

> In an ideal world we probably would have split the whole thing, politically it was never going to happen ... if the last government had embarked down that path promptly ... but by the time the Vickers Commission had been established, the situation had by then stabilized, a lot of the momentum behind really drastic action had dissipated by that point.

Whether it was lack of financial knowledge and institutional naivety, the power of the banking lobby or simply a matter of pragmatism, wider critical debate was squeezed to the margins.[28]

There is another reason why a more radical questioning and overhaul of the financial and economic system didn't take place. This was the development of an alternative narrative about what went wrong. This didn't completely deny the ideological and political issues, but it did emphasize the technical, institutional and procedural failings of banking and regulation. And ultimately, it was this view which then helped deflect calls for a fundamental inquiry, instead offering more limited technical answers.

The technical narrative begins with the reorganization of financial regulation that took place in 1997. For years regulation had tended to be spread across multiple, fairly toothless agencies. Gus O'Donnell talked about the struggle to amalgamate 11 different regulators into one FSA, at a time when the priority focus was on setting up the independent Bank of England. Paul Tucker, former deputy governor of the Bank of England, agrees. It all came down to designing a system that the Treasury and New Labour had too little understanding of:

> It's about organizational dynamics and institutional design, but Treasury policymakers were careless about institutional design ... And I think that the design in '97/98 was dreadful. There are friends of mine involved. They were very capable but I don't think they'd thought about the financial stability side, whereas I think they'd thought very carefully about the design of the monetary policy part of an independent monetary authority.

As various interviewees and post-mortems of the crisis explained, there were two obvious problems. The first was one of jurisdiction. Responsibility for financial stability and banking supervision fell between the three bodies, with none having sole responsibility.[29] The second issue was a lack of enforcement tools, even in the new FSA. As Andy Haldane recalled, while his part of the Bank had the data, 'We didn't have the regulatory tools that would have enabled us to rein in that risk taking, to rein in that leverage in the banks.' James Sassoon, who later reviewed the system for David Cameron's Conservatives when in opposition, explains the breakdown: 'There was this divide of responsibility between the Bank of England who were still doing the analysis, and the FSA who had all the tools, albeit inadequate ones, for getting the banks and other financial institutions to do what was necessary.'

Another technical issue came down to the mainstream economic models used in the Treasury. The historical data used in contemporary modelling only went back so far. It didn't incorporate previous crisis periods and so virtually excluded their future possibility. As Gus O'Donnell explained.

> This is the nature of economic models. They're all based on past data. Well, our past data didn't involve any crises. So, they really didn't work very well ... given the models we had at the time, the sorts of things that happened, for example the volatility in the stock market, was something that should happen once in the life of the universe. That's how much our model predicted it would happen and I think it happened twice in a week.

The models being used also excluded multiple elements of the economy, from financial markets to the housing bubble. Thus they didn't show any signs of distress. In effect, data-driven models were developed in line with flawed theory. Both had reinforced each other in the minds of technocrats. Consequently, as Nicholas Macpherson, among others, explained: 'This didn't have the look or feel of some massive boom in 2005, 2006, 2007. The economy was growing broadly in line with its historic average, inflation was under control and ... actually revenue growth was pretty anaemic.'

In this shifted narrative, one can detect a very technocratic sort of mea culpa emerging. The problem of

Treasury economic policy was not its broader philosophy but its outdated and limited models. The problems of the banking system were not corrupt, unaccountable financiers but a poor regulatory system. In this more technocentric version, there are clearly identifiable institutional, technical and organizational problems. Fixing those, ipso facto, will fix everything else.

This technical approach to diagnosing the crisis dictated the terms of reference for the Vickers Commission and Report of 2011. Its conclusions were in line with wider technocratic thinking. None of those I interviewed supported the more radical recommendations of these inquiries. Each took a pragmatic approach to change, believing there was too much at stake. Officials and politicians alike talked of the importance of Britain's 'world-leading financial sector' to the UK economy. Punishing banks too much would be damaging at a time when the country needed bank lending to push the recovery. All rejected the idea of breaking up banks or even ringfencing them.

Having talked to many of those officials operating in the eye of the financial and political storm, it seems evident that they lacked allies to pursue more radical reforms, even if they had wanted them. International support for larger-scale change was muted. Paul Tucker and Andy Haldane of the Bank of England explained that the country could not go it alone and impose harsher measures if rival economies didn't. For different reasons, neither Labour nor the Conservatives were prepared to punish and substantially reform big finance, let alone address wider economic issues.

The technocrats then did what they normally do in such circumstances: they took the path of least resistance and made pragmatic decisions. Having successfully charted their way through the crisis and prevented a banking collapse and depression, they continued 'fixing' things in much the same way. Keynesian-style measures were deployed to stimulate activity once again.[30] Meanwhile, out of sight of mainstream media coverage, they began to alter the organizational, technical and regulatory mechanisms for finance now deemed previously lacking. The finance division of the Treasury, from almost nothing, was expanded to number in the hundreds and, even after the crisis was over, remained a substantial division.[31] The tripartite system itself was dismantled and reconstituted via the 2012 Financial Services Act. In 2013 the FSA was shut down and an alternative set of regulatory bodies were created, each with a similar sounding (but different) acronym: the PRA (Prudential Regulation Authority), the FPC (Financial Policy Committee) and the FCA (Financial Conduct Authority).

New regulations to make banks safe again were based on a mix of the Vickers Report recommendations and Basel III.[32] Large banks were now obliged to ringfence their investment and consumer parts off from each other. Capital reserve requirements were substantially raised, with extra conditions attached if derivatives trading was taking place. From now on, banks would be regularly stress-tested. All of these measures were designed to substantially lower the risks that bank CEOs had been oblivious to before.

Looking back, most of those I interviewed about what happened sounded fairly confident that the measures put in place had left banks far more resilient than before. They believed that they were now far better placed to survive the dual threats of Brexit and COVID. I asked several of those who had been critical at the time about the failure to achieve a more radical paradigm shift. They all sounded hopeful while also admitting that the same core foundations were still in place. None appeared to be moving beyond the technical and organizational levels of change required to offer something more disruptive to the dominant UK economic model of the past four decades.

Adair Turner was perhaps the most critical of it all. He hasn't held back from denunciations of 'socially useless' big finance and an economy built on creating ever more debt. In his books he advocates the adoption of rather more extreme measures. Asked about getting his ideas more accepted by economic institutions, his answer is telling. It explains just how technocrats, even the most critical, open-minded ones, operated as they did during the crisis:

> I feel the need to push the envelope of thinking some-
> times as a deliberate exercise. But ... if you had recordings
> of me, transcripts of our meetings in 2008, you would
> not see me saying 'Guys, don't worry about the money
> let's do helicopter money.' Because right in the crisis I

don't think you can suddenly say 'I'm just going to change the whole terms of reference' ... it's very difficult if you're literally staring down the barrel of a gun and RBS is about to crash. This does tend to produce a bit of a bias to conservatism in the reactions that people have within the crisis, because those crises are so difficult and complicated and fast moving to deal with.

A former political grandee was less genteel and considered about what had transpired. He and those around him had fought hard for more concerted change and to get justice for all those impacted by big finance. Years later he sounded bitterly disappointed:

I like to be prepared for something but to be honest emotionally, intellectually, I've left this behind, because to me the shits have won, you know, because the institutional memory has gone. If you look at banking now, banking's bigger now than it was before the 2008 crisis, so they've more than regained their position. The shits have won.

Conclusion

The financial crisis showed as never before that the economic system being used to manage the UK economy was deeply flawed. If there was a time for a radical rethink it was then. Previous crises of such magnitude had produced important paradigm shifts in economic management: 1929, 1945 and 1976 had each forced the Treasury and UK government to go back to first principles and make large-scale changes. Not so now. In Martin Wolf's view, 'The Establishment view of the world was discredited in the financial crisis. There's no question about it … there wasn't a new coherent established view of how to run things after the financial crisis.'

This political and institutional failure to engage with the deeper problems or even acknowledge them properly was to have profound, long-term consequences. It allowed a flawed economic model to continue, one which stabilized the banking system but left the real economy that most people operated in stagnating and directionless. Finance got bigger, banking scandals continued alongside bankers' bonuses, and the extremely rich became super-rich. And people began to wonder about the independence and knowledge of 'experts' and career technocrats, questioning if they were any more trustworthy than politicians or bankers.

7

Austerity, spin and the road to Brexit: posh boys take charge

This final full chapter begins in May 2010 with the new Coalition government and ends with the Brexit vote in June 2016. In 2010 the new Conservative-led administration and Treasury found themselves dealing with a struggling economy and a bulging budget deficit. They found common cause in their desire to hack back public expenditure and get the finances under control. John Maynard Keynes, after a brief reappearance in the final Brown years, was dispatched and TINA[1] was back on the scene.

The period in question was very much a time when Generation P took charge: privileged, posh, professionalized politicians. David Cameron, George Osborne and Nick Clegg typified the new generation of frontbench politicians. Each had flitted between political party work, media and public relations before launching their Westminster careers. They played the tennis match of news management as well as they did the parliamentary pastime of snakes and ladders. Unfortunately, none seemed well versed in any modern games of economics (although partial to a bit of Monopoly: Ultimate Banking Edition). Having the posh boys in charge contributed to two problematic developments: a limited, detached view of the real economy, and an ability to over-sell that view through the media.

Their understanding of the economy was very much a business elite one. Their approach to economic management combined Thatcher style trickle-down economics with New Labour pseudo-Keynesian forms of boosterism. The consequence was to exacerbate the glaring social inequalities and structural economic imbalances of the UK. Big finance and services in London and the South-East flourished. But elsewhere salaries were not recovering, housing costs were shooting up, precarious working conditions were on the rise, and regional communities and economies were collapsing faster than ever.

The other key factor of the period was the Coalition's ability to dictate the media narrative on the economy. The national news media, as London-bound as the ministers and City economists they took their leads from, were happy to agree with the Coalition's decrees about the economy.

The basis of posh boy rule was shown to be the misty mirage it was during the EU referendum in 2016. When Osborne's Treasury rolled out the news about an impending economic disaster should Brexit come to pass, there was a collective shrug in many regions. Similarly, clever media management only worked when the Conservative leadership and the press were on the same page. When it came to Europe and Brexit they weren't even in the same library. People not only had had enough of expert economists, but they were also turning away from establishment politicians, national news media and all things London.

The rise of Generation P (posh professional politicians)

The May 2010 General Election saw the end of thirteen years of New Labour and brought in the UK's first Coalition government since the Second World War. There is much to be made in the way of comparison between 1979 and 2010. Both years saw a Conservative-led government, with a new-mould Tory leader, take charge following a period of national economic crisis. The new administrations each inherited a humbled Treasury determined to take control of public spending. Both involved a seemingly radical change of economic policy, which began with institutional reform, years of widespread economic pain and extensive cuts to the public sector.

The Coalition inherited an economic mess as well as a crisis of confidence in governing institutions and the banking sector. Come 2010, the Treasury budget with its deficit equivalent to 10% of GDP had got seriously out of control. Everyone agreed, Labour included, that whoever won the election would have to confront the overspend as a priority. As Nicholas Macpherson recounts: 'whoever won the 2010 election was bound to have a fiscal consolidation plan … in the end the outcome of his [Osborne's] consolidation was the same as Alistair Darling was planning'.

What was equally important was restoring the authority of UK state institutions. The banking system had failed. The regulatory system had failed. The budget deficit was spiralling up. And now there was a hung parliament. International markets were worried. Behind the scenes, confidence in the Treasury had also been dented. As Michael Fallon, a senior figure on the Treasury Select Committee during the 2000s, explained:

> The Treasury understood that two very big things had gone wrong. Financial supervision had gone wrong … and the public finances had gone badly wrong. So, my impression was that there was a degree of humility in the Treasury. These things had gone wrong on Gordon Brown's watch and that they needed to be put right fairly urgently, otherwise we would end up back in the hands of the IMF as we did in '76.

Public and Establishment trust, in theory, was restored by the removal of the Labour government, now blamed for the financial crisis, and through reform of the banking sector (see Chapter 6). Less obviously, the Treasury was effectively punished by losing some of its responsibilities to other institutions. The newly created financial regulatory bodies were placed under the sole control of the Bank of England. There was also the creation of the OBR (Office for Budget Responsibility) to produce independent forecasts and analysis of government economic data. This was to give confidence that future chancellors and

Treasury staff would not be able to manipulate forecasts according to political expediency.

However, there were also vital differences between 1979 and 2010. Most fundamental of these for me was the relationship between media, politics and economics. National economic policy has always been more intertwined with politics, Treasury needs and media debate than economists care to admit. But the balance in 2010 was very different from that of 1979. In 1979 there was an alternative economic theory and direction of travel that underpinned the politics of the Thatcherites. Economic ideas, no matter how thinly sketched out, drove the new political project and public debate.

In 2010 it was the reverse. There were no new economic ideas. Politics and media coverage instead were used to maintain an old and discredited economic policy framework packaged up as something new. The Coalition's arrival marks a sort of tipping point in the balance of forces; a point where economics became an entirely fluid and subservient puppet to whatever politicians, officials and media moguls wanted it to be.

Much of this comes down to the professional 'posh boy' politicians who found themselves in charge of the Coalition government in 2010.[2] David Cameron, George Osborne and Nick Clegg, as well as some of their key advisors and Treasury officials, shared a number of traits. One of these was being members of the British elite higher circle, the kind marked out by money, family peerages and titles, Clarendon public school educations and Oxbridge degrees.[3] Both Nicholas Macpherson, the Treasury permanent secretary, and Rupert Harrison, Osborne's chief of staff, also went to Eton and Oxford.

Having such similar backgrounds is relevant to this account because it helped cohere the contrasting organizational representatives now in charge of the economy: the senior officials of the Treasury and the leaderships of the Conservative and Liberal Democrat parties. This background offered a recognized cultural hinterland of mores, sensibilities and pre-established forms of engagement, of the kind that had been absent in the New Labour years of Brown and Balls. It brought a common view of the world and interpretation of its economic problems and solutions.

The other factor uniting the four core members of the Coalition's decision-making 'Quad' (Danny Alexander being the fourth) was that they could all be described as typifying a new generation of centrist, professionalized politicians: Generation P. Looking back now, the 2000s was probably the high point of Generation P. Various observers have noted that as parties morphed into 'electoral-professional' parties in the late twentieth century, so senior UK politicians took very different career pathways to the top.[4] The new generation were more likely to have a PPE degree, designed for aspiring leaders. They sidestepped the usual apprenticeship stints on local councils, the lengthy careers in law, business or campaigning. Previous work experience was likely to have been in a junior party backroom role, in journalism or public relations and lobbying. They became

MPs far younger and were elevated to their respective (shadow) cabinets at least a decade earlier than previous cohorts. Many were also rather more ideologically flexible, which suited them to campaigning on the political centre ground. The New Labour cabinets were chock-full of Gen P figures.

In 2010 all four members of the new ruling Coalition Quad excelled in their Gen P-ness: educational pathways, junior party roles after university, media experience, ideologically flexible, young and each rapidly elevated to shadow cabinet positions. David Cameron, at 43, was the youngest prime minister for almost two centuries and George Osborne, at 38, the youngest chancellor in almost a century. The longest any had served as an MP was nine years.

In talking to each of them, I never sensed that economics was more than a political means to an end. There was no sense of excitement about economic ideas. Those who had been part of the New Labour regime, such as Ed Balls, Dan Corry or Gus O'Donnell, got rather excited when speaking about economics, even with a non-economist academic. It was the same with Alan Budd, Terry Burns and Nigel Lawson when talking about the Thatcher years. But for those leading the Coalition, economics was just another consideration in the wider matrix of Westminster party strategizing and news lobby management.

George Osborne typified this shift. He had never studied economics, worked on economic research briefs or taken on junior Treasury roles prior to becoming shadow chancellor aged just 33. When we talked, he got more animated about political strategy than about economics. He struggled to recall his guiding economic theory – something 'based out of Harvard, the name has escaped me', or basic economic principles – 'my economic thinking is very classical … you would call it a small "l" liberal'. At one point he laughed in embarrassment at the fact that he had gained a senior academic position in a subject he knew little about: 'I even … ha ha ha … managed to become an honorary professor of economics.'

My personal view of Osborne is reinforced by several other interviews and political biographies. News accounts of the time refer to him as a 'part-time chancellor'[5] who seemed more involved in election tactics and spent more time at Number 10 meetings. A Radio Four profile referred to Rupert Harrison as 'the real chancellor'.[6] By all accounts, Cameron and Osborne almost did a 50:50 job share as both PM and chancellor.[7]

Thatcherism 101 seems to have been the default position of a collection of leaders with only a passing interest in economics. Both Osborne and Cameron were self-confessed fans of Thatcher. In developing their economic plans, they worked closely with Oliver Letwin and Terry Burns, two stalwarts of the 1980s Thatcher governments. Cameron's autobiography notes that at a young age he found inspiration in IEA[8] publications and that 'right from the start it was the radical monetarists and free marketeers who seemed to have the new and exciting ideas'. And austerity, beneath all the rhetoric, was just an accounting principle that dovetailed neatly with basic Thatcherite economics. Shrink the state that is 'crowding out' and impeding the private sector with its size, regulations and taxes and, hey presto, the economy will take off.

Rupert Harrison, 'the real chancellor', was a 26-year-old PhD student when he first began advising Osborne and Cameron. In several accounts, he is lauded in glowing terms. 'One of the most talented economists of his generation', states Cameron. 'Brilliant', comment Seldon and Snowdon.[9] I've never seen anything to explain this conclusion. When I asked him directly about the broader inspirations of his economic thinking, Harrison responded that he had no interest in macroeconomic thought. His policy views were 'shaped by more general reading' and by being 'a centre-right leaning person'. His economic framework is summed up as 'fiscal responsibility, monetary activism and supply side reform'. These simply translate into the Thatcherite staples of tax cuts, boosting the money supply and deregulation. Harrison comes across as a very competent economist and a personable individual. But that's it.

While the new Quad leaders were not that engaged with economic management, it was a different story when it came to media management. Cameron had spent seven years in PR as director of communication at the TV company Carlton. His PR and journalism skills were undoubtedly key to his success when, in 2005, as a virtual unknown, he ran a masterful media campaign to become leader of the Conservatives.[10]

Osborne, a budding part-time journalist before joining the Conservative Research Department, was his campaign manager at the time. His first post-politics job was editor of *The Evening Standard*. Nick Clegg's pre-MP work experience included stints as a journalist and at GJW Government Relations. He now has a senior lobbying/PR role at Meta (Facebook). Danny Alexander had over ten years experience as a press officer and director of communications before being elected.

Extensive efforts went into their media management strategies. Cameron conducted hundreds of meetings a year with political journalists and editors.[11] His core advisory team always contained seasoned national journalists and PR experts. Osborne, similarly, went to great lengths to sell his economic ideas, budgets and broader economic narratives. A senior economic advisor told me about Osborne's regular media strategizing in opposition and his carefully crafted budget-day sound-bites. Another insider relayed to me Osborne's extensive media preparation in advance of each budget day:

> He had such a big team, the budget was his time to shine so he took over the news agenda a week in advance, he had a story to brief every day for a week, he did certain set interviews then he did the budget ... George Osborne would have aimed for releases Friday, Saturday, Sunday, Monday, Tuesday and then the budget's on Wednesday.

In effect, Osborne was probably the least economically interested and informed of the chancellors covered in this book; but he was also one of the most politically and media astute ones. For him, economic arguments were merely tools to be skilfully deployed in the service of larger political goals: winning elections, destroying Labour Party credibility, holding the Coalition together and managing the Cameron–Osborne brand. This mattered because that ability to sell economic arguments through the media created various myths. These had a much greater purchase with the political and media classes than actual professional economists did.

Selling austerity economics: the myths of change, recovery and togetherness

A number of public narratives evolved in the Coalition years and gained significant traction across the political and media establishment. Labour profligacy rather than out-of-control bankers had crashed the economy. Britain had been living beyond its means and close to bankruptcy.[12] Each of these lines have their advocates and critics.

There are four further narrative lines that came to be generally accepted, but that are all contested here. The first is that there was professional consensus in support of austerity. Second, although austerity was painful, 'we were all in this together'. Third, Coalition economic policy enacted a radical policy shift from the New Labour years. Fourth was that Coalition policy, after a few difficult years, gained moderate success and was responsible for restoring the health of the UK economy. Each of these is far more myth than reality.[13]

The defining economic policy of the Coalition, readily embraced by both political parties and the Treasury, was, of course, austerity, aka 'fiscal consolidation'. This was very much presented as a fait accompli. Remarkably, there seems to have been little debate about either the scale and pace of the cuts, or whether an alternative balance of spending cuts and tax rises would be more desirable. I asked all those who were there, and gaining agreement on both of these issues seems to have been a very smooth process.

The key reason for this was that austerity was the central policy area uniting the two parties and the Treasury. Cameron, Osborne and Co. were essentially Thatcherite small staters when it came to economic policy. Eight of the nine Liberal Democrat authors of the 2004 Orange Book,[14] a strongly pro-market collection of essays, ended up in the Coalition cabinet at one point or another. According to Seldon and Snowdon, 'centre-leaning, pragmatic Conservatives' shared ideological territory with 'right-leaning Liberal Democrats'.[15] In the varied Coalition negotiations between the two parties, the most consistent point of consensus turned out to be an agreement on making big cuts. In one senior advisor's recollection:

> The Coalition negotiations were definitely influenced by that environment, so there was a sort of shared commitment by Conservatives and the Liberal Democrats to securing credibility for the UK public finances, concern around the kind of market environment … that definitely created buy-in, and if you read the Coalition agreement

that fiscal responsibility was absolutely a kind of glue
that anchored the entire Coalition agenda.

For the Treasury, the large-scale cuts were not simply
about pleasing its new political masters or needing to
stave off a 1979-style cull of senior mandarins. It wanted
them as much as the new Coalition leaders. The one
enduring first principle of the Treasury is that budgets
should always be balanced, unless dealing with a crisis.
By 2010, as all recall, two years after the banking collapse, the Treasury was more than ready for a return
to its basic *raison d'être*. For Cameron: 'The weight of
Treasury opinion, of Nick Macpherson, Tom Scholar,
of those sorts of people were "this is the right thing to
do."' In fact, the Treasury imposed the biggest single
department cuts on itself (33%) and Macpherson made
great efforts to reduce his own civil service headcount.
In Danny Alexander's recollection, the Exchequer wanted
to go even further:

> In the Treasury there'd been quite a lot of frustration
> over quite a few years under the previous government,
> that public expenditure hadn't been controlled … and
> Nick Macpherson joined him [Osborne] at one stage,
> made a pitch in 2012, for substantial further cuts above
> and beyond those we'd already planned, because the
> numbers had drifted so far away. And they came to the
> Quad and said, 'look we think that we need to go further,
> we need to have an extra ten or twenty billion pounds
> worth of savings', and we said 'no'.

'The most aggressive austerity programme of any
G7 country'[16] was initiated with a mix of 80% public

spending cuts and 20% tax rises. It began with an emergency 2010 budget in which £6.2 billion of cuts were announced. Later spending reviews and budgets set out how £115 billion of further cuts were to be phased in over the course of the Parliament. This resulted in an average 25% budget reduction per Whitehall department, local council funding cuts of almost a third, and an £18 billion slice off the welfare budget. It included the loss of over 600,000 public-sector jobs, a public-sector pay freeze and a block on civil service hiring. In consequence, government spending as a percentage of GDP was cut from 45% to 40% over five years, a percentage reduction that Thatcher took eleven years to implement.[17]

Having developed a policy consensus, it was then down to selling it to the media and public. Part of that was a fear-driven TINA line. Britain was going to be the next Greece, brought down by its debts. International confidence in UK Plc would collapse. International investors would flee, and no one would buy UK debt, thus bankrupting the country.

They also sought out professional and industry endorsement, to present a sense of mainstream economic consensus on austerity measures. They latched on to recent work by Carmen Reinhart and Kenneth Rogoff (that 'something from Harvard') that argued that, as a country's debt levels rose, so its growth rates declined.[18] This study, itself very controversial, was used by many politicians and commentators to argue for austerity policies.[19] Osborne also tried to recruit Rogoff to be his chief economic advisor. A public letter from 20 economists backing cuts was organized. Pro-austerity opinions from the IMF, OECD and business groups were fed to the press.

Osborne and Cameron also made sure to let the British public know that the burden of austerity was to be evenly shared. In opposition and during the 2010 election they had made great play of the Conservatives' break with 'the nasty party' of old. Once in power, the phrase 'we are all in this together' was a feature of many speeches. Certain measures supported the presentation. For the first three years they did not reduce top rates of tax. They raised the minimum wage. They maintained the overseas aid and NHS budgets while cutting all other sectors. Talking to both of them and Rupert Harrison, long after they had departed Westminster, they were still keen to stress their one-nation view and progressive intentions at the time. Cameron talked of his goals of 'job creation' and 'sharing the proceeds of growth between public spending increases and tax reductions'. Osborne told me, 'The longer I was chancellor, the more I felt we needed to make sure that the rewards of the economic turnaround were being more widely felt.'

Having set in motion its Plan A, the Coalition got on with a number of other market-oriented policy goals and waited for the economic shoots of recovery to arrive. A clear official chronicle has evolved over time regarding this. It was fleshed out in several interviews. The story is one of those where everything looks increasingly grim, but the heroes hold strong and, just when catastrophe nears, victory is snatched from the jaws of defeat.

In more detail, in 2010 the economy was struggling to shake off the effects of the financial crisis. Banks were more interested in rebuilding their balance sheets than lending to anyone. A massive crisis in the Eurozone economy was pulling the UK down with it. For almost three years there was no discernible GDP growth. Brand Osborne took a major hit in the 2012 Omnishambles budget. He was booed at the London Olympics. Then the UK lost its highly valued AAA credit rating (one of the justifications for austerity). The number of international critics of austerity grew, including OECD and IMF technocrats. Confidence in Plan A was dropping. By January 2013 things were looking particularly grim. As Charles Roxburgh, who had only recently been appointed to the Treasury, recalled:

> I remember the Chancellor opened the session at Dorneywood as we all sat round his table, and he said something like: 'Look here's what we are facing. The economy is flatlining. We're three years into this programme, and there's no sign of growth on the horizon. We might be about to have a triple dip recession. So, if you guys joined the Treasury to do serious economic policy making, now is the time to come up with some bright new ideas. And we've got a budget in six weeks' time, so we need to get moving.' I thought well, things really are pretty bleak, how is it all going to come together in time?'

In all of this, the Quad held steady. Rupert Harrison pulled others through with a burst of optimism and his 'gangbusters moment'. He convinced the team that other economic metrics were actually looking promising. The economy would be surging forward in a matter of months. The story has become folklore, relayed in several accounts.[20] He repeated it for me both times that I interviewed him. I heard the same from another senior economic advisor in the room that day:

> There was a low point which I remember at Davos in January 2013. We just had the Q4 GDP number came out and it was negative. It's since been revised to be positive but there was all this 'would we have a triple dip?' And we had a sort of crisis meeting after that. It was probably early February at Downing Street and I remember Rupert saying 'just got to hang tough, the economy will be going gangbusters by July', and everyone laughed and actually, Ed Llewellyn, David Cameron's chief of staff wrote that down in his diary and made him sign it.

As the official story continues, Harrison was proved right. The Eurozone crisis ended. Revised ONS figures came out showing that the economy was not dipping again but turning to growth ('I feel like suing the statistics office', said Cameron). Employment rose rapidly with more private-sector jobs created than public-sector ones lost. Banks began lending again. Consumer and investor confidence and house buying returned. By 2014 the UK had leapt ahead of many of its rival economies. David Cameron beamed as he confidently sketched out the achievements to me:

> By 2015 we had the fastest growth in the G7. We had this amazing record of job creation, and we'd been able

to prove the doubters wrong. People said 'You'll never replace the public sector jobs.' We did. 'You'll never get the economy growing.' We did ... post-tax income for most people was actually increasing and that, combined with the high minimum wage, we can argue that it was a recovery people could feel in their pockets ... what we did between 2010 and 2016 showed you could get the deficit down and get the economy growing and get unemployment falling.

Seldon and Snowdon agreed: 'The economic recovery of 2010–15 defined the character of the Coalition ... his [Osborne's] piloting Britain through profound economic weakness back to economic vitality, will be his greatest achievement.' So did most media commentators come the election. The Conservatives increased their lead over Labour as the party most trusted to run the economy. A Conservative majority followed.

Myths and reality: K-shaped recovery and the asset economy

Unfortunately, what the above account really shows is that there are lies, damn lies and official political biographies. While there are some core elements of truth, much of the official and media narratives about the period are more myth than reality.

First, much of the TINA line of professional economic consensus around austerity is not supported. There may have been close agreements on cuts among senior Treasury officials and the Quad, but things were not so assured beyond it. No one really thought the UK was similar to Greece or that the markets were about to stop buying government debt. There was no clear consensus that austerity was the correct approach. A sizeable minority supported the policy in 2010, but those numbers declined, and by 2013, 80% of academic economists were against it in an *FT* survey.[21] Cutting clearly conflicted with standard Keynesian responses to economic crises, as multiple high-profile economists pointed out (Paul Krugman, Joseph Stiglitz, Martin Wolf, Simon Wren-Lewis). As one senior official explained, the UK austerity policy response was far from universally adopted:

> We were some ways out of line with the international consensus, in particular in those years with the G7, it was just an endless pitched battle between the Germans and the Americans, in which the Americans under Obama were fiscally expansionary, and the Germans were, well German. And we were very German at that time.

Second, there is ample evidence to suggest that the recovery was muted at best in 2013. Actual GDP per capita growth, as opposed to growth, did not return to pre-crisis levels until 2015.[22] Again, senior officials there at the time sound very sceptical about the upturn. One spontaneously laughed out loud when I mentioned the Harrison 'gangbusters' anecdote: 'Ha ha ha. It wasn't quite gangbusters! But it came good, started to get positive quarterly growth, something like 0.3 one quarter. Everyone got very excited', he said with a nod and a wink.

By 2015 the indicators were clearer, but few economic historians would claim this was a 'strong recovery'.

Productivity growth was consistently lower than it had been at any point since 1965.[23] The same OBR that Osborne set up to deliver objective analysis consistently stated that austerity delayed the recovery. The Institute for Fiscal Studies concludes that the period was record breaking for all the wrong reasons: 'record low earnings growth, record low interest rates, record low productivity growth, record public borrowing followed by record cuts in public spending'.[24] By 2016 the budget deficit had been reduced to 3.3% but was still very much there. The UK debt to GDP ratio of 63.84% in 2010 had reached 81.35% in 2016.[25]

In fact, what prompted the semblance of a recovery was a return to the same kinds of pseudo-Keynesian activities that previous administrations had been engineering for decades (see Chapter 4). Cameron and Harrison refer to this as 'monetary activism', which was basically finding ways to create and circulate large amounts of capital in parts of the economy without it appearing to be government spending. Interest rates were kept very low and, in July 2012, another round of QE to the value of £175 billion took place. The Bank of England estimated that the value of equities on the London Stock Exchange over 2008–14 was 25% higher than it would have been without QE.[26]

Osborne continued with PFI schemes, to the tune of £6.9 billion in his first year in office, before creating PF2 for further projects. The Coalition also did its best to push the housing market once again. As a senior economic advisor explained, the intentions here were clearly not to officially increase government spending but to stimulate economic activity by other means:

> Monetary activism initially was conceived of as QE, but we increasingly came to see that QE was not being effective because essentially the financial transmission mechanism was impaired ... So, it was Help-to-Buy [2013], it was the infrastructure loan guarantees that the Treasury launched. I would include the Funding for Lending [2012] scheme within that. So, it wasn't the government spending more money directly through fiscal policy, as we were very keen to stick to the consolidation plan. But we were using the government balance sheet in other ways to stimulate the economy.

Despite all the political rhetoric of a big change in policy, 'rebalancing the economy', a 'March of the Makers' and the 'Northern Powerhouse', very little actually changed. Manufacturing continued its decline, losing some 200,000 jobs, while finance continued to grow, gaining a similar amount. Manufacturing as a percentage of output fell from 10.9% in 2007 to 9.7% in 2014, while finance and insurance increased from 7.4% to 9.9%.[27] At the same time, London and the South-East continued to outstrip the rest of the country in terms of incomes, productivity, living standards, asset wealth, infrastructure investment and so on. In 2016 London's GVA (Gross Value Added) per head was 72% higher on average than the rest of the nation.[28]

For several critics things had barely changed. This was the same old economic policy in action, but this time with severe public-sector cuts. The things most responsible for boosting growth and the economy in artificial and damaging ways were, once again, being deployed: pushing big finance, firing up the housing market, debt-based consumer spending and magic money trees. As Adam Tooze concluded: 'In economic terms "rebalancing" was a myth.'[29] Craig Berry refers to the austerity years as a period of 'radical continuity' and an 'illusion of change' used 'to justify the resurrection of the UK's pre-crisis growth model'.[30]

Third, we were never all in it together; quite the reverse in fact. Much of this came back to the Quad and Treasury mandarin view of the economy and how it was best boosted. Simply put, this saw multinational businesses, the City and international investment as being the drivers of growth, employment and tax income. Hence, what top CEOs expected, requested, pleaded for, was what needed to be done to spur the economy on. Looking back over my interviews with key figures, this basic world view shone through in various ways. As Osborne explained:

> The essential environment you have to create is one in which businesses want to invest and create jobs in a world where capital's highly mobile and, indeed, very sought-after people are highly mobile. So, you have to attract business to these shores. And I went out of my way to pick up the phone to get companies to move their headquarters here, as well as creating an environment in which they might want to, like reducing corporation tax.

Compliance with business expectations meant an adherence to trickle-down economics in all its guises.

Quantitative easing as a policy for stimulating economic activity is entirely trickle-down in conception.[31] Something similar was evident in their 'Laffer Curve' thinking about reducing the top rates of income and corporation tax. The rate of corporation tax dropped steadily in each annual budget, from 28% in 2010 to 20% in 2015. The top rate of personal income tax was also lowered from 50% to 45%. Cameron and others confidently told me that these measures brought in more tax overall. The OBR was not so sure.

What also became clear when talking to Quad members and economic advisors was their focus on financial markets. Osborne told me that keeping 'financial markets happy and reassured' was one of his top priorities when delivering his budget speeches. As Philip Hammond remembers: 'George was more concerned about markets, was always nervous about the way markets would view the UK economy and its performance.' When I asked how Harrison had known that a 'gangbusters' period for the economy was on the way, the advisor relating the story reeled off a series of metrics, all of which sounded of greatest interest to international investors: 'The reason was that we in the Treasury were very optimistic because we had seen bank funding, we'd seen credit growth start to move, we'd seen business confidence in surveys starting to come back. We'd seen that reflected in a lot of market pricing about UK.' According to these indicators, the UK economy did appear to be improving in the last years of the Coalition. Growth had returned, unemployment was rapidly declining, the financial and housing markets were buoyant once again, and business and financial market confidence was riding high. Those metrics, from the Quad and Treasury vantage point, equalled economic recovery and success.

But from multiple other perspectives, the aggregate data didn't reflect many people's day-to-day experience of the economy. In fact, for certain groups it was a matter of being subjected to a triple financial hit: in their employment conditions, in the direct impact of cuts, and in the housing market.

Starting with employment, by the end of the Parliament unemployment had dropped under 6% and was below that of most EU countries. However, two-thirds of the new private-sector jobs that had replaced lost public-sector ones were in low-skilled and low-paid sectors. Many were also precarious in that they were part-time, fixed-term, self-employed and zero-hours in nature. By the start of 2017 three million jobs, or one-third of the workforce, were now in such forms of employment.[32] In the first three years of the Coalition, British workers saw a drop in real wages of 8.5%, the fourth largest drop of the 27 EU member states.[33] This explains why the UK was the only leading economy to record both GDP growth and a fall in real wages between 2007 and 2015.[34]

The second element of the financial hit came from the large cuts to public services and the changing tax regime. This primarily affected the poorer parts of society. By the end of the Coalition's term, 89% of fiscal consolidation was achieved by such cuts.[35] The one tax that was raised was VAT, from 15% to 20%, a tax which disproportionately affected those at the bottom. The cuts in public-sector and regional support also hit some of the poorest regions most.

The third financial hit came in housing. During the financial crisis and for a couple of years after, house prices suffered a major fall. But as the 2010s proceeded, the combination of ultra-low interest rates, QE, tax changes and new Treasury schemes all encouraged housing investors, and associated costs then leapt up. The Bank of England calculated that the hundreds of billions in QE money had helped push this rise and that house prices in 2014 would have been 22% lower without it.[36] In 1997 median house prices were 3.44 times median annual earnings in England and Wales, but by 2017 that had risen to 7.57 times.[37] Clearly, for those whose income was either static, precarious or in decline, rising rental and mortgage costs were an increasing problem. Yet this issue seemed to have bypassed many in the Treasury and the Quad. Harrison thought this was a limited 'side-effect'. Osborne called it a 'high-quality problem'.

For much of the 2010s, forecasters and commentators discussed whether the UK economy was going to have a U-, V- or W-shaped recovery. The predictions were invariably wrong. What rarely came up was the fact that the shape of the recovery in Britain, whenever it arrived, was more likely to be K-shaped. From mid-2013 onwards, key demographics and parts of the economy saw a steady upward turn, with a select group experiencing almost a 'gangbusters' period. But for others, a lengthy period of stagnation and slow decline, which had begun well before the financial crisis, then took a very pronounced downward shift.

For several heterodox economists, these growing disparities across the nation exacerbated longer-term trends towards Britain's 'rentier' or 'asset' economy. Thomas Piketty, Guy Standing and Brett Christophers each apply slightly different terms in their analysis.[38] But each agree that capitalist economies, particularly more neoliberal ones, have re-reached a particular tipping point where more money is being made from varied types of rentier activity and assets than from producing, distributing and selling real goods and services. Such conditions existed prior to the 1929 Wall Street Crash, and then began to develop once again in line with neoliberal policies in the late 1970s.

Rentier activity does not simply apply to profits from renting land or property but also to rents extracted from intellectual copyright, digital platforms, financial market structures and products. Marketization and deregulation have also meant that rentiers are more able to extract excess profits by virtue of owning and exploiting private monopoly positions, whether in outsourced government contracts[39] or in natural resources. Multiple economic conditions pushed these trends further in the post-financial crisis years. Loose monetary policy, with low interest rates and QE, beneficial tax systems and continued financial innovation, have all encouraged varieties of rentier-type activity. They have also encouraged what Adkins and others call the 'asset economy',[40] whereby the accumulation of profit-bearing assets, such as property and shares, has become a primary goal of wealthy individuals and companies, non-financial as well as financial.

By 2016 the post-financial crisis economy of the UK had barely recovered. The recovery that did exist was based on the same artificial and short-term boosts to wealthy individual and corporate asset holders. As with previous such activities, the larger macro picture is one of redistributing capital upwards, to certain financial and professional services sectors, to London and the South-East. Those not in these categories were paying the price.

And then came the EU referendum.

Caught in the Brexit crossfire?

On 23 June 2016 the UK voted to leave the European Union. The EU referendum result was an event that was as damaging to the Treasury as the 1976 IMF bailout. Even more than the catastrophic attempt to join the ERM (1992) or the failures of the great financial crisis (2007–08), Brexit dealt a devastating blow to the institution.

The referendum was originally called to end a decades-long conflict in the Tory Party. The expectation was of a decisive vote to remain. The reasons why the Leave campaign won have been chewed over in numerous accounts.[41] All note the role of the Treasury in the events, but few see it as playing more than a reluctant supporting part in the action. As with all Treasury-linked disasters, the Exchequer is happy to go along with that narrative. Senior civil servants prefer to present the institution as an innocent party, one that didn't cause the mess but worked admirably to clear it up afterwards. A senior Treasury official put the formal institutional position on Brexit to me:

> The Treasury never declared for remain at all, the Treasury is just a government department. The government did, the chancellor did, and there were some aspects of that that were quite unfortunate … the Treasury that I grew up in was I would say a deeply Eurosceptic institution.

The Treasury was increasingly pulled into the debate because of the campaign line taken by Cameron, Osborne and the Remain side. The key argument of Remain, pretty much the only argument of Remain, was that British economic prosperity relied on EU membership. Leaving would lead to economic disaster. This same strategy worked well in the 2014 Scottish independence referendum and the 2015 General Election, only with Scottish independence and a Miliband government being potentially disastrous for the nation's economy. As David Cameron explained, this same argument was the one that gained most traction with the 20–30% of wavering voters: 'People in the middle who were undecided, the evidence showed that the thing that drove them most was economic arguments … we had a very strong economic case and every time we were on the economy we were winning, and you can tell that from the daily polls.'

So, the Exchequer was forcibly seconded on to the campaign by Osborne and Cameron to make official assessments of what leaving the EU would do to the economy. In April there was a long-term forecast, talking of a 6.2% GDP drop, families being £4,300 worse off, and a £36 billion black hole in the nation's finances that would have to be covered with a big rise in income tax. In May that was followed by a 90-page short-term immediate impact assessment by the Treasury, adding in some more 'severe shock scenario' forecasts.[42] This was followed in mid-June by Osborne's suggestion of an emergency ('punishment') leave budget with increased taxes and cuts to services.

By various accounts, Osborne pushed the neutral civil servants of the Treasury into participating in what Leave quickly labelled 'Project Fear'. This undermined its independence and authority as well as posing questions about its competence in forecasting. According to one economic advisor, 'George made them put out this economic analysis which showed Brexit would be economically damaging.' For another mandarin, no official wanted to be linked with it, and they were concerned with what they were asked to do: 'George was frustrated that the long term one hadn't been shocking enough and wanted something that was more shocking, but it was always a bit suspicious … And that short term forecast did us terrible reputational damage.'

However, for me, this doesn't quite ring true. Treasury officials may have been dragged into the public arena against their will, but I believe they were always very much on the Remain side. Treasury officials had played a key role in the establishment of the single market in the 1980s. Leaving went counter to decades of Treasury orthodoxy on internationalism, free trade and free markets. British industry had become heavily inter-twined with supply chains and markets that criss-crossed between Continental Europe and the UK. International corporations had been enticed to Britain with the promise of frictionless access to Europe. For politicians and economic advisors, there was no question about where the Treasury stood on the issue. As one former advisor says, 'It was massively Europhile. They thought it was a desperately damaging decision to leave the European Union.' 'They were pro Britain's membership of the EU. I don't remember getting any pushback on that', states Cameron.

It is at this point that I feel a need to make a con-troversial and contradictory statement. The Treasury was not only against Brexit, but it also strongly con-tributed to that outcome. How can I come to such a conclusion?

For one, I hold the Treasury (and successive govern-ments) responsible for ushering in an economy that was so unbalanced and unequal. Years of trickle-down economics, and years of favouring finance over manufacturing, large foreign multinationals over home-grown companies, large asset-holders and rentiers over others, London over the regions, monetary rather than fiscal activism had had a cumulative impact. Austerity economics only exacerbated such trends, with several commentators linking that to the vote outcome.[43]

More than that, Osborne, Cameron, the City and much of the press had spent years telling people that the economy was doing splendidly, and that they were all better off now. They patently weren't in many cases. So, when the Treasury set out its alarming forecasts and abstract data, the dismissal of Project Fear gained traction. When Michael Gove remarked that people had had 'enough of experts', meaning economists, while there was outrage across the London intelligentsia, there was a lot of nodding elsewhere. And when Osborne and a few rich captains of industry said a vote to leave would mean great financial hardship, no one really listened. As Robert Peston puts it, being told 'that things would only get shittier if we left the EU' was never a winning argument, especially when presented by 'the posh boys'.[44]

And then there was the role of the British right-wing press, whose owners actually thought the EU was holding back the national economy. For decades a majority of the UK print media, including the *Daily Mail*, *Daily Express*, the *Sun*, *The Times*, the *Telegraph* and their Sunday equivalents, had strongly supported the Conservatives at every election. The thought of a non-Blairite

Labour leader or Scottish nationalist in power was enough for them to go all out for Cameron in 2010, 2014 and 2015. But on Europe things were different. These same titles had been overtly critical of the EU for many years. They had never been particularly taken with Osborne and Cameron, nor forgiven Cameron for acceding to public demand for the Leveson Inquiry into the press. And in 2016, if it was a choice between backing Cameron or backing an opportunity to leave the hated EU, they didn't hesitate.

All Cameron and Osborne's skilful media management and economic fear arguments were far less effective when countered directly by their normally supportive press. Loughborough University's news content analysis of the referendum found that most coverage contained biased reporting which was heavily skewed towards the Leave side. If adjusted for circulation, 82% of that biased coverage came down in favour of Brexit.[45]

But Remain's loss was not just about their lack of credibility on economic arguments as they related to ordinary people. It was also that Leave's arguments about sovereignty and immigration had a stronger purchase on undecided voters (yeah, OK, and that lying NHS bus too). As Cameron acknowledged: 'Every time we were on the immigration issue we were effectively losing.' But on these issues, decades of Treasury economic policy were also a strong contributory factor. As Chapter 5 showed, the internationalist philosophy of the Exchequer meant that Britain had become one of the nations that did least to protect its own industries, to support UK company exports, or to nurture and invest in emerging new sectors. It had proved itself to be remarkably relaxed about UK-based companies moving jobs and investment abroad, or international companies relocating profits back to home headquarters or international shareholders. Arguments about sovereignty, when it came to the economy, were roundly rejected.

And then there was the immigration issue. The Exchequer, in line with most studies, had always encouraged immigration, believing it to be good for growth, productivity and largely positive for the economy. What was not part of its accounting was the social and welfare costs of immigration in terms of investing in services and infrastructure in areas where migrant numbers were increasing. In effect, it was happy to reap the economic benefits and tax income of migrants but didn't want to provide the extra funding for schools, health and transport that were then required.

With the benefit of Brexit hindsight, many now point a finger at New Labour's move to allow citizens from the new Eastern Bloc members of the EU to gain UK residency early in 2004.[46] In the 2010s, and despite tough talk from Cameron about limiting immigration, annual net migration into the UK continued to be in the hundreds of thousands. In fact, over the decade 2010–20, the UK population grew by 4.5 million, usually unevenly distributed and often concentrated in particular areas. Two-thirds of the new jobs in precarious work sectors created in the Coalition years went to such new immigrants.[47] Much of this migration at the time came from Europe as the Eurozone crisis unfolded. And in 2015–16 net migration reached 333,000, the second highest figure on record.[48]

Looking back, the members of the Quad and Treasury mandarins, although refusing to recognize the part played by austerity in the Brexit vote, do admit they got something wrong when it came to issues of sovereignty and immigration. David Cameron and Nicholas Macpherson lament the Treasury's 'naivety' and blind spot on the issue. Another senior official offers more detailed mea culpa reflections:

> In my view, we completely misunderstood the mood of the nation. We misunderstood the mood outside of London and we didn't recognize the very legitimate counter case to the purely economic argument, which is the sovereignty case … We also didn't appreciate the social impact of migration. The Treasury had long argued that migration was a good thing, which economically it undoubtedly is. But I think we had been insensitive to the social impact of a sudden rise in migration, as happened in the years before the referendum, and particularly if that migration was regionally concentrated … The fact that free movement of people might be good for the flexible labour market and all that good economic stuff, well, those theoretical arguments meant nothing to families who couldn't get their kids into the local schools or see their GPs because the population in their town had grown so fast. I think a fair criticism is that, under successive governments, the Treasury had advocated free movement without committing the money to expand public services to cope with the resulting increase in population, especially where it was regionally concentrated.

Conclusion: truth, lies and experts

Of course, there were many reasons that Brexit came about, and many heroes and villains involved. So, is it fair to hold the Treasury to account for the outcome and make it a more central player? This seems a little counter-intuitive and unfair, especially since the Treasury, willingly or not, was part of the Remain campaign. Treasury orthodoxy, in various ways, meant the institution had an awful lot of buy-in into the EU, and not just the single market element.

But that is precisely the issue that needs deconstructing. The Treasury's insular nature and abstract mode of thinking has been a major contributor to wider socio-economic problems as they have developed over time across the UK; something it can rarely see for itself as it battles endlessly to try and balance the nation's books. And that includes all manner of consequences that the Treasury never wanted, such as Brexit.

The other counter-intuitive point to make, something that I really became more aware of in writing this book, relates to the political and media-management trends that built from New Labour to the Coalition government to the Johnson administration. It's easy to mark out Boris Johnson's Brexiteers as markedly different from the Coalition leaders or the New Labour government that went before; to see Johnson, Farage and their followers as 'irrational', 'ignorant', 'liars', 'fantasists', 'self-interested' and 'opportunistic', manipulating the new world of celebrity politics. However, looking back, one can see these self-same elements in the Osborne and Cameron Coalition years or even in Blair and Brown's time. They may have used charm rather than crude culture war rhetoric, experts and rationality rather than pushing knee-jerk emotions, but in many ways the result was the same. Self-interested claims were spun, misleading narratives were built up, and the rich got richer while the poor got poorer, just at a faster rate. Economics and experts could be just as wrong, self-serving and fantastical as colourful populists.

The reckless opportunists who took over after 2016 did not come out of nowhere. They had a clear political genealogy.

8

Brexit and COVID postscript: reckless opportunists gain control

Originally Brexit was going to be this book's punchline. It neatly marked the end of forty years of Treasury history, starting with one existential crisis for the institution and ending in another. It also seemed to mark forty years of the rise and fall of Britain's particular neoliberal experiment. The Exchequer had played a vital role in shaping that system, positioned as it had been at the centre of an intellectual and institutional nexus, connecting British elites from Whitehall to the City. But since the referendum, there have been several big shifts in the Treasury's fortunes, making a postscript seem essential.

Since the 2016 Brexit vote, the Treasury has experienced both a rapid decline and a renewal of fortunes. The downward spiral began with the lost vote. The result marked the end of both Establishment unity and relative policy consensus, as well as a powerful strike against Exchequer power itself. Into the power vacuum walked Britain's own reckless opportunists.[1] Boris Johnson and a makeshift alliance of politicians, media moguls and corporate leaders had all seen the EU referendum as an opening too good to miss. Nothing, including the Union, several decades of excess profits or the endurance of the Tory Party itself, was going to get in their way. Neither was the Treasury and its orthodoxy.

Initially, throughout the Theresa May years of Westminster trench warfare, a weakened Exchequer was left struggling and blindfolded as it attempted to regain influence. The arrival of the Johnson government offered a further challenge and a direct threat to the Whitehall mandarins themselves. The new administration sold itself on tearing up austerity and balanced budgets in favour of costly intervention. The pandemic crisis then provided cover for Johnson's populist spending plans. The weakened Treasury had little choice but to return to levels of economic intervention not seen since the 1970s.

But at the time of writing (early 2022), the Exchequer is once again in the ascendancy. Rishi Sunak and the Treasury have had a good pandemic, performing rather better than Matt Hancock and the rest of the cabinet. Partygate has finally cut through Johnson's Teflon coating in a way that his other failings have not. Sunak and other leadership contenders are far more in tune with traditional Treasury small-state instincts, as levelling up is quietly dug over again.

But such is the current dysfunction of British politics and mainstream economic policy that it's unclear how enduring the emerging ruling coalition might be.

Brexit and the breakdown of the Treasury-centred establishment consensus

Brexit devastated the Treasury on multiple levels, some more visible than others. First was the immediate fallout from the referendum itself. One senior official's account of what was happening inside the institution the day after the vote reveals the sense of chaos and disarray that followed:

> The day of the referendum was an extraordinary day in the Treasury … I woke up again at four o'clock and I went into the Treasury … when everyone else came to work, it was quite shocking and the leaders of what we call the EMB, we all went out and talked to different teams, did stand up meetings and we were very keen to reassure people … But there were a lot of people in tears. There were a lot of people, who did take it as a personal criticism. George Osborne disappeared. We didn't see him again until the following Monday. The prime minister resigned. So, by 9.30 on the day of the biggest political shock in modern British history we didn't have a chancellor because he'd gone AWOL, but the prime minister had just resigned. It was kind of bizarre. The adult, the supervising adult for the financial system was Mark Carney who had made an extremely accomplished, almost presidential statement from the Bank [of England]. Nobody understood what it meant, but he had a very big number.

The damage went rather deeper and was more long-lasting. The Treasury was very obviously on the losing side of a huge fight. Under Cameron and Osborne, the relationship between 10 Downing Street and the Treasury had been exceptionally harmonious. But even in the difficult Blair–Brown years, the Treasury had been a commanding government presence with a very powerful patron. Now it was sent spinning and leaderless. For one senior advisor at the time, the Exchequer remained both isolated and in the denial stage of grief for some time:

> The Treasury was quite bruised when we got there, by having to engage with the referendum, by losing it, by losing George and losing George's very closeness with David the prime minister, and having a more difficult relationship between 10 and 11. So it was seen as it being clipped … they were feeling Brexit was the wrong decision for the country. And I spoke to one very senior official whose plan basically was to drop out of the EU, into the EEA for a few years, and then re-join the EU.

What the campaigns also showed was the fact that the British Establishment had violently fractured over the issue. With the Brexit vote, the Treasury lost its dominant, facilitating position in the institutional nexus of national economic management. The Leave side of the Tory Party, Establishment and country had won. A vote for Brexit was also a vote of no confidence in economic experts and Treasury authority. From Martin Wolf's perspective:

> Brexit was a project carried through by people against the overwhelming view of the economics profession. So, Brexit has almost by definition had to say, 'economists are useless because they disagree with us', and since this government is still really only united by Brexit, economists and economic thinking just doesn't fit into their ideology.

Consequently, Treasury orthodoxy and authority were much diminished. Within the Conservative government there was no longer an economic consensus or agreed plan. The Treasury was now one player among many, jostling with enemies on all sides. For one senior official: 'The impact on the standing of the institution I think was significant ... there were certain individuals and maybe even sections of the governing party who continued to view the Treasury with enormous suspicion.'

It wasn't just the Conservative Party that was pulling apart Establishment cohesion during the post-referendum years of political limbo. Hitherto, the Treasury could find common cause with the City, big business, most of the Conservative-supporting national press and the Blairite wing of the Labour Party. They all broadly agreed on the key elements of economic policy. But the EU was something else, as was any agreement on the future of EU–UK relations.

Many of Britain's business and financial elite, despite their strong concerns about leaving the EU, were reluctant to get involved publicly in the 2016 campaign. This remained so when it came to making the soft Brexit case. As Philip Hammond admitted: 'Across business more generally I was really quite shocked ... whenever I addressed the business audience, I could not assume that my audience was all going to be of the same view as myself and they weren't.' As several in and around the Treasury commented, CEOs constantly turned up, armed with alarming research to lobby against leaving the EU and a hard Brexit. But many calculated that public campaigning for Remain or a soft Brexit contained as much business risk as leaving. As one advisor explained:

> That drove me mad and some of the others as well. They'd come into the Treasury, and they'd complain and complain and complain. They'd provide this sharp harsh data, and we'd think great, write a letter, publish it in *The Times*. 'Oh, we can't do that.' They didn't want the risk … from a business perspective they'd done the right thing, but they all came in and complained.

And then there was the British news media. They had been highly critical of the EU for years. They were also inclined to savage any frontbench politician when it suited them, but they normally ignored the grey, backroom officials of Whitehall. Not so now. Along with judges, woke academics and Remoaner MPs, Treasury officials were placed in the ranks of the 'enemies of the people'.[2]

Under Theresa May, the antagonism between Number 10 and the Treasury grew. No one, including Philip Hammond and all the advisors and officials I talked to, quite knew what May's intentions were on Brexit. They were all blindsided by her 'Brexit means Brexit' speech, her decision to trigger Article 50,[3] and shocked by her complete lack of understanding of the economic implications of leaving the single market.[4] Hammond continued to battle for the status quo; that is, balancing the budget and aiming for the softest Brexit possible. However, May, pushed on by the Brexiteers and her aides Nick Timothy and Fiona Hill, instead veered towards a hard

Brexit. They also directly challenged the Treasury, attempting to wrest control of economic policy from it. As one top official recalls:

> Nick Timothy genuinely hated the Treasury, genuinely hated us and saw us as the root of all evil, and his creation of BEIS[5] was a straight up attack, meant to recreate the department of economic affairs, to pull the economics part out of the Treasury, give it to a department for business, energy and industrial strategy, and to shift the centre of economic policy making debate.

Both the Treasury and Philip Hammond looked increasingly isolated in their position. Few were prepared to take their side within Westminster or outside. They seemed to be hanging on by default amid the wider turmoil of government.

The Treasury's revival through crisis

Three major crises have pushed the Treasury's recovery from its 2016–17 nadir (as this book indicates, the Exchequer does crisis exceedingly well). The first, devastating to the nation's politics, was the June 2017 election. The second, devastating to its health, was the 2020 arrival of COVID. The third was more localized and personal, but no less significant: Partygate and the breakdown of Johnson's temporary ruling coalition.

The 2017 election result, debilitating as it was for May, probably saved both Hammond's position as chancellor and the Exchequer from a more major assault. Instead of Hammond being sacked, as had been widely touted before the election, it was Nick Timothy and Fiona Hill who were dispatched. Gavin Barwell, May's new chief of staff, was far better disposed to the Treasury and to gaining working consensus across government. For all May's and Hammond's differing views on Brexit and spending, Hammond was rather easier to deal with than the many reckless opportunists now taking up cabinet seats. As a senior official reflected: 'Theresa May realized that Philip Hammond, for all the challenging aspects of that relationship, was basically the only member of the cabinet that remained consistently loyal and respectful to her and didn't brief against her.'

The Treasury also regained a degree of economic management authority. This was partly because none of the department's enemies offered an alternative economic vision or were able to influence Exchequer policy. As one former economic advisor states: 'Brexiteers like Boris basically had no coherent position or argument, frankly. They didn't understand the trade-offs that were inherent in Brexit.' Thus, Hammond was able to keep them at arm's length.

Hammond and the Treasury were then quietly able to regroup and continue pursuing the as-you-were strategy of balancing the budget, maintaining international investor confidence and pushing for a softer Brexit. Although they eased up a bit on deficit reduction, Hammond was entirely attuned to the previous orthodoxy. He had backed the cuts strategy of the Coalition before and strongly believed in retaining access to the single market now.[6]

Then, after three and a half years of Brexit treacle, May was finally checkmated by Johnson's collection of Leavers and reckless opportunists. The Exchequer once again found itself in danger as Johnson ruthlessly began dispatching Conservative Party malcontents. He removed the party whip from 21 MPs including Hammond, and purged many of May's ministers. Johnson was then returned with a clear majority at the election at the end of 2019. He consolidated his position by hacking away at any dissenting Establishment institutions and voices, from Parliament to the judiciary and the BBC. A hard Brexit was achieved. He made a point of firing any cabinet colleagues who might either offer a hint of opposition or, worse still, appear more competent than him. As one former Treasury advisor put it to me: 'And we all know what happens if you say no to the prime minister. You get whacked.'

Sajid Javid, Johnson's first chancellor and a popular figure in the Treasury, was whacked less than six months after being appointed. Rishi Sunak, then just another unknown Goldman Sachs graduate, fell into line. Dominic Cummings, Johnson's whacker-in-chief, was set on ejecting many senior mandarins, with Tom Scholar, the Treasury permanent secretary, at the top of his list. Then, just as Cummings was preparing the hits, Johnson, in true Robert De Niro (or perhaps Michael Gove) style, clipped Cummings instead. Surprisingly, once he was secure as PM, Johnson dropped his attacks on anti-Brexiteers and Whitehall. Peerages were quietly doled out and whips restored. Peace was made with Number 11. In one mandarin's view:

> Once he [Boris Johnson] became prime minister, he has never turned that flak on us. I mean he's actually worked well with the Treasury … I genuinely think we've recovered from it, and I think that the current prime minister and chancellor are both very, very committed Brexiteers, who hold the Treasury in very high regard, and we've moved on, and that institutional damage has been repaired.

Key to the better relationship was the fact that the Treasury and its new chancellors, Javid and then Sunak, accepted Johnson's Brexit and big spending agendas. On the Brexit side, talking to those in and around the Treasury in 2021, there appeared to be a greater willingness to engage with the Leave position. Voting Leave hadn't made much sense to them at the time. They now acknowledged the issues of sovereignty, immigration and regional economic disparities, keenly felt beyond the London bubble. A new office is being set up in Darlington with an expectation of eventually employing some two to three hundred Treasury staff there.[7]

There was also a recognition that austerity had gone on too long and that there was a need to actively support those regions left behind. A move away from austerity was already being signalled after the 2017 election. After his 2019 triumph, Johnson made great efforts to distinguish his administration from Cameron's and May's with tens of billions of additional public spending and by setting up an infrastructure investment bank. As one official explains in relation to this: 'The private sector is, at least our institutional investors are, very risk averse. And they won't invest in unproven technology or early-stage technology and so … you need public sector risk appetite to get it going.'[8] All of which sounds very un-Treasury and un-Tory.

I asked several Conservatives to explain this sudden shift of party and Exchequer policy and got varied explanations. Some talked of the levelling up agenda and the need to secure those new northern 'red wall' seats gained from Labour in 2019. For others, like Michael Fallon and Philip Hammond, the Tories can spend pragmatically when circumstances require it, and the party has always had its interventionists. According to Hammond: 'Boris has always been an interventionist. Boris as Mayor of London was always trying to get money to intervene in things … Boris is a Tory in the Heseltine mode, believes in government and intervention.'

For others, the spending has no larger economic policy coherence but is purely about Johnson's populist instincts. It was aimed at changing the Tory brand and maintaining Johnson's voter appeal. Its future is therefore limited, clashing as it does with more traditional Conservative world views. As one advisor put it:

> He tells everybody what they want to hear. He just says yes. He just tells people what they want. It was a slightly childish but not illogical approach to levelling up. He full-throatedly accepted that austerity was over. His policy was to level up. He got that that meant local

spending on schools and buses in the way that Theresa's administration hadn't quite arrived at yet. And then of course Boris Johnson went too far … like all prime ministers they want to spend, their answer to everything is spend. A vote? Spend, spend, spend. They have absolutely no concept of where it comes from.

And then, just as the officials in the Treasury started to feel distinctly uncomfortable with the new grand outlays, there came the COVID pandemic. This event, probably the most devastating for the general public's lives since the Second World War, was both punishing for the Treasury and one of its finest hours.

While Boris Johnson and Matt Hancock dithered about the correct health response, Sunak's Exchequer moved remarkably quickly. People and businesses had to be persuaded that they could go into lockdown without starving or going bankrupt. That entailed an economic intervention of a scale not seen in peacetime. For Tom Scholar, as with the 2008 move to shore up the banks, 'both of those interventions would have been unthinkable until they became inevitable'. Senior officials combined with the Bank of England to ignore usual practices and dream up solutions to problems they had never thought about. As one official admitted: 'Some countries have existing furlough schemes, we had nothing, we didn't even know what the name meant.' As another tells the story, the speed and responsiveness were extremely impressive:

> Our tax teams and HMRC invented and implemented furlough at incredible speed. At its peak, we had a third

of the British workforce on our payroll. We were paying 80% of the salaries of nearly ten million out of a workforce of thirty million. We created a whole new large corporate banking capability from scratch, which no one's really noticed. With the Bank of England, we extended £100 billion of credit facilities for larger companies. We guaranteed several multi-billion-pound loans to strategically important UK companies to support them through the crisis. With BEIS and the British Business Bank, we guaranteed new small business lending supporting over 1.5 million SMEs. And we did it all with our colleagues working remotely from their bedrooms, living rooms and kitchen tables … It was a truly unprecedented series of interventions on a breadth, scale and speed that would have been completely unthinkable before the pandemic.

As of September 2021, the National Audit Office estimated the total expenditure on COVID management to amount to £370 billion. This included £154 billion in support for business, £84 billion for health and social care and £60 billion for individuals. Roughly two-thirds of the finance came from the Treasury and one-third from Bank of England loans and guarantees.[9] In early 2022, unfortunately, it's also becoming clear that the emergency operation has lost tens of billions in waste and fraud.[10]

Between Brexit and COVID, the Treasury once again became indispensable in government. In addition to dealing with economic support schemes during the pandemic, it also had to take on many new administrative roles to replace those previously done at the EU level. These included covering gaps in trade policy, tariffs, financial services regulation and competition policy. Under Nicholas Macpherson, Treasury headcount had been steadily reduced to just under 1,200 people. Expanding to deal with the new functions pushed that back up to over 2,000.[11]

And, as with previous crises, with many urgent demands on government funds, the Treasury's hand was strengthened by holding the purse strings. Whatever Johnson and other cabinet ministers thought of the department, they were too reliant on its abilities and practical administrative tools to take it on. As one former advisor put it: 'there is now a certain level of co-dependency … in a way COVID sort of saves their political union'.

But as the effects of the pandemic stretched out into a second year, evident tensions began to build. The question was how long the Treasury would be prepared to maintain such levels of emergency spending, let alone be willing to fund Johnson's interventionist agenda. Large parts of the private sector continued to suffer from the impacts of Brexit, COVID or both. Similarly, many parts of the public sector are in desperate need of greater resources to maintain vital services. As Tom Scholar reflected: 'I think there are big questions confronting the Treasury and the chancellor. One is what to do about all of the debt that's been incurred in the last 18 months, over what time-frame and with what target to start … Every country in the world's got that question.' Speaking to another senior official, his cheery demeanour disappeared as he reeled off the impossible list of essential things to be funded:

> There's huge tension around the fiscal pressure to spend. We've got a huge health backlog. Getting to net zero isn't free … levelling up, big investment, depending on what it is, but the deprived communities are not going to think levelling up means anything unless they see some money that they wouldn't otherwise have seen. And we've also got rising debt interest on the bigger stock of debt … and we've got an ageing population. So, you can make yourself all quite gloomy on the fiscal outlook and if you read the fiscal risks report, because you can say that the debt's going ever upwards unless we do something about it.

It was also clear that Rishi Sunak's economic thinking mixed traditional Tory small statism with investment banker detachment. His views had clearly been disseminated across the Exchequer, as one senior official told me:

> Sunak is much more in the mould of a more traditional 1980s Conservative. Look at his speech to the party conference last year, where he talked about some classic Conservative things, like the government trying to get out of people's economic lives and low regulation, low tax, high enterprise economy.

Towards the end of 2021 it looked as though a showdown was coming. Johnson and the big spenders would declare new measures for levelling up. The Treasury would respond with a Liam Byrne-style empty coffer.[12] HS2's north-eastern leg scrapped. No public money to fix high-rise building cladding. No new Treasury money for levelling up in Michael Gove's White Paper. More health and social care but with little additional funding. Johnsonian interventionism was suffering slow death by a thousand Exchequer refusals.

And then came Partygate. As Johnson's poll ratings dropped, so his 80-strong majority and Establishment coalition was shown to be nothing but a confidence-and-supply agreement, temporarily held together by a demand for a hard Brexit (now done). Various self-serving factions began airing their grievances and plotting revolution by WhatsApp. And, with Starmer's Labour Party going full Mandelson, even the Tory press felt secure enough to start attacking their Brexit hero.

As so often in the past, and again now, when crises hit and governments are in disarray, the default Treasury position exerts itself. So too, with recent periods of Conservative Party fracture, the fall-back position of aspiring Tory leadership contenders is a return to 1980s Thatcherism. The combination suggests that in early 2022, the Exchequer is returning to full strength.

Impossible dilemmas and paradigm shifts?

However, whatever the current state of Treasury power and influence is, I would argue that it remains very precarious. While moving to stronger political ground, and shoring up its Whitehall position, there are a number of wider intellectual and social challenges ahead. These all strongly contest the key elements of Treasury orthodoxy and mainstream economic policy that have been widely adopted in many nations: free trade, free markets, monetary over fiscal activism and balanced budgets.

In early 2022 there appears to be a light at the end of the COVID tunnel, but no one is quite sure how far away it actually is. As of December 2021, 5.3 million people had died worldwide, including over 146,000 in the UK. If looking at excess deaths figures, the global death toll is four times the official COVID one.[13] Despite the roll-out of vaccines, poorer nations have very low rates of vaccination, and vaccine hesitancy is surprisingly high in countries such as the US. New, more transmissible variants, Omicron being the latest, keep appearing. The risk is that, sooner or later, these will reduce vaccine efficacy, although, as with Omicron, they may be less virulent. All nations continue to go through cycles of restrictions and lockdowns and, increasingly, militant and destabilizing protests.

One clear Treasury principle, which looks to have been undermined by events, is that of internationalism and free trade. Since the financial crisis protectionism has grown globally, with the WTO being sidelined and many international trade disputes following. Brexit was the UK's very public rejection of certain aspects of globalization. Since then, COVID has put further barriers up as nations have tightened borders and restricted movement, as well as competing aggressively over vaccine production and distribution. The pandemic also revealed that too much dependence on international supply chains was extremely problematic amid a global crisis. As one Treasury official explains in more detail:

> We couldn't even manufacture a plastic glove in the UK. And so, we had a shocking dependence on PPE from around the world … Now Treasury orthodoxy before would have been: 'Oh well, you know, free market, it's protectionism to have national preference, you can always buy these plastic guards from the cheapest provider, and someone will make them somewhere else.' But I think it's a bit of a wake-up call for all of us … there's a sort of general economic zeitgeist. America's always been far more interventionist than the myth of free market capitalism that America is. Europe has been very dirigiste and is getting more so. China's obviously highly dirigiste.

But more generally, the wider intellectual rationales that have guided UK economic policy, as in many capitalist economies, appear increasingly confused. Governments everywhere have intervened in their economies to degrees unprecedented since the Second World War. This completely goes against decades of consensus about minimal levels of state economic intervention. Such interventions and practices, adopted during the 2007–08 financial crisis, were supposed to be temporary and later unwound. They weren't. Now similar actions, from huge government bond buying by central banks to emergency funding of the private sector, make the temporary the norm. For Daniela Gabor, the new financial shift means that 'we are living through a revolution without revolutionaries … Central banks have quietly put in place a shadow monetary financing regime since the global financial crisis. This is Minsky without Keynes.'[14]

And behind all this lurks the issue of rising inflation. Textbook monetarism says that interest rates need to rise to head off inflation, but even modest rises will have a very hard impact on the economy. Quite apart from inhibiting economic recovery, ballooning individual, corporate and government debt levels, already huge prior to COVID, will become unserviceable. Potential collapses and domino effects could be a lot worse than those experienced in 2007–08. Several officials and advisors voice their concerns here. Ken Clarke sets out the problem clearly:

> The idea of free money and that the big state can stem populism is growing like mad and the level of debt we're running up is absolutely horrifying ... because once you get real inflation come back then this burden of debt is going to be an absolute crisis for many countries and many businesses.

On the other hand, the success of Sunak and the would-be Thatcherites, coupled with an increasingly strong Treasury with a determination to balance budgets again, indicates that austerity 2.0 is on the way. As we know, that didn't end well in 2016.

Such dilemmas, of course, reach far beyond the UK. But the UK and the Treasury, like many other nations and finance departments, must be wondering how to cope and how to retain credibility. Sticking to conventional economic thinking of the kind that has dominated since the late 1970s does not seem sustainable. In fact, the actions of central banks and finance departments everywhere demonstrate that the iron economic certainties of mainstream economic policy have proved to be as malleable as soft butter when needs must. But this also suggests that they are discredited and untenable in the long term. Quite possibly, we are seeing the end of four to five decades of neoliberalism, at least as a vaguely coherent ideological position.[15]

On the other hand, throwing up key policy norms and once indisputable practices to be replaced by a radical paradigm shift in thinking and economic management seems equally implausible. This is either for lack of new ideas or lack of political support. Into the vacuum are emerging variations on authoritarian capitalism with a nationalist-populist appeal; something that looks to be the direction of travel of the Conservative government and opposition Republicans in the US.

9

Conclusion: an institutional perspective on UK economic history

One of this book's key objectives was to document the part played by the Treasury in the evolution of the UK's economy. Political and economic histories tend to focus on big ideas and leading political actors or dramatic events and shifting global economic forces. Somewhere in between lie institutions, linking actors and forces and facilitating more enduring changes. The Treasury is the most significant economic institution in the UK, far more powerful than its public visibility suggests. As such, whether destabilizing or defending the status quo, its mundane institutional orthodoxies and practices, professional cultures and networks have played a very substantial role.

Thus, this book has attempted to look at forty-five years of the UK's political and economic history through Treasury eyes. The narrative arc of the book began with one momentous national and institutional crisis, the 1976 IMF bailout, and ends with two more, Brexit and COVID. The first crisis spelled the end of one form of national economic management and ruling elite constellation. It remains to be seen where the second two will lead.

The year 1976 effectively signalled the end of the Keynesian interlude that had shaped Treasury and post-war government thinking and practice since the late 1930s. Labour's Denis Healey initiated the first changes. The new Conservative government in 1979 then pushed ahead zealously, culling the top tiers of Treasury officials and battering through a new regimen. Thatcherism set out a new set of broad economic principles and priorities to deliver the UK's particular version of neoliberalism.

However, as argued throughout, ideas had to be turned into realizable policies and practices, and the Exchequer was the institution to facilitate this. Beneath the big political personalities and momentous confrontations operated the institutional knowhow of the Treasury. To effect change, it relied as much on itself, its orthodoxics and contacts, as on the vaguer ideologies of its transient political ministers.

As Chapter 2 explains, behind the 1980s political fireworks two fundamental organizational changes were taking place within the Treasury that proved key to the practical implementation of Thatcherite ideas. One was the increase in Whitehall power handed to the Treasury. This enabled it to achieve its primary historical goal of getting public expenditure under control while also forcing rival departments to follow its policy pathway. The second was the rise to prominence of a new generation of economists in the Exchequer, focused more on microeconomics and modelling than on national macroeconomic management. So was set in motion the long journey towards state withdrawal, not only from direct forms of economic intervention and management, but from national macroeconomic management altogether.

Looking back from the present it is easy to assume the existence of a clear pathway for achieving many of the fundamental shifts we now associate with Thatcherism. But in many elements, from privatization to applying monetary policy, there was no such pathway. Something had to step in to replace the state's role in managing and stimulating the economy. But who and what was unclear. Indeed, the ways and means by which this happened evolved in erratic circumstances. The only thing that was apparent was that the new system was going to operate without the mechanisms and economic actors that were central before: Keynesianism, unions and leaders of British industry.

So, the Exchequer and successive chancellors turned elsewhere. While ministers drew on their own life experiences and political leanings, Treasury officials harked back to older department defaults, networks and linked institutions. Chapters 3, 4 and 5 focused on three of the alternative means of economic management that emerged. Thus, Chapter 3 recorded the Thatcherites looking towards the City and financial markets to take over the ownership and financing of UK corporations. Chapter 5 followed them as they encouraged international investors and big foreign multinationals to come in and invest in new industries and markets in the UK. Chapter 4 showed how the Exchequer and successive governments found multiple alternatives to stimulate economic activity that avoided government intervention and Treasury expenditure.

As these same chapters showed, each of these policies, while boosting economic growth in various ways, also had consequences that policymakers and politicians alike could not foresee (or didn't want to see). Some of these issues, such as increasing debt levels and market bubbles, then exploded spectacularly in the financial meltdown of 2007–08 and the recession that resulted. As Chapter 6 revealed, no great paradigm shift followed this. Conceptually, the problems and solutions were reduced to an issue of banking, with the answers being bailouts and stronger regulation. But the larger instabilities and imbalances of the UK economy were not confronted. Indeed, policy responses went to extreme lengths to maintain a crumbling and discredited system. Chapter 7 shows that the Coalition government did more of the same. Austerity policies, directed by Treasury orthodoxies and Thatcherite small statism, hobbled any substantial recovery and hit the poorest hardest. When combined with monetary activist policies that primarily boosted wealthy asset holders, inequalities and imbalances were exacerbated. So followed political and economic breakdown and division, most obviously signalled by the vote to leave the EU.

Brexit marked the end of four decades of consolidated Treasury power and orthodoxy, economic consensus and trust in economists, relative Establishment cohesion, and public acquiescence to a technocratic, centrist political system. Each were shown to be rather more tenuous than they appeared to those inhabiting the prosperous London bubble. Chapter 8 revealed that, despite a recovery of Exchequer strength and a new governing elite coalition, both remain unstable. Dealing with a pandemic has temporarily reinforced both but also shown their glaring flaws and precarity.

The question is: is this the start of a real political change and economic paradigm shift, as experienced in the 1930s and 1970s, or have we merely witnessed a temporary putsch? The Johnson government offers no alternative, sustainable economic vision. But a return to the UK's entirely discredited post-1970s model would be absurd. And there seem few signs of a radical new paradigm shift that would gain enough political and institutional support to be enacted. In early 2022 it remains to be seen what impact Partygate and Russian military action in Ukraine will have on British politics and Treasury fortunes. The only thing that is clear is that further bloody Establishment conflicts lie ahead.

Stability and change at the Exchequer

In researching and writing this book I explored several larger questions. What have been the continuities and changes that have happened over the period? How have the contradictions and conflicts at the heart of the

Treasury impacted on policymaking and the national economy? Do any of these continuities or contradictions mean that the Treasury requires radical reform, both for its own good and the good of the nation? I shall return to this issue at the end.

There is much to suggest that no change is best. The Treasury is the oldest department of government. It has been around for the best part of a millennium. On a day-to-day level it deals with a series of demands and complex tasks with an enduring force of will. This includes pulling together the nation's annual budget, akin to playing four-dimensional chess with a blindfold, all while juggling party political agendas, unstable markets and erratic currency movements. It holds the line against all of them. A phrase I hear often in relation to the machinations of British politics is that officials of the Treasury were and are 'the adults in the room'.

Everyone I asked, minister, advisor, institutional official from outside the department, said the same thing. The Treasury has the brightest and best, not just in comparison to other government departments, but also to far better paid private-sector professionals. George Osborne, among many others, talks of a 'culture of excellence' there, concluding that the officials he worked with 'are some of the most creative policymakers and thinkers that I've come across'. Charles Roxburgh, currently second permanent secretary, who spent most of his career in the private sector, dispels many private-sector myths about a slow, stodgy civil service:

The quality of the people at the Treasury was just as good or slightly better than the quality of the people I had worked with in the private sector – all my new colleagues were extremely high quality, really smart, hard-working and energetic, and with very strong values. I also found the pace much faster in the Treasury than in the private sector … I was genuinely struck by the number of really major decisions flowing through any senior official's in-tray or any minister's box on a daily basis. I was really impressed by the speed with which these big, complicated decisions got resolved.

Most impressive is how the Exchequer operates in a crisis. In traumatic times, its senior officials leap into action. They throw off their doddery boffin personas and become action heroes, rather like Q discarding his glasses and picking up a 007 issue Walther PPK. Time and time again, the quick thinking and adaptability of the institution has indeed secured the nation. This happened after the 1992 ERM debacle, when the dot. com boom burst in 2000, during the financial market crash in 2007–08, after the Brexit vote in 2016 and again when COVID struck in 2020. Where would the nation be without the Treasury in such situations?

Despite disagreeing with many things about the Exchequer, I have nearly always felt a sense of committed public service from the senior figures I've interviewed there. Many gave up much better salaries in the private sector to be there. Officials displayed a surprising level of self-reflection and a desire to try new things, to modernize and reform. And the institution has indeed continued to evolve and 'modernize' in various ways since the mid-1970s.

In the 1970s the Exchequer was very privately educated and Oxbridge, very hierarchical, white and male. Its structure and culture probably resembled the elite public schools from which many of its officials had come. Coming from the right Oxbridge college was more important than having professional expertise or experience. Those elements are still there, but rather less so. Recent mandarins have made a point of reducing bureaucratic layers and casting the talent net wider, consciously looking to achieve a more representative demographic. It is now looking to move some of its operations outside London. The proportion of women and ethnic minorities in senior roles in the Exchequer has grown steadily, although we are still waiting for the Treasury's first female permanent secretary and chancellor.

Another change has been the growing political power of the Treasury over the period. Its influence has waxed and waned historically. But from the 1970s it most definitely consolidated its authority across Whitehall. Influence over senior civil service appointments and new financial controls have helped it impose itself on other departments. It decimated its main economic policymaking rival, the DTI, as well as its successors. It has continually cut off or scaled back grander economic strategic plans and resisted attempts to devolve budgetary controls beyond London.

Part of its growing political power has also been a consequence of the ambitious endeavours of some strong chancellors. Nigel Lawson, Gordon Brown and George Osborne, in particular, used their position to wield expansive influence over other ministers and policy briefs. Several of those I spoke to expressed concern about how far the Treasury had extended its authority over other policy areas. Many a non-Treasury minister or official spoke of the 'bully-boy' tendencies they had had to endure.

In contrast to its increased political power, the institution has been weakened considerably when it comes to economic management and influence. At one level this is an obvious consequence of the UK state's withdrawal from economic management. But a less obvious point is that it has shifted away from macroeconomic analysis and management. The direction of travel has been towards microeconomics and supply-side reforms, tax breaks to nudge market behaviour rather than tax to spend and invest or intervene. And there is a greater focus on accounting methods and personnel.

This weakening has been accompanied by the giving away of functions and economic calculating power to other entities. Since Keynes and fiscal activism were disregarded, the main macro instrument of economic management had become the setting of interest rates to maintain low and stable inflation. This task, and all the analytical power that went with it, was transferred to the Bank of England in stages, becoming fully realized when New Labour made the Bank independent in 1998.

After the financial crisis, Exchequer oversight of financial regulation was also handed over to the Bank. In 2010 the Coalition then set up the Office for Budget Responsibility, taking forecasting and more intellectual capacity away too. As Paul Tucker, previously at the Bank of England, now reflects: 'It is true that in macroeconomic policy the centre of intellectual gravity moved hugely from the Treasury to the Bank [of England]. So that when I started out in 1980 the Treasury had more human capital than the Bank. I mean that's just not remotely true any more.'

Whether intended or not, the Treasury has become more a finance than an economics department. Its actions have ensured that it has both eradicated rival department sources of economic thinking and analysis, while also reducing its own capabilities and analytical power.

The continuities of Treasury orthodoxy: ideology and practice

While the Exchequer has evolved professionally in various ways, there remain strong continuities. Above all else, these are to be found in the Treasury orthodoxy, a set of enduring ideas, principles and practices.

When asked, everyone is convinced that there is an orthodoxy, although which elements are emphasized varies. The first element of the orthodoxy, which almost doesn't need saying, is the Treasury's focus on balanced budgets. It often seems as though it is the Treasury set against the rest of Whitehall. As Adair Turner explains it: 'deep in the Treasury's ethos is the belief that every other department left to itself will relentlessly increase government expenditure. And they're the only guys who can lean against that pattern.' The reality doesn't quite match up. In the 45-year period considered here only a handful of years have produced an annual surplus.

The next three beliefs, repeated by many, are clearly identified in Nicholas Macpherson's 2014 speech on 'The Treasury View'.[1] His presentation suggests that each of these became more institutionalized during William Gladstone's tenure in the second half of the nineteenth century. They have endured since. They are support for free trade, the promotion of market mechanisms and the need to achieve price stability (in terms of a stable currency and steady, low inflation).

Talking to the officials who have been there for the last five decades, all four of these Exchequer goals are mentioned frequently. Tom Scholar typically explains two of them when asked:

> I would say there is an enduring belief in the power of markets and market conditions. That's not to say we're blind to the possibility of market failure but the belief that very often that's the best way. And there is an attachment to free trade and reducing barriers to trade and economic activity.

How these aims have been achieved and the tools utilized have changed, going one way during the Keynesian interlude and then another from Thatcher onwards. However, ignoring subtle differences, both

Conservative and Labour (and Coalition) governments of the last forty-five years have supported these goals, at least overtly.

There is an obvious fifth point of continuity and consensus in the period of this book, something that clearly marked the break with the Keynesians. That is the decline of fiscal activism, to be replaced by monetarist thinking in various forms. This was publicly spelled out by Nigel Lawson in the 1980s while being modelled and operationalized by Alan Budd and Terry Burns inside the Treasury. New Labour kept with this after 1997. Following a brief post-financial-crisis flirtation with Keynesianism again, the monetarist norm was quickly re-established.

Each of these aims has endured regardless of the party in power since 1979. I've asked many ministers and mandarins about the continuities and differences between Labour and the Conservatives on economic policy. Politicians usually think for a few seconds before concluding, sometimes with a wry smile, that for all their shows of political opposition and conflict, the differences were relatively small. Officials do the same without the hesitation or the smile. Nicholas Macpherson, who worked in the Treasury for over thirty years, holding senior positions from the mid-1990s to Brexit, summarizes his experience:

> They all denied that they had these things in common, because politics is all about difference, but their basic world view was quite similar ... implicit in all of these policies was a view that monetary policy was the main

instrument of achieving stability, minimizing the amplitude of the cycle. Fiscal policy generally was there to support monetary policy ... The Tories were more committed to reducing tax rates. Labour was slightly more interested in addressing poverty. But they weren't particularly interested in pursuing equality of outcomes per se. So, economic policy evolved through this period, and it changed with the political complexion of governments, but it didn't change very much ... if you look at what [George] Osborne's growth policy was, it was pretty much identical to Gordon Brown's.

This is hardly surprising given certain persistent cultural and institutional patterns. Many party leaders, including ministers and advisors in the Exchequer, had the same PPE degrees from Oxford, with the same tutors who mentored them. Following the cull of officials in the early Thatcher years, there has been a high degree of continuity among the senior officials who were retained from government to government. New Labour inherited many up-and-coming juniors in 1997, who they then promoted to the top. In 2010 George Osborne was content to keep most of those who were there from Brown and Darling's time (and on Alistair Darling's advice).[2]

Few people refer to these principles of orthodoxy as being ideological. Certainly not officials, who are quick to take offence if you suggest that they are wilfully taking a 'political' position. Nor economic advisors, who see these things as being accepted professional norms that are not up for debate. But for me, such iron, unquestionable precepts must have ideological and political components. This seems all the more so when huge levels of political and economic capital have been expended to defend these principles over the last decade.

Looking back, there have been three more areas of continuity, instigated in the period considered in this book, but each now more enduring. These have marked out and guided the UK's particular manifestation of neoliberalism. Although having an ideological component, I also see them as developing in a more ad hoc way. Ideas and inspirations, often initiated to solve an immediate problem, have since become more mundane Treasury preferences and practices, ultimately becoming part of the everyday institutional machinery. These were spelled out in Chapters 3, 4 and 5.

As Chapter 3 argued, the Treasury repeatedly chose finance and professional services over manufacturing. Privatization usually involved selling off the nationalized industries via the London Stock Exchange, to be traded by financiers who prioritized shareholder value. Changes in regulation and taxation further strengthened the control of the financial sector vis-à-vis UK industry. In contrast there was a very clear cutting of ties and support to manufacturing and the regions. By the time New Labour arrived, it was evident that the City was a major source of national income and a big contributor to Treasury coffers. So they continued to indulge big finance.

Thus, the UK ended up with the biggest financial sector relative to its economy of any major economy. Its manufacturing base shrank faster over the period than that of any of its rivals too. Arguably, Britain's low levels of productivity and research and development spending are directly related to this decades-long sectoral imbalance. And arguably, this is linked to the fact that the Treasury has far more dealings with the City and the Bank of England than it does with the non-financial areas and regions of the economy.

Chapter 5 similarly revealed that successive UK governments have embraced the globalization and free trade agenda more than most nations. Treasury officials, as a matter of principle, rejected any preferencing of UK-based companies and sectors, whether through protection or investment. Instead, whether it was in relation to big finance, property or manufacturing, policy has been to offer all manner of enticements to international investors and foreign multinationals to set up in Britain. Thus, it has become much easier in the UK than in most rival economies to take over companies, buy and sell UK property from abroad, hide and transfer vast capital flows in and out, and so on. And again, much of this follows on from past Treasury practices, when imperial preference operated, and with a closeness to international finance and global economic institutions.

The third area of continuity, documented in Chapter 4, is what might be termed pseudo- or privatized Keynesianism. This has involved various attempts to use state mechanisms to stimulate market activity through markets rather than official expenditure. These began with the mass sell-off of state assets and deregulation of the financial sector, thus enabling private credit creation on a much larger scale. It continued with the regular puffing-up of the property market, a variety of off-balance-sheet ruses such as PFI, and creating new public money out of thin air with quantitative easing.

This reflects the dominance of monetary policy thinking and the rejection of fiscal tools and anything that might be termed 'state intervention'. Successive chancellors and Treasury officials have gone to great lengths to maintain this increasingly elaborate and costly sleight of hand. As with the embrace of financialization and globalization, the Exchequer's institutional preferences, practices and networks have been a driving force. The Treasury's desire to balance its books, to be seen to be keeping out of markets, as well as the revolving doors between the Treasury and the financial sector have each played a part.

Defending the status quo orthodoxy at all costs

Among those who were there in the late 1970s and 1980s, no one was quite clear where it was all going. Many shifts in policy and practice were new and experimental. Some failed and others came to be standard procedure. For several interviewees looking back, the new economic system really established itself and reached its high point in the decade or two after Thatcher had departed. For Ken Clarke, 'The really successful period was the early 1990s until the financial crash in 2007–08. During which time, globally as well as nationally, we made the most remarkable progress in raising living standards.'

Since 2007–08, however, it has been all about shoring up this failing economic policy regime. As part of successive governments, the Treasury and other institutions appear to have done whatever it took to maintain an increasingly discredited means of national economic management. Consciously or not, such ideas and practices have done more to sustain UK elite wealth than they have to promote national prosperity and wider public well-being.

The defence of the Establishment status quo and Treasury orthodoxy has been conducted on several fronts. On the public level, successive chancellors and their advisors have become increasingly adept at media management. The spinning of budgets, forecasts and economic data has a long history, but has advanced considerably in the era of public relations democracy.[3] Documenting the period, I've observed the regular creation of dubious narratives, fake fiscal rules, logic-defying sleights of hand and grandiose but meaningless soundbites; and much of it to shore up failing policy pathways.

Brown persuaded everyone that he had conquered boom and bust, while helping to create housing and financial market booms, then blaming the mother of all busts on others. Cameron and Osborne talked compassionate conservativism and Northern Power-houses, while creating greater inequality and regional disparity than ever. And Johnson's levelling-up lies are as implausible as his many Brexit claims.

Conclusion

Much of the defence of the prevailing economic policy and Treasury orthodoxy has also been at a very technical level. Any scan over historical forecasts and evaluations of national economic health reveals that the metrics and figures used are highly malleable. How income and expenditure are classified, how growth is measured and how inflation is calculated have been extremely variable, selective and subject to political expediency.

In the 1980s the sale of state assets (nationalized industries) was treated as 'negative expenditure' so that the Thatcher governments could falsely claim they were reducing state spending. Under Brown, PFI was done to keep state spending projects off the balance sheet, so that New Labour could pretend it wasn't tax-and-spend Old Labour. Treasury forecasts frequently change in the lead-up to budgets, suddenly enabling new expenditure (the back of the Treasury sofa, like Dr Who's Tardis, operates beyond the laws of time and space). GDP and public-sector spending numbers alternate between headline and per capita figures, real and inflation-adjusted totals, and hand-picked time periods. CPI and RPI measures of inflation are adopted according to preference. Switching interest rate setting to the Bank of England and forecasting to the Office for Budget Responsibility has only partly ameliorated these issues.

Perhaps the thing I find most puzzling is the ongoing attempts to adhere to monetarist policy in all its guises and regardless of the evidence. The original idea of controlling the money supply to control inflation was never workable. Chancellors and officials who were there at the time denied that it was ever a practical policy. Blowing the regulatory lid off finance and embracing globalization did the exact opposite of restricting the money supply.

Inflation rates continued to exclude both housing costs and financial assets for much of the period. This is one reason why the huge bubbles in property and financial markets never registered as problematic before the financial crash hit. But of course, the rise and fall of such sectors has a big impact on other parts of the economy as well as people's personal finances. Likewise, inflation rates based on the changing costs of goods and services may be significantly affected by the ups and downs of global commodity prices rather than official interest rates.

Most recently, since interest rates have remained low (below 1%) for over a decade, the main tool of macroeconomic management has effectively been neutralized. Instead, there was the turn to QE, supposedly a temporary measure taken in the wake of the financial crisis. What began with £200 billion of bond purchases in 2009 had reached a total of £895 billion by November 2020. In early 2022 inflation was getting out of control, reaching levels not experienced for decades. Officially, interest rates should be jumping up to counter this, but central banks, including the Bank of England, know that this would be catastrophic to an economy now built on such huge debts.

This vast QE expenditure is itself to be added to other similarly large quantities of debt, all created with the pretence of keeping the charade of monetary policy working and denying the reality of government interventions in the economy: the hundreds of billions of long-term liabilities connected to PFI contracts, the hundred billion of outstanding debt building up from student loans, the hundreds of billions suddenly created to keep the COVID economy running, the hundreds of billions of corporate tax breaks, and the hundreds of billions of 'contingent liabilities' where government has guaranteed to cover the risks of banking loans to private companies and house buyers.

What does it take to admit that this mainstay of national macroeconomic management, so dominant for several decades, is no longer fit for purpose?

Consequences, costs and institutional change?

There have been multiple consequences that can be connected to the power and sustained influence of Treasury orthodoxy on both UK economic policy and public expenditure control. These have been detailed through each of the chapters of this book.

Picking financial services over manufacturing so concertedly has undermined the development of new industries and supply chains. Productivity levels and research and development budgets have suffered. Too many UK companies have been bought up, dismantled and sold off for quick profits. There is too little appetite for taking on the risk of investing in new technologies and sectors, especially when there are easier routes to gaining healthy, low-risk profits (housing, utility monopolies, PFI, outsourcing contracts, financial markets, tax evasion, to name a few). Encouraging international financiers and CEOs to invest in the UK while disregarding the needs of home-grown industries has left the economy insecure and at the mercy of fickle international capital, multinational demands and geopolitics. Brexit and COVID have revealed the dearth of productive capacity in multiple sectors, the broken supply chains and the huge skills gaps. War in Europe will likely show just how over-reliant the UK is on international fossil fuel supplies.

Picking London and the South-East over the rest of the UK has created growing regional imbalances and inequalities. Choosing monetary over fiscal policy and free markets over states, regardless of circumstances and economic conditions, has generated growing wealth disparities between classes, regions and generations. Labour's share of income has declined, from 70% in the 1970s to 55% now.[4] Economic policy has ultimately come to be something that does more to secure the wealth of the top tiers, particularly the top 0.01%, than the rest. The chosen indicators and targets of national economic success relate far more to those at the top than the mass of the population. It's not just 'Your bloody GDP, not ours!',[5] it's also 'your inflation', 'your stock market', 'your house prices', 'your employment rates' and 'your business sentiment'. All too often Treasury mandarins, unable to look beyond their London-centric bubble, have missed all this, just as they were blindsided by Brexit.

Picking free markets over other forms of economic management, as a default and regardless of circumstances, means that private, exploitative monopolies have replaced public, inefficient ones. Financialized, platform and rentier forms of capitalism have flourished as high streets and local economies have slowly withered. Property has become another investment market and source of Treasury income rather than simply providing homes for people to live in. Too many parts of the economy have come to resemble free-flowing Ponzi-schemes, funnelling money to their creators and first movers, and leaving the costs and debts to everyone else: small businesses, pension funds, individuals and state balance sheets. And markets and commercial players, left to themselves, will never seriously engage with global warming, environmental and energy crises, pandemics and other grander and more long-term crises.

Many old hands who were there from the 1980s onwards now look back with a certain amount of regret regarding where we have ended up today. A retired former permanent secretary, who excitedly embraced the changes in her department under Thatcher, now thinks the UK went much too far in its free-market transition. Terry Burns acknowledged that the UK economy had left itself way too open to global economic forces. Nigel Lawson said he didn't foresee how changes in the 1980s would lead to the kind of merged, highly risky banking of today and thought banks should be forcibly split. Gordon Brown now declares to me that 'economics – and the teaching of it – has to change'. Ken Clarke, an ever-present leading figure in the Thatcher and Major cabinets, sounds particularly sad about how long-running policies have left the UK so fractured and unbalanced:

> Free market principles, competition and all that sort of thing did foster a period of quite remarkable economic rise, but the average worker, the average employee scarcely rose at all in real terms. We were creating an ever-increasing number of multi-millionaire chief executives and well-paid executives at all levels. The top 10% were seeing their living standards surging quite spectacularly, and we were relying on trickle down too much … I am a great believer in the independence of our private-sector companies, but our shareholder democracy doesn't work. Corporate governance doesn't work … The market has various weaknesses and I think it remains a very big problem now, because it's produced so much populism. The Western democracy that I've known has broken down.

Of course, such developments can't all be put down to the Treasury, not by a long shot. So many ideas and practices have been created elsewhere and adopted across the globe. So much that happens in the international economy impacts upon the UK. Establishment rule stretches far and wide beyond Whitehall. Prime ministers and their senior ministers have driven particular initiatives, appointed and pushed out top officials. Chancellors continually impose choices on officials to suit particular party-political goals. Successive senior officials have fought losing battles against pre-election giveaways, off-balance-sheet schemes, ministerial vanity projects, quick-fix housing policies and so on.

But at the same time, long-running Treasury orthodoxies, institutional practices, policy levers and networks have made their contribution. They have helped shape the UK's own particular form of neoliberalism. Many free-market economies have followed different pathways and their varieties of capitalism have proved more successful than the UK's. Several have higher levels of taxation and state intervention and equality, while also generating more per capita wealth and reducing their carbon footprints more effectively. The British economy of today as much reflects the enduring principles of Treasury belief systems as it does Thatcherism, Brownism or Osbornism. And those same tenets and practices have helped shore up the system, despite its glaring contradictions and growing precarity.

The need for a paradigm shift was made clear after the 2007–08 crash but it never came. Both Brexit and COVID have made that need stronger than ever. But no such shift appears remotely in sight in the UK. That's three great crises that have gone to waste without bringing substantial change or even political inspiration.

As Chapter 8 concluded, it's looking as though post-COVID economic policy responses are edging back to the status quo defence again. There is little emerging from the leaderships of the main political parties that suggests something that is both cogent and that will generate a parliamentary majority. For Martin Wolf:

> Boris doesn't have of course a coherent view. His instincts
> are those for power. He's not attached to any ideology
> apart from Boris … the Thatcherite view of the world,
> free market, small government, the nineteenth-century
> state, that's really ridiculous, obviously completely
> inconceivable as a policy doctrine to win elections now.
> Just as, in my view, the sort of left-wing policy that
> Corbyn offered was also a policy that would only attract
> the fevered support of a third of the electorate, and that's
> it! … basically, the government now is, to put it bluntly,
> and I think the opposition is too, they're intellectual
> wastelands.

Radical transformation is unlikely to come from within the Treasury itself either. As Robert Peston commented to me, the institution is very resistant to substantial change: 'a paradigm shift will never be driven by the Treasury because that's just not within the culture. It's an inherently conservative culture.' If anything, recent crises have done more to maintain Exchequer power than they have to enact intellectual and system change. This suggests that the centralized power of the Treasury is part of the reason for a failure to look outside its Whitehall box. The Exchequer, with its dominant spending and management control over all other civil service departments, and its positioning within networks of international institutions and finance, is too invested in the existing paradigm, too buried in the system, to see beyond it.

So what next? Coming up with inspired, original economic thinking to 'fix' the UK economy is beyond the scope of this book (and me personally). But since the focus has been on the Treasury and related institutions, I can speculate on what might bring real change on a governmental and institutional level. And here my findings lead me to think, on the one hand, about rejuvenating macroeconomic policymaking in central government but, on the other, curtailing existing Treasury power and the centralized, institutional elite nexus in which it operates. Personnel and ideas can shift, but if structures and wider systems of control remain, substantial change is unlikely. If all roads, Keynesian, monetarist, Old Labour or New Labour, Thatcherite or populist Tory, lead back to the same dominant institutional and Establishment structures, then all we get is 'radical continuity'.

So, at one level, government needs to make a variety of more national, strategic interventions and to creatively explore the tools that are deployed for that. Governments as diverse as China, Germany and the US continue to make a range of such economic interventions far more than the UK does. Whether attempting to improve productivity, infrastructure, redistribute resources across regions, take investment risks that the private sector won't, or make considerable investments in particular sectors, it's no longer sufficient to leave macroeconomic policy to the Bank of England and free-flowing markets.

It also needs to be asked how effective are the current mechanisms of economic management at the disposal of the Treasury and how many should it have control of? There are obviously clear disagreements on the balance and efficacy of deploying fiscal and monetary levers. Government policymakers long ago rejected fiscal tools, but monetarist ones seem quite useless or even dangerous to deploy now. How is messing around with interest rates alone, or creating endless new tranches of Monopoly money, going to combat runaway inflation without crashing and burning an economy built on massive piles of debt? Even if such a regime still made sense, refusing to use fiscal tools while handing over monetary ones to less accountable technocrats elsewhere, while crushing all possible rival sources of macroeconomic thinking across Whitehall, seems particularly limiting.

On the other hand, while wanting more state innovation and intervention, putting more power in Treasury hands and the London–City centred nexus has to be avoided. An Exchequer that is fixed on iron control of government spending is never going to facilitate the evolution of an innovative, competitive national economy. A Treasury that is London-centred and inward-facing, with far stronger links to international institutions and finance than to its own regions, industrial sectors and local economies, will always have very limited horizons. If we are to get the radical paradigm shift we need, a rethink about a separation of functions is essential.

One route would be a clear division of finance and economic policy functions. Such a split has been tried and abandoned in the past, most famously when the Wilson government created the Department of Economic Affairs in 1964. Periodically, the option has been explored again, usually under Labour governments. Recent attempts have not got far. Theresa May and Nick Timothy tried and failed before the 2017 election. In 2017 the Kerslake Review concluded that, on balance, the Treasury should be reformed, and its wings clipped, but that structural separation would be too costly and disruptive.[6] Sheffield's political economy research institute (SPERI), a long-running critic of UK economic policy and the Treasury, came to a similar conclusion.[7] Unsurprisingly, no one I've talked to in the Treasury in recent years, minister or official, agreed that it would be appropriate to divide the institution.

But many others think some kind of split is essential, even if they are not sure how that would work. How the separation would happen, and whether it should be 'economics' and 'finance' departments, needs further exploration. Instead of an 'economics department' there might just as well be a wider policy unit that works on macroeconomic thinking, productivity and other strategic spending initiatives; one that involves the prime minister and other senior ministers and officials, and has a strong say on the overall spending envelope and key priorities. The finance-oriented Treasury then operationalizes this. The point is that, however the functions are divvied up, they need separating, because all such debates and decisions cannot be confined within the opaque operations of the Exchequer alone.

Just as important, and 'far more useful, probably, than splitting the Treasury', says Robert Peston, would be 'a much more devolved structure … in a variety of hubs' beyond London. Or, to take a step further, giving substantial financial independence to Scotland, Wales and Northern Ireland, and also to the regions of England. This doesn't just mean token funds doled out by the Treasury and on Treasury terms, but instead the devolution of real tax and spend powers, an ability to borrow and invest locally and according to particular need. In effect, a genuine form of multi-level governance should be evolved that empowers institutions and regions, rather than tying everything rigidly to an elite nexus centred on Whitehall, Westminster and the City.

Too radical? Too impractical? Maybe. But without something more far-reaching, the direction of travel doesn't look promising: the break-up of the United Kingdom, economic stagnation, extremes of inequality and widespread poverty, populist and exploitative leadership, violent protests, authoritarian or fascist-style capitalism and an increased chance of military conflict. And I'm pretty sure that, whatever else, the public-minded officials of the Treasury most definitely don't want any of that.

List of interviewees and their Treasury-linked positions

Sixty interviews were conducted with 55 people; 49 of them are listed here. The other six did not want to be listed as an interviewee. Some who are here only wanted their comments reported anonymously. The large majority were happy to be reported on the record with the odd quote given off the record. All interviews were in person, the majority being face to face with one third being via online video platforms. Three were by phone and one (Gordon Brown) by email correspondence.

Alexander, Sir Danny, Chief Secretary to the Treasury 2010–15

Balls, Ed, economic advisor to Gordon Brown 1994–97, Chief Economic Advisor at the Treasury 1997–2005, Economic Secretary to the Treasury 2006–07

Beckett, Dame Margaret, Secretary of State for Trade and Industry, 1997–98

Bender, Sir Brian, career civil servant mainly in the Department of Trade and Industry 1973–2009, Permanent Secretary at the DTI/Business Enterprise 2005–09

Brown, Gordon, Shadow Chancellor 1992–97, Chancellor of the Exchequer 1997–2007, Prime Minister 2007–10

Budd, Sir Alan, economic advisor at the Treasury 1970–74 and 1979–81, Chief Economic Advisor to the Treasury 1991–97, founding member of Bank of England Monetary Policy Committee 1997, Interim Chairman of Office for Budget Responsibility 2010

Burns, Lord Terry, economic advisor at the Treasury 1976–79, Chief Economic Advisor to Treasury and Head of the Government Economic Services 1980–91, Treasury Permanent Secretary 1991–98

Byers, Stephen, Chief Secretary to the Treasury 1998, Secretary of State for Trade and Industry 1998–2001

Cable, Sir Vince, Secretary of State for Business, Innovation and Skills 2010–15

Cameron, David, Leader of the Conservative Party 2005–16, Prime Minister 2010–16

Clarke, Lord Ken, Chancellor of the Exchequer 1993–97

Corry, Dan, Treasury civil servant 1986–89, Labour Party economic advisor 1989–92, economic advisor at DTI 1997–2001, Chair of Council of Economic Advisors Treasury 2006–07, senior economic advisor for Gordon Brown 2007–10

Darling, Lord Alistair, Chief Secretary to the Treasury 1997–98, Secretary of State for Trade and Industry 2006–07, Chancellor of the Exchequer 2007–10

Fallon, Sir Michael, on Treasury Select Committee 2001–10, Minister of State for Business and Enterprise 2012–14

Gieve, Sir John, career civil servant, mainly in the Treasury 1978–2001, including being private secretary to several chancellors and Second Permanent Secretary in the Treasury, Deputy Governor of the Bank of England 2005–09

Haddrill, Sir Stephen, career civil servant including at Department of Trade and Industry 1994–2005, Director General at the Financial Reporting Council 2009–18

Haldane, Andy, Bank of England economist 1989–2021, much of it as Chief Economist

Hammond, Lord Philip, Shadow Chief Secretary to the Treasury 2007–10, Chancellor of the Exchequer 2016–19

Harrison, Rupert, Chief Economic Advisor to George Osborne 2006–10, Chief of Staff to George Osborne and Chair of the UK Council of Economic Advisors 2010–15

Heseltine, Lord Michael, Secretary of State for Trade and Industry 1992–95

Howe, Lord Geoffrey, Shadow Chancellor of the Exchequer 1975–79, Chancellor of the Exchequer 1979–83

Kerslake, Lord Bob, Head of Home Civil Service 2012–14

Interviewees

Kingman, Sir John, civil servant in Treasury on and off 1990–2016, including as Second Permanent Secretary and first CEO of UK Financial Investments

Lamont, Lord Norman, Minister of State for Trade and Industry 1981–85, Financial Secretary to the Treasury 1986–88, Chief Secretary to the Treasury 1989–90, Chancellor of the Exchequer 1990–93

Lawson, Lord Nigel, Financial Secretary to the Treasury 1979–81, Chancellor of the Exchequer 1983–89

Lindley, Dominic, advisor to Treasury Select Committee, 2002–06, and to Future of Banking Commission 2009

Macpherson, Lord Nicholas, civil servant in the Treasury 1985–2016, including as Permanent Secretary 2005–16.

McCourt, Duncan, Chief of Staff for Philip Hammond, 2016–19

McFall, Lord John, Lord Commissioner of the Treasury 1997–98, Chair Treasury Select Committee 2001–10

Middleton, Sir Peter, Treasury civil servant 1961–91, including as Permanent Secretary 1983–91

O'Donnell, Lord Gus, career civil servant on and off in the Treasury 1979–2005, including as Permanent Secretary 2002–05, Cabinet Permanent Secretary and Head of Home Civil Service 2005–11

Osborne, George, Shadow Chancellor of the Exchequer 2005–10, Chancellor of the Exchequer 2010–16

Parkinson, Lord Cecil, Paymaster General 1981–83, Secretary of State for Trade and Industry 1983

Peston, Robert, business, financial and political journalist and editor 1983 to present, including at *The Financial Times*, *The Times*, *The Telegraph*, BBC and ITN

Pryce, Vicky, Chief Economic Advisor at the Department for Trade and Industry (Business, Innovation and Skills) 2002–10, Head of Government Economic Services 2004–10 (Joint Head 2007–10)

Ramsden, Sir Dave, Treasury civil servant 1988–2017, including as Head of Government Economic Services 2007–17 (Joint Head 2007–10), Deputy Governor of Bank of England 2017 to present

Robinson, Geoffrey, Paymaster General 1997–98

Robson, Sir Steve, Treasury civil servant 1969–2001, including as Second Permanent Secretary

Roxburgh, Charles, Treasury civil servant 2013–present, including as Second Permanent Secretary Treasury since 2016

Sassoon, Lord James, Treasury civil servant 2002–08, advisor to George Osborne 2008–10, Commercial Secretary to the Treasury 2010–12

Scholar, Sir Tom, Treasury civil servant on and off since 1992, Second Permanent Secretary 2009–13, Permanent Secretary 2016 to present

Timms, Stephen, Financial Secretary to the Treasury 1999–2001, 2004–05, 2008–10, Chief Secretary to the Treasury 2006–07

Troup, Sir Edward, tax advisor to Ken Clarke 1995–97, Treasury civil servant 2004–17

Trowbridge, Poppy, business journalist 2006–16, Director of Communication for Philip Hammond 2016–19

Tucker, Sir Paul, central banker at Bank of England 1980–2013, including as Deputy Governor of the Bank of England 2009–13

Turnbull, Lord Andrew, career civil servant on and off in Treasury 1970–2002, including as Permanent Secretary 1998–2002, Cabinet Secretary and Head of Civil Service 2002–05

Turner, Lord Adair, Director of Confederation of British Industry 1995–99, Chairman of the Financial Services Authority 2008–13

Wales, Chris, tax advisor to Gordon Brown 1994–2003

Wolf, Martin, economist and *Financial Times* journalist 1987 to present, including as chief economics commentator since 1996, member of Independent Commission on Banking 2010–11

Abbreviations

BEIS	Business, Energy and Industrial Strategy (department)
CPI	Consumer Price Index (measure of inflation)
DTI	Department of Trade and Industry
ECOFIN	Economic and Financial Affairs Council of Europe
EEA	European Economic Area
ERM	European Exchange Rate Mechanism
FSA	Financial Services Authority (regulatory body)
FTSE 100	Financial Times Stock Exchange 100 (index)
G7	Group of Seven (intergovernmental forum including UK)
GDP	Gross Domestic Product (measure of the economy)
GES	Government Economic Services
HMRC	Her Majesty's Revenue and Customs

Abbreviations

IEA	Institute of Economic Affairs (think tank)
IMF	International Monetary Fund
IPPR	Institute for Public Policy Research (think tank)
LSE	London Stock Exchange
MBS	mortgage-backed securities
MPC	Monetary Policy Committee
OBR	Office for Budget Responsibility
OECD	Organisation for Economic Co-operation and Development
ONS	Office for National Statistics
PFI	private finance initiative
PPE	Philosophy, Politics and Economics (degree)
PSBR	public sector borrowing requirement
QE	quantitative easing
RPI	Retail Price Index (measure of inflation)
UKTI	United Kingdom Trade and Investment (department)
WTO	World Trade Organization

Notes

Notes to Introduction

1 Well, according to Dominic Cummings at least, in Select Committee testimony. Although not a reliable witness, much of his evidence sounds plausible and has other sources to support it.

2 The best book I read on the Treasury was Simon Jenkins' *Thatcher and Sons: A Revolution in Three Acts* (London: Penguin, 2006). Although Jenkins' book is about the political continuities between the Thatcher and Blair administrations, rather a lot of it focuses on the Treasury and economic policy. Robert Peston's various books on British politics do something similar. His *WTF?* (London: Hodder and Stoughton, 2017) is particularly incisive here.

3 You can get a glimpse here: https://social.shorthand.com/hmtreasury/32EEikq966/the-treasury-building-a-surprising-history (accessed 15 February 2022).

4 An issue most recently explored in Lord Kerslake, *Rethinking the Treasury: Kerslake Review of the Treasury* (London: Labour Party, 2017).

5 See Tom Sasse and Emma Norris, *Moving On: The Costs of High Staff Turnover in the Civil Service* (London: Institute for Government, 2019).

6 Examples here include Colin Thain and Maurice Wright, *The Treasury and Whitehall: The Planning and Control of Public*

Expenditure, 1976–1993 (Oxford: Oxford University Press, 1995); Maurice Mullard, *The Politics of Public Expenditure*, 2nd edn (London: Routledge, 1993).

7 For example, much work in International Political Economy, Science and Technology Studies and Actor Network Theory.

8 See, for example, Philip Mirowski and Dieter Plehwe (eds), *The Road to Mont Pelerin: The Making of the Neoliberal Thought Collective* (Cambridge, MA: Harvard University Press, 2009).

9 See, for example, Adam Tooze, *Crashed: How a Decade of Financial Crisis Changed the World* (London: Penguin, 2018).

10 See Peter Hall and David Soskice (eds), *Varieties of Capitalism: The Institutional Foundations of Comparative Advantage* (Oxford: Oxford University Press, 2001).

11 See Gretta Krippner, *Capitalizing on Crisis: The Political Origins of the Rise of Finance* (Cambridge, MA: Harvard University Press, 2011).

12 Yanis Varoufakis, *Adults in the Room: My Battle with Europe's Deep Establishment* (London: Random House, 2017).

13 A K-shaped recovery describes an economic recovery where different sectors, regions or groups recover at different times or some don't recover at all.

14 MMT is modern monetary theory, the idea that governments with their own currency can bypass the limits of taxation and borrowing by simply printing as much money as they need.

Notes to Chapter 2

1 The Bretton Woods Agreement, negotiated in 1944, was an international system for governing monetary relations between states, offering fixed exchange rates that were pegged to the US dollar and gold reserves. The US withdrew from this in 1971 and the system broke down.

2 There are several interpretations of why the Keynesian formula broke down. Presented here is the Burns and Budd version.

3 See the account in Richard Roberts, *When Britain Went Bust: The 1976 IMF Crisis* (London: OMFIF Press, 2016).

4 The recognised definitive insider account of this event is deemed to be Douglas Wass's *Decline to Fall* (Oxford: Oxford University Press, 1976). See also Leo Pliatzky, *The Treasury under Mrs Thatcher* (Oxford: Blackwell, 1989) and Simon Jenkins, *Thatcher and Sons: A Revolution in Three Acts* (London: Penguin, 2006).

5 Although the switch to monetarism is associated with Thatcherism, it began with Denis Healey and the Labour government. While downplaying this shift in public, Healey and Callaghan were already making substantial moves in this direction. This is something noted in some key historical accounts and by all interviewees who were there.

6 Quoted from John Ranelagh's *Thatcher's People: An Insider Account of the Politics, the Power and the Personalities* (London: Fontana, 1992).

7 The prestigious Mais lectures have taken place annually at City, University of London since 1978. Several chancellors, prime ministers and governors of the Bank of England have given them.

8 Nigel Lawson, 'The Fifth Mais Lecture: The British Experiment', speech to City Business School, 18 June 1984.

9 See scathing contemporary critiques such as Nicholas Kaldor's *The Scourge of Monetarism*, 2nd edn (Oxford: Oxford University Press, 1985) and William Keegan's *Mrs Thatcher's Economic Experiment* (London: Penguin, 1984).

10 See, for example, Christopher Johnson, *The Economy under Mrs Thatcher 1979–1990* (London: Penguin, 1991); Alec Cairncross, *The British Economy since 1945* (Oxford: Blackwell, 1992).

11 Howard Davies, *The Chancellors' Tales: Managing the British Economy* (Cambridge: Polity, 2006).

12 See Johnson, *The Economy under Mrs Thatcher*; Cairncross, *The British Economy since 1945*; and various chancellors' accounts in Davies, *The Chancellors' Tales*.

13 See, in particular, Pliatzky, *The Treasury under Mrs Thatcher*.

14 See accounts in Jenkins, *Thatcher and Sons*; and Andrew Gamble, *The Free Economy and the Strong State: The Politics of Thatcherism*, 2nd edn (Basingstoke: Palgrave, 1994).

15 Colin Thain and Maurice Wright published a number of journal articles on the subject, including a two-part journal piece in *Public Administration*. C. Thain and M. Wright, 'Planning and Controlling Public Expenditure in the UK, Part I: The Treasury's Public Expenditure Survey', *Public Administration*, 70 (1992): 3–24; C. Thain and M. Wright, 'Planning and Controlling Public Expenditure in the UK, Part II: The Effects and Effectiveness of the Survey', *Public Administration*, 70 (1992): 193–224; and a book, *The Treasury and Whitehall: The Planning and Control of Public Expenditure, 1976–1993* (Oxford: Oxford University Press, 1995).

16 See accounts in Maurice Mullard's *The Politics of Public Expenditure*, 2nd edn (London: Routledge, 1993); and, in relation to the DTI, Aeron Davis and Catherine Walsh, 'The Role of the State in the Financialization of the UK Economy', *Political Studies*, 64.3 (2016): 666–682.

17 Gamble, *The Free Economy and the Strong State*.

18 Henry Gibbons, *Privatization Yearbook 1997* (London: Privatization International, 1997).

19 See Johnson, *The Economy under Mrs Thatcher*, p. 153.

20 Figures in Pliatzky, *The Treasury under Mrs Thatcher*; Jenkins, *Thatcher and Sons*; and Cairncross, *The British Economy since 1945*.

21 Peter Riddell describes him as 'one of the most adventurous of outsider appointments' in *The Thatcher Government*, 2nd edn (Oxford: Blackwell, 1985).

22 Nigel Lawson, *The View from Number 11: Memoirs of a Tory Radical* (London: Bantam Press, 1992).

23 See Peter Barberis, *The Elite of the Elite: Permanent Secretaries in the British Higher Civil Service* (Brookfield, VT: Dartmouth, 1996). It is also a background feature of past Establishment accounts such as Anthony Sampson, *Anatomy of Britain* (London: Hodder and Stoughton, 1962).

24 Cairncross, *The British Economy since 1945*; Kevin Theakston, 'Whitehall and British Industrial Policy', in D. Coates and J. Hillard (eds), *UK Economic Decline: Key Texts* (London: Prentice Hall, 1995), pp. 300–313.

25 David Lipsey, *The Secret Treasury* (London: Viking, 2000).

26 See figures and details in Aeron Davis, 'The New Professional Econocracy and the Maintenance of Elite Power', *Political Studies*, 65.3 (2017): 594–610.

27 Isaac Asimov's *Foundation Series* was first published in the 1940s and 1950s, with further volumes in the 1980s. Asimov was himself inspired by Edward Gibbon's *The History of the Decline and Fall of the Roman Empire*.

28 Lawson, *The View from Number 11*.

29 See Davies, *The Chancellors' Tales*. See also Davis, 'The New Professional Econocracy'.

30 See former chancellors' views given in Davies, *The Chancellors' Tales*.

31 Eddie George then being the governor of the Bank of England.

32 Ken Clarke told me that every chancellor bar John Major had been frustrated by party political pressure to change interest rates for short-term political gain, and that he had argued for such a move.

33 See overviews in Jenkins, *Thatcher and Sons*; and Polly Toynbee and David Walker, *The Verdict: Did Labour Change Britain?* (London: Granta, 2010).

34 This view was expressed by Pliatzky, *The Treasury under Mrs Thatcher*; Theakston, 'Whitehall and British Industrial Policy'; Peter Hall, 'The State and Economic Decline' in D. Coates and J. Hillard (eds), *UK Economic Decline: Key Texts* (London: Prentice Hall, 1995), pp. 265–286; and Johnson, *The Economy under Mrs Thatcher*.

35 Jenkins, *Thatcher and Sons*, p. 192.

Notes to Chapter 3

1 For a history of neoliberalism, see David Harvey, *A Brief History of Neoliberalism* (Oxford: Oxford University Press, 2007); Philip Mirowski and Dieter Plehwe (eds), *The Road to Mont Pelerin: The Making of the Neoliberal Thought Collective* (Cambridge, MA: Harvard University Press, 2009).

2 Pinochet's Chile applied them earlier than this.

3 For an introduction to financialization, see Gerald Epstein (ed.), *Financialization and the World Economy* (Cheltenham:

Notes

Edward Elgar, 2005); Thomas Palley, 'Financialization: What it is and Why it Matters', Working Paper No. 525 (London: Levy Economics Institute, 2007).

4 Nigel Lawson, *The View from Number 11: Memoirs of a Tory Radical* (London: Bantam Press, 1992).

5 Nigel Lawson, 'The Fifth Mais Lecture: The British Experiment', speech to City Business School, 18 June 1984.

6 See Morrison Halcrow, *Keith Joseph: A Single Mind* (London: Macmillan, 1989).

7 See historical accounts in Keith Middlemas, *Power, Competition and the State, Vol 3: The End of the Post-War Era* (London: Macmillan, 1991); Sidney Pollard, *The Development of the British Economy 1914–90*, 4th edn (London: Edward Arnold, 1992).

8 Figures in Maurice Mullard, *The Politics of Public Expenditure*, 2nd edn (London: Routledge, 1993); see also Colin Thain and Maurice Wright, *The Treasury and Whitehall: The Planning and Control of Public Expenditure, 1976–1993* (Oxford: Oxford University Press, 1995).

9 Christopher Johnson, *The Economy under Mrs Thatcher 1979–1990* (London: Penguin, 1991).

10 See Hugo Young, *One of Us* (London: Macmillan, 1989).

11 The term used by Mirowski and Plehwe (eds), *The Road to Mont Pelerin*.

12 See account in Kevin Theakston, 'Whitehall and British Industrial Policy', in D. Coates and J. Hillard (eds), *UK Economic Decline: Key Texts* (London: Prentice Hall, 1995), pp. 300–313.

13 Stuart Hood, 'The "New Public Management" in the 1980s: Variations on a Theme', *Accounting, Organizations and Society*, 20.2/3 (1995): 93–109; and Michael Moran, *The British Regulatory State: High Modernism and Hyper-Innovation* (Oxford: Oxford University Press, 2003).

14 See Geoffrey Ingham, *Capitalism Divided? The City and Industry in British Social Development* (Basingstoke: Palgrave, 1984); P. J. Cain and A. G. Hopkins, *British Imperialism 1688–2000*, 2nd edn (Harlow: Pearson Education, 2002).

15 Henry Gibbons, *Privatization Yearbook 1997* (London: Privatization International, 1997).

16 See study by Gregory Jackson and Hideaki Miyajima, 'Varieties of Capitalism, Varieties of Markets: Mergers and Acquisitions in Japan, Germany, France, the UK and USA', *RIETI Discussion Paper Series* 07-E-054 (London: RIETI, 2007).

17 See, for example, Will Hutton, *The State We're In* (London: Vintage, 1996); Ha Joon Chang, *23 Things They Didn't Tell You about Capitalism* (London: Allen Lane, 2010).

18 Figures in Hutton, *The State We're In*, p. 8.

19 See accounts in Johnson, *The Economy under Mrs Thatcher*; and Grace Blakeley, *Stolen: How to Save the World from Financialization* (London: Repeater Books, 2019).

20 See Hansard UK Parliament HC Deb, 20 March 1990, 169 c1014–1015.

21 See D. Coates and J. Hillard (eds), *UK Economic Decline: Key Texts* (London: Prentice Hall, 1995).

22 See Johnson, *The Economy under Mrs Thatcher*.

23 See Polly Toynbee and David Walker, *The Verdict: Did Labour Change Britain?* (London: Granta, 2011); Simon Jenkins, *Thatcher and Sons: A Revolution in Three Acts* (London: Penguin, 2006).

24 Ed Balls, *Speaking Out* (London: Arrow Books, 2016)

25 See Blakeley, *Stolen*, p. 12.

26 See history in Anthony Seely, *Takeovers: The Public Interest Test*, House of Commons Standard Note SN 05374 (London: House of Commons, 2012).

27 David Coates, 'UK Underperformance: Claim and Reality', in D. Coates and J. Hillard (eds), *UK Economic Decline: Key Texts* (London: Prentice Hall, 1995), pp. 3–24.

28 Chang, *23 Things They Didn't Tell You about Capitalism*.

29 Coates, 'UK Underperformance'.

30 Chang, *23 Things They Didn't Tell You about Capitalism*.

31 Johnson, *The Economy under Mrs Thatcher*.

32 See figures in Nicholas Comfort, *Surrender: How British Industry Gave up the Ghost, 1952–2012* (London: Biteback, 2012); and Toynbee and Walker, *The Verdict*.

33 See accounts by Coates, 'UK Underperformance'; Hutton, *The State We're In*; Chang, *23 Things They Didn't Tell You about Capitalism*; and Peter Hall, 'The State and Economic Decline', in D. Coates and J. Hillard (eds), *UK Economic*

Decline: Key Texts (London: Prentice Hall, 1995), pp. 265–286. See also Peter Hall and David Soskice, *Varieties of Capitalism: The Institutional Foundations of Comparative Advantage* (Oxford: Oxford University Press, 2001).

34 Andrew Haldane, 'The Contribution of the Financial Sector: Miracle or Mirage?', speech at the Future of Finance Conference, LSE, 14 July 2010.

Notes to Chapter 4

1 See *London Stock Exchange Fact File* (London: London Stock Exchange, 1998).

2 See Christopher Johnson, *The Economy under Mrs Thatcher 1979–1990* (London: Penguin, 1991), p. 149.

3 See Henry Gibbons, *The Privatization Yearbook 1997* (London: Privatization International, 1997).

4 See Johnson, *The Economy under Mrs Thatcher*, p. 153.

5 See Andrew Gamble, *The Free Economy and the Strong State: The Politics of Thatcherism*, 2nd edn (Basingstoke: Palgrave, 1994); Leo Pliatzky, *The Treasury under Mrs Thatcher* (Oxford: Blackwell, 1989); Alec Cairncross, *The British Economy since 1945* (Oxford: Blackwell, 1992); Colin Thain and Maurice Wright, *The Treasury and Whitehall: The Planning and Control of Public Expenditure, 1976–1993* (Oxford: Oxford University Press, 1995).

6 See Pliatzky, *The Treasury under Mrs Thatcher*; Cairncross, *The British Economy since 1945*; and Thain and Wright, *The Treasury and Whitehall*.

7 See Pliatsky, *The Treasury under Mrs Thatcher*, p. 150.

8 See Anna Minton, *Big Capital: Who is London For?* (London: Penguin, 2017), p. 28.

9 See Ann Pettifor, *The Coming First World Debt Crisis* (Basingstoke: Palgrave Macmillan, 2006).

10 See, variously, Colin Crouch, 'Privatized Keynesianism: An Unacknowledged Policy Regime', *British Journal of Politics and International Relations*, 11 (2009): 382–399; Adair Turner, *Between Debt and the Devil: Money, Credit and Fixing Global Finance* (Princeton, NJ: Princeton University Press,

2016); Steve Keen, *Can We Afford Another Financial Crisis?* (Cambridge: Polity, 2017); Grace Blakeley, *Stolen: How to Save the World from Financialization* (London: Repeater Books, 2019).

11 See Janine Wedel, *Shadow Elite* (New York: Basic Books, 2009); Janine Wedel, *Unaccountable* (New York: Pegasus Books, 2014).

12 National Air Traffic Services and British Nuclear Fuels.

13 An account of this can be found in Geoffrey Robinson, *The Unconventional Minister: My Life Inside New Labour* (London: Penguin, 2001).

14 See accounts in Stuart Hood, 'The "New Public Management" in the 1980s: Variations on a Theme', *Accounting, Organizations and Society*, 20.2/3 (1995): 93–109; Michael Moran, *The British Regulatory State: High Modernism and Hyper-Innovation* (Oxford: Oxford University Press, 2003).

15 Simon Jenkins' account is very insightful here: Simon Jenkins, *Thatcher and Sons: A Revolution in Three Acts* (London: Penguin, 2006).

16 See Robinson, *The Unconventional Minister*, ch. 8.

17 See the *Guardian*'s summary analysis at https://www.theguardian.com/news/datablog/2012/jul/05/pfi-contracts-list (accessed 15 February 2022).

18 There are several critical accounts of PFI and its consequences, including several National Audit Office reports; see https://www.nao.org.uk/report/pfi-and-pf2/ (accessed 15 February 2022).

19 Andrew Sparrow, 'George Osborne Backs 61 PFI Projects despite Earlier Doubts over Costing', *The Guardian*, 18 April 2011, https://www.theguardian.com/politics/2011/apr/18/george-osborne-backs-pfi-projects (accessed 15 February 2022).

20 PSND is public sector net debt.

21 See Andrew McGettigan, *The Great University Gamble: Money, Markets and the Future of Higher Education* (London: Pluto Press, 2013); and also his blog at https://andrewmcgettigan.org/ (accessed 15 February 2022).

22 See Paul Bolton, 'Student Loan Statistics', Research Briefing CBP01079, December 2021 (London: House of Commons Library, 2021).

23 See Guy Standing, *The Corruption of Capitalism: Why Rentiers Thrive and Work Does Not Pay* (London: Biteback, 2021, Kindle edition), pp. 14, 36.

24 See lengthy accounts in Minton, *Big Capital*; and Johnson, *The Economy under Mrs Thatcher*.

25 Figures in Turner, *Between Debt and the Devil*, pp. 7, 50.

26 See Mariana Mazzucato, *The Value of Everything: Making and Taking in the Global Economy* (London: Allen Lane, 2018), p. 130.

27 See, in particular, Manuel Aalbers, 'The Financialization of Homes and the Mortgage Market Crisis', *Competition and Change*, 12.2 (2009): 148–166; and Colin Crouch, 'Privatized Keynesianism', *British Journal of Politics and International Relations*, 11.3 (2009): 382–399.

28 Aalbers, 'The Financialization of Homes', pp. 151, 155.

29 CPI is the Consumer Price Index and RPI is the Retail Price Index.

30 See Minton, *Big Capital*, p. 30.

31 See, in particular, Keen, *Can We Afford Another Financial Crisis?*; Ann Pettifor, *The Production of Money: How to Break the Power of Bankers* (London: Verso, 2017); and Turner, *Between Debt and the Devil*.

32 DSGE or dynamic stochastic general equilibrium models.

33 See Keen, *Can We Afford Another Financial Crisis?*, pp. 192–193.

Notes to Chapter 5

1 For a wide-ranging discussion of the links between nationalism and economic decline in Britain and the US, see Anthony Barnett, *The Lure of Greatness* (London: Unbound, 2017).

2 See Nicholas Macpherson, speech entitled 'The Origins of the Treasury', 16 January 2013, https://www.gov.uk/government/speeches/speech-by-the-permanent-secretary-to-the-treasury-sir-nicholas-macpherson-the-origins-of-treasury-control (accessed 15 February 2022). See also account in W. Lowndes and D. Gill, 'The Treasury, 1660–1714', *The English Historical Review*, 46.184 (1931): 600–622.

Notes

3 See Eric Hobsbawm, *Industry and Empire: The Birth of the Industrial Revolution* (London: Penguin, 1999); J. Holland Rose, A. P. Newton and E. A. Beniani, *The Cambridge History of the British Empire, Volumes I and II* (Cambridge: Cambridge University Press, 1940).

4 Geoffrey Ingham, *Capitalism Divided? The City and Industry in British Social Development* (Basingstoke: Palgrave, 1984); P. J. Cain and A. G. Hopkins, *British Imperialism 1688–2000*, 2nd edn (Harlow: Pearson Education, 2002).

5 For Ingham, *Capitalism Divided?*, the essentials of Treasury economy policy, as they emerged in the early 1980s, had a lot in common with those set out in Gladstone's time.

6 Nicholas Macpherson, speech to the Mile End Group entitled 'The Treasury View: A Testament of Experience', 17 January 2014, https://www.gov.uk/government/speeches/speech-by-the-permanent-secretary-to-the-treasury-the-treasury-view-a-testament-of-experience (accessed 15 February 2022).

7 See Geoffrey Howe, *Conflict of Loyalty* (London: Pan Macmillan, 1995).

8 See the account in Simon Jenkins, *Thatcher and Sons: A Revolution in Three Acts* (London: Penguin, 2006).

9 Figures in Alec Cairncross, *The British Economy since 1945* (Oxford: Blackwell, 1992).

10 A reference to Mervyn Peake's *Gormenghast* trilogy (London: Eyre and Spottiswoode, 1946, 1950, 1959).

11 Maurice Mullard, *The Politics of Public Expenditure*, 2nd edn (London: Routledge, 1993).

12 ECOFIN is the Economic and Financial Affairs Council of Europe.

13 See Philip Hammond, published interview for UK in a Changing Europe, 20 November 2020, https://ukandeu.ac.uk/brexit-witness-archive/philip-hammond/ (accessed 15 February 2022)

14 Ken Clarke, *A Kind of Blue: A Political Memoir* (London: Macmillan, 2016); Gordon Brown, *My Life, Our Times* (London: Bodley Head, 2017); David Cameron, *For the Record* (London: William Collins, 2019); Janan Ganesh, *George Osborne: The Austerity Chancellor* (London: Biteback, 2014), p. 266.

15 Interview with Ed Balls, *New Statesman*, 20 March 2006.

16 Ed Balls, *Speaking Out* (London: Arrow Books, 2016).

17 See Ed Balls's own contribution 'Open Macroeconomics in an Open Economy', Centre for Economic Performance, Paper No. 13 (London: London School of Economics, 2007), https://ideas.repec.org/p/ehl/lserod/28748.html (accessed 15 February 2022).

18 For an optimistic account of the fall and rise of British manufacturing in the period, see Geoffrey Owen, *From Empire to Europe: The Decline and Revival of British Industry since the Second World War* (London: Harper Collins, 1999).

19 See accounts in Tony Golding, *The City: Inside the Great Expectation Machine* (London: Prentice Hall, 2003); and Philip Augar, *The Death of Gentlemanly Capitalism* (London: Penguin, 2000).

20 See accounts in Peter Hall, 'The State and Economic Decline', in D. Coates and J. Hillard (eds), *UK Economic Decline: Key Texts* (London: Prentice Hall, 1995), pp. 265–286; Will Hutton, *The State We're In* (London: Vintage, 1996).

21 Figures from the Office for National Statistics (London: ONS, 2014).

22 Nicholas Comfort, *Surrender: How British Industry Gave up the Ghost, 1952–2012* (London: Biteback, 2012).

23 See CRESC, 'Rebalancing the Economy (or Buyers Remorse)', CRESC Working Paper Series No. 87 (Manchester: CRESC, 2011).

24 See, for example, *The Cox Review: Overcoming Short-Termism within British Business: The Key to Sustained Economic Growth* (London: Labour Party, 2013); *The Kay Review of UK Equity Markets and Long-Term Decision-Making* (London: Department of Business, Innovation and Skills, 2012); Ewald Engelen et al., *After the Great Complacence: Financial Crisis and the Politics of Reform* (Oxford: Oxford University Press, 2011).

25 See Reuters report at https://www.reuters.com/business/finance/london-banking-job-exodus-eu-slows-despite-brexit-2021-12-20/ (accessed 15 February 2022).

26 See figures in annual reports from the Society of Motor Manufacturers and Traders (SMMT).

27 BBC, 'UK Car Production Slumps to Lowest Level since 1984', 28 January 2021, https://www.bbc.com/news/business-55817920 (accessed 15 February 2022).
28 For figures and general accounts of elite mobility, see Chrystia Freeland, *Plutocrats: The Rise of the New Global Super-Rich* (London: Penguin, 2012); John Urry, *Offshoring* (Cambridge: Polity, 2014).
29 See details of the international financialization of the UK economy in Aeron Davis and Catherine Walsh, 'Distinguishing Financialization from Neoliberalism', *Theory, Culture and Society*, 34.5–6 (2017): 27–51.
30 See figures in John Urry, 'The Super-rich and Offshore Worlds', in J. Birtchnell and J. Caletrio (eds), *Elite Mobilities* (Abingdon: Routledge, 2014), pp. 226–240.
31 See Anthony Seely, *Tax Avoidance and Tax Evasion*, House of Commons Library Report No. 7948 (2021).
32 See Tax Justice Network report on the UK (2021), https://taxjustice.net/country-profiles/united-kingdom/ (accessed 15 February 2022).

Notes to Chapter 6

1 See Colin Crouch, *The Strange Non-Death of Neoliberalism* (Cambridge: Polity, 2011).
2 'The great moderation' was a term coined by many economists and policymakers to describe the relatively stable period of economic growth from the mid-1980s until the 2007–08 crisis. Its advocates usually link it to central bank independence, inflation targeting and free-market policies.
3 See, for example, Andrew Ross Sorkin, *Too Big to Fail: Inside the Battle to Save Wall Street* (London: Penguin, 2010); Gillian Tett, *Fool's Gold: How Unrestrained Greed Corrupted a Dream, Shattered Global Markets and Unleashed a Catastrophe* (London: Abacus, 2010).
4 See, for example, Vince Cable, *The Storm: The World Economic Crisis and What it Means* (London: Atlantic Books, 2009); Martin Wolf, *The Shifts and the Shocks: What We've Learned – and Have Still to Learn – From the Financial*

Crisis (London: Penguin, 2015); Adam Tooze, *Crashed: How a Decade of Financial Crisis Changed the World* (London: Penguin, 2018).

5 See, for example, Paul Krugman, *The Return of Depression Economics and the Crisis of 2008* (London: Penguin, 2008); Larry Elliott and David Atkinson, *The Gods that Failed: How the Financial Elite Have Gambled Away Our Futures* (London: Vintage, 2009); Charles Ferguson, *Inside Job: The Financiers Who Pulled Off the Heist of the Century* (Oxford: Oneworld, 2012).

6 See figures in Ferguson, *Inside Job*, for the US, and Cable, *The Storm*, for the UK.

7 See UNCTAD, *The Global Economic Crisis: Systemic Failures and Multilateral Remedies*, UNCTAD/GDS/2009/1 (New York/Geneva: United Nations Conference on Trade and Development, 2009), p. 13.

8 See Elliott and Atkinson, *The Gods that Failed*, p. 52.

9 See Cable, *The Storm*, p. 34.

10 See Aditya Chakrabortty, 'Barclays Libor Scandal: How Can We Change Banking Culture?', *The Guardian*, 2 July 2012, https://www.theguardian.com/business/2012/jul/02/barclays-libor-scandal-change-banking-culture (accessed 15 February 2022).

11 Such figures include Michael Hudson, Steve Keen, Ann Pettifor, Raghuram Rajan, Nouriel Roubini, Peter Schiff and a small number of eclectic traders who did well out of betting on the collapse, as documented in Michael Lewis, *The Big Short: Inside the Doomsday Machine* (New York: W. W. Norton, 2010).

12 Howard Davies came up with a list of 38 different culprits in his book *The Financial Crisis: Who is to Blame?* (Cambridge: Polity, 2010).

13 See accounts in Gordon Brown, *Beyond the Crash* (London: Simon and Schuster, 2010); and Ed Balls, *Speaking Out: Lessons in Life and Politics* (London: Arrow Books, 2016).

14 See also insider accounts in, for example, Brown, *Beyond the Crash*, and Alistair Darling, *Back From the Brink* (London: Atlantic Books, 2011).

15 In December 2008 Brown in a slip of the tongue claimed to 'have saved the world'. While ridiculed by some for this, others claimed he stepped up to the crisis ahead of other world leaders. See William Keegan, *Saving the World? Gordon Brown Reconsidered* (Cambridge: Searching Finance, 2012).

16 Matt Taibi, 'Why isn't Wall Street in Jail?', *Rolling Stone*, https://www.rollingstone.com/politics/politics-news/why-isnt-wall-street-in-jail-179414/ (accessed 15 February 2022).

17 See Thomas Piketty, *Capital in the Twenty-First Century* (Cambridge, MA: Harvard University Press, 2014); Brett Christophers, *Rentier Capitalism: Who Owns the Economy and Who Pays for It?* (London: Verso, 2020); Guy Standing, *The Corruption of Capitalism: Why Rentiers Thrive and Work Does Not Pay* (London: Biteback, 2021).

18 See accounts in, for example, John Kay, *Other People's Money: Masters of the Universe or Servants of the People?* (London: Profile Books, 2016); Adair Turner, *Between Debt and the Devil: Money, Credit and Fixing Global Finance* (Princeton, NJ: Princeton University Press, 2017); Mariana Mazzucato, *The Value of Everything: Making and Taking in the Global Economy* (London: Penguin, 2018).

19 See Robert Shiller, *Irrational Exuberance* (Princeton, NJ: Princeton University Press, 2001); Robert Aliber and Charles Kindleberger, *Manias, Panics and Crashes: A History of Financial Crises*, 7th edn (Basingstoke: Palgrave Macmillan, 2015); Krugman, *The Return of Depression Economics*.

20 See also accounts in Kevin Theakston, 'Whitehall and British Industrial Policy', in D. Coates and J. Hillard (eds), *UK Economic Decline: Key Texts* (London: Prentice Hall, 1995), pp. 300–313; David Lipsey, *The Secret Treasury* (London: Viking, 2000).

21 Both Gordon Brown, *Beyond the Crash*, and Ed Balls, *Speaking Out*, are fairly critical of Mervyn King in their biographies.

22 David Davis, *The Future of Banking Commission* (London: Which?, 2010).

23 Bob Wigley, *London: Winning in a Changing World* (London: Merrill Lynch Europe, 2008); Win Bischoff and Alistair Darling, *UK International Financial Services – The Future: A Report*

from UK Based Financial Service Leaders to the Government (London: HM Treasury, 2009).

24 See Aeron Davis, *Promotional Cultures* (Cambridge: Polity, 2013), p. 180; Bureau of Investigative Journalism Online at http://www.thebureauinvestigates.com (London: 2012)

25 Davis, *The Future of Banking Commission.*

26 John Vickers, *Independent Commission on Banking* (London, 2011).

27 CRESC Working Paper No. 108, 'Groundhog Day, Elite Power, Democratic Disconnects and the Failure of Financial Reform in the UK' (Manchester: CRESC, 2011), p. 9.

28 See critical accounts of the City lobby and the closing down of wider debate in Ewald Engelen et al., *After the Great Complacence: Financial Crisis and the Politics of Reform* (Oxford: Oxford University Press, 2011); and a series from 2011 from Manchester Business School's CRESC Unit: Working Papers – Centre for Research on Socio-Cultural Change –University of Manchester, https://www.cresc.ac.uk/publications/working-papers/ (accessed 15 February 2022).

29 Such problems are also documented in Brown, *Beyond the Crash*, and Davies, *The Financial Crisis.*

30 Interest rates were reduced rapidly from 5% to 0.5% in 2008, VAT was cut, and quantitative easing introduced (£200 billion in 2008).

31 John Kingman interview.

32 See Basel III: A global regulatory framework for more resilient banks and banking systems, revised version June 2011, at https://www.bis.org/publ/bcbs189.pdf (accessed 15 February 2022).

Notes to Chapter 7

1 TINA or 'There is no alternative' was the key phrase used by Thatcher in the 1980s to bludgeon critics of her market reforms.

2 Nadine Dorries, a Conservative backbench MP, during a low point in the Coalition years, called out Cameron and Osborne for being two out-of-touch 'arrogant posh boys'.

Notes

3   Cameron, Osborne and Clegg each had at least one baron(ness) in their close families, and each went to one of the nine most exclusive public schools as identified by the Clarendon Commission (Eton, St Paul's, Westminster).

4   See Aeron Davis, *Political Communication and Social Theory* (Abingdon: Routledge, 2010); but also accounts in Colin Crouch, *Post-Democracy* (Cambridge: Polity, 2004); Peter Mair, *Ruling the Void: The Hollowing Out of Western Democracy* (London: Verso, 2013).

5   For example, Fraser Nelson, 'Ever Wondered how George Osborne Can be a Part-time Chancellor?', *The Daily Telegraph*, 16 March 2012, https://www.telegraph.co.uk/news/politics/georgeosborne/9148687/Ever-wondered-how-George-Osborne-can-be-a-part-time-Chancellor.html (accessed 15 February 2022); Ed Jacobs, 'Chancellor's Constituents Call on him to End "Part-time Role"', *The Guardian*, 13 March 2013, https://www.theguardian.com/uk/the-northerner/2013/mar/13/george-osborne-tatton-opinion-poll-chancellor-of-the-exchequer-budget (accessed 15 February 2022).

6   Mary Ann Sieghart, Radio 4 profile of Rupert Harrison, 16 March 2014.

7   See David Cameron, *For the Record* (London: William Collins, 2019).

8   The Institute of Economic Affairs, a think tank that did much to support Thatcherite policies in the 1980s.

9   Cameron, *For the Record*, p. 186; Anthony Seldon and Peter Snowdon, *Cameron at 10: The Inside Story 2010–2015* (London: William Collins, 2015), ch. 42; see also Janan Ganesh, *George Osborne: The Austerity Chancellor* (London: Biteback, 2014), p. 162.

10 See account in Aeron Davis and Emily Seymour, 'Generating Forms of Media Capital inside and outside the Political Field: The Strange Case of David Cameron', *Media, Culture and Society*, 32.5 (2010): 1–20.

11 Cameron's extensive media dealings were highlighted during the Leveson Inquiry, available at https://www.gov.uk/government/publications/leveson-inquiry-report-into-the-culture-practices-and-ethics-of-the-press (accessed 15 February 2022).

12 For a wider discussion of the political and media myths that evolved in the Coalition years, see Jack Mosse, *The Pound and the Fury: Why Anger and Confusion Reign in an Economy Paralysed by Myth* (Manchester: Manchester University Press, 2021).

13 Probably the most consistent critic of austerity economics and its largely supportive media coverage comes from Simon Wren-Lewis's *Mainly Macro* blog (https://mainlymacro.blogspot.com), reproduced in *The Lies We Were Told: Politics, Economics, Austerity and Brexit* (Bristol: Bristol University Press, 2018). See also regular media columns by Paul Krugman, Martin Woolf and Joseph Stiglitz; and Laura Basu, Steve Schifferes and Sophie Knowles's edited collection *Austerity and the Media: Comparative Perspectives* (London: Routledge, 2018).

14 Paul Marshall and David Laws (eds), *The Orange Book: Reclaiming Liberalism* (London: Profile Books, 2004).

15 See Seldon and Snowdon, *Cameron at 10*, ch. 2.

16 See Ganesh, *George Osborne*, p. 266.

17 See Seldon and Snowdon, *Cameron at 10*. Other figures in Cameron, *For the Record*; Polly Toynbee and David Walker, *The Lost Decade 2010–2020, and What Lies Ahead for Britain* (London: Guardian-Faber, 2020).

18 Carmen Reinhart and Kenneth Rogoff, *This Time is Different: Eight Centuries of Financial Folly* (Princeton, NJ: Princeton University Press, 2009); Carmen Reinhart and Kenneth Rogoff, 'Growth in a Time of Debt', *American Economic Review*, 100.2 (2010): 573–578.

19 In 2013 it was subject to a telling critique which showed glaring methodological errors in the study: Thomas Herndon, Michael Ash and Robert Pollin, 'Does High Public Debt Consistently Stifle Economic Growth? A Critique of Reinhart and Rogoff', UMASS PERI Working Paper Series No. 322 (2013).

20 In Cameron, *For the Record*; Ganesh, *George Osborne*; and Seldon and Snowdon, *Cameron at 10*.

21 Figures and summaries in Simon Wren-Lewis, 'What Brexit and Austerity Tell Us about Economics, Policy and the Media', SPERI Paper No. 36 (2016), pp. 2–4.

22 See Craig Berry, *Austerity Politics and UK Economic Policy* (Sheffield: SPERI-Palgrave-Macmillan, 2016), p. 5.

23 See Robert Peston, *WTF?* (London: Hodder and Stoughton, 2017), p. 128.

24 Cited from Toynbee and Walker, *The Lost Decade*, p. 21.

25 Figures in Sean McDaniel and Craig Berry, *Macroeconomic Policy Change Since the Financial Crisis: A Literature Review* (Sheffield: SPERI, 2017), p. 24.

26 See Guy Standing, *The Corruption of Capitalism: Why Rentiers Thrive and Work Does Not Pay* (London: Biteback, 2021, Kindle edition), p. 14.

27 See SPERI, 'Has the UK Economy Been "Rebalanced"?', Brief No. 4 (July 2015), p. 2.

28 See Daniel Harari, 'Regional and Local Economic Growth Statistics', House of Commons Briefing Paper 05795 (HMSO: London, 2016).

29 See Adam Tooze, *Crashed: How a Decade of Financial Crisis Changed the World* (London: Penguin, 2018), p. 544.

30 See Berry, *Austerity Politics*, pp. 109–110.

31 See, for example, Berry, *Austerity Politics*; Standing, *The Corruption of Capitalism*; Lisa Adkins, Melinda Cooper and Martijn Konings, *The Asset Economy* (Cambridge: Polity, 2020).

32 See Anjum Klair, 'Insecure Work is up by a Quarter since 2011', TUC Briefing Note (London: TUC, 2017).

33 See Jeremy Green and Scott Lavery, 'Britain's Post-Crisis Political Economy: A "Recovery" Through Regressive Distribution', SPERI Paper No. 11 (2014), pp. 12–14.

34 See Simon Wren-Lewis, 'Why it's your bloody GDP, not ours', https://mainlymacro.blogspot.co.uk/ (accessed 15 February 2022).

35 Toynbee and Walker, *The Lost Decade*, pp. 81–82.

36 See Brett Christophers, 'The Rentierization of the United Kingdom Economy', in *Environment and Planning A: Economy and Space* (2019): 1–33 (p. 30). See also House of Lords, Built Environment Committee, *Meeting Housing Demand*, HL Paper 132 (London: House of Lords, 2022).

37 See Brett Christophers, *Rentier Capitalism: Who Owns the Economy and Who Pays for It?* (London: Verso, 2020), p. 105.

38 Thomas Piketty, *Capital in the Twenty-First Century* (Cambridge, MA: Harvard University Press, 2014); Christophers, *Rentier Capitalism*; Standing, *The Corruption of Capitalism*.

39 See Andrew Bowman et al., *What a Waste: Outsourcing and How it Goes Wrong* (Manchester: Manchester University Press, 2015).

40 Adkins, Cooper and Konings, *The Asset Economy*.

41 Probably the most-read insider account being Tim Shipman's *All Out War: The Full Story of Brexit* (London: William Collins, 2016). For accounts looking at the longer-term political, economic and cultural trends that resulted in Brexit, see also Fintan O'Toole, *Heroic Failure: Brexit and the Politics of Pain* (New York: Apollo, 2018); Peston, *WTF?*; and Maria Sobolewska and Robert Ford, *Brexitland: Identity, Diversity and the Reshaping of British Politics* (Cambridge: Cambridge University Press, 2020).

42 HM Government (April 2016), *HM Treasury Analysis: The Long-Term Impact of EU Membership and the Alternatives* CM 9250; HM Government (May 2016), *HM Treasury Analysis: The Immediate Economic Impact of Leaving the EU*, CM 9292.

43 See, for example, Toynbee and Walker, *The Lost Decade*; Peston, *WTF?*; Tooze, *Crashed*; and Standing, *The Corruption of Capitalism*.

44 See Peston, *WTF?*, p. 18.

45 See Loughborough University 'EU Referendum Research', 2016, https://blog.lboro.ac.uk/crcc/eu-referendum/ (accessed 15 February 2022).

46 A factor noted by Shipman, *All Out War*; Toynbee and Walker, *The Lost Decade*; and Philip Hammond, published interview for UK in a Changing Europe, 20 November 2020, https://ukandeu.ac.uk/brexit-witness-archive/philip-hammond/ (accessed 15 February 2022).

47 See Toynbee and Walker, *The Lost Decade*, pp. 20, 77.

48 See Tooze, *Crashed*, p. 553.

Notes to Chapter 8

1 See Aeron Davis, *Reckless Opportunists: Elites at the End of the Establishment* (Manchester: Manchester University Press, 2018).

2 See the *Daily Mail* front page headline from 4 November 2016, referring to the decision of High Court judges that Parliament should be allowed to vote on the triggering of Article 50. James Slack, 'Enemies of the People', *The Daily Mail*, https://www.dailymail.co.uk/news/article-3903436/Enemies-people-Fury-touch-judges-defied-17–4m-Brexit-voters-trigger-constitutional-crisis.html (accessed 15 February 2022). For visual image of the print edition front page, see the Wikipedia article, https://en.wikipedia.org/wiki/Enemies_of_the_People_(headline) (accessed 15 February 2022).

3 Robert Peston, *WTF?* (London: Hodder and Stoughton, 2017), p. 22, says May's decision to trigger Article 50 was 'the most wilful act of vandalism by a serving prime minister'.

4 See Philip Hammond's published interview for UK in a Changing Europe, 20 November 2020, https://ukandeu.ac.uk/brexit-witness-archive/philip-hammond/ (accessed 15 February 2022).

5 Department for Business, Energy and Industrial Strategy.

6 See Philip Hammond interview, 20 November 2020. Hammond was part of the original deficit reduction discussions with Osborne and Cameron.

7 From interview with Charles Roxburgh.

8 A position argued for by Mariana Mazzucato in several books, including *The Entrepreneurial State: Debunking Public vs Private Sector Myths* (London: Penguin, 2013).

9 National Audit Office (September 2021), 'Covid-19 Cost Tracker', https://www.nao.org.uk/covid-19/cost-tracker/ (accessed 15 February 2022).

10 See, for example, Public Accounts Committee, 23 February 2022, 'Covid-19 Cost Tracker', HC 640, House of Commons.

11 From interview with Charles Roxburgh.

12 In 2010, when the Coalition government took over in the wake of the financial crisis, Liam Byrne, the Labour Chief Secretary to the Treasury, left a note for his successor David Laws saying 'I'm afraid there is no money.'

13 In December 2021 the global death toll related to COVID, based on excess deaths, stood at 20.9 million. *The Economist*, https://www.economist.com/graphic-detail/coronavirus-excess-deaths-estimates (accessed 16 December 2021).

14 See Daniela Gabor, *Revolution Without Revolutionaries: Interrogating the Return of Monetary Financing* (2021), Transformative Responses to the Crisis, pp. 4–5, https://transformative-responses.org/wp-content/uploads/2021/01/TR_Report_Gabor_FINAL.pdf (accessed 15 February 2022).

15 See such arguments made by, for example, Adam Tooze, *Shutdown: How Covid Shook the World's Economy* (London: Penguin, 2021); James Meadway, 'After Neoliberalism', podcast on *Politics, Theory, Other*, https://soundcloud.com/poltheoryother/after-neoliberalism-w-james-meadway (September 2021).

Notes to Conclusion

1 Nicholas Macpherson, speech to the Mile End Group entitled 'The Treasury View: A Testament of Experience', 17 January 2014, https://www.gov.uk/government/speeches/speech-by-the-permanent-secretary-to-the-treasury-the-treasury-view-a-testament-of-experience (accessed 15 February 2022).

2 Interviews with George Osborne and Alistair Darling.

3 See Aeron Davis, *Public Relations Democracy: Public Relations, Politics and the Mass Media in Britain* (Manchester: Manchester University Press, 2002).

4 See Brett Christophers, *Rentier Capitalism: Who Owns the Economy and Who Pays for It?* (London: Verso, 2020), p. 63.

5 This refers to Anand Menon's (2016) review of Brexit and an anecdote about a member of the public throwing back the Remain campaign's claims about a drop in GDP if Britain left the EU. Anand Menon, '2016: A Review', *UK in a Changing Europe*, https://ukandeu.ac.uk/2016-a-review/ (accessed 15 February 2022).

6 Lord Kerslake, *Rethinking the Treasury: Kerslake Review of the Treasury* (London: Labour Party, 2017).

7 SPERI, 'Reforming the Treasury, Reorienting British Capitalism', British Political Economy Brief No. 21 (Sheffield: SPERI,
2017), http://speri.dept.shef.ac.uk/2016/03/21/reforming-the-
treasury-reorienting-british-capitalism-new-speri-brief/
(accessed 15 February 2022).

Index

Note: 'n' after a page number indicates the number of a note on that page